Immigrant Acts

ON

ASIAN AMERICAN

CULTURAL

POLITICS

IMMIGRANT ACTS

LISA LOWE

DUKE

UNIVERSITY

PRESS

Durham and London   1996

© 1996 Duke University Press
All rights reserved
Printed in the United States of America on acid-free paper ∞
Typeset in Scala by Tseng Information Systems, Inc.
Library of Congress Cataloging-in-Publication Data appear
on the last printed page of this book.

for my students

Contents

Preface

Understanding Asian immigration to the United States is fundamental to understanding the racialized foundations of both the emergence of the United States as a nation and the development of American capitalism. This is far from claiming that Asians are the only group to have been racialized in the founding of the United States but rather to suggest that the history of the nation's attempt to resolve the contradictions between its economic and political imperatives through laws that excluded Asians from citizenship—from 1790 until the 1940s—contributes to our general understanding of *race* as a contradictory site of struggle for cultural, economic, as well as political membership in the United States. To this end, I have engaged in a materialist critique of the institution of citizenship, not to discount the important struggles through which Asian immigrants have become, after the 1940s, citizens and in that capacity have widened the meaning of "rights" in democratic society, but to name the genealogy of the legal exclusion, disenfranchisement, and restricted enfranchisement of Asian immigrants *as* a genealogy of the American institution of citizenship. I have sought to link this particular genealogy of citizenship to the importance of Asia in the development of Western capitalism globally and the use of Asian labor in the development of capitalist America. The failure of citizenship to guarantee truly equal rights to all the nation's citizenry is not only an index of the historical and persistent racial, class, and gender contradictions of American society but also a condition exacerbated since World War II by the contradiction between U.S. national institutions and the imperatives of the global economy.

In the period from 1850 to World War II, Asians entered the United States along the economic axis, while the state has simultaneously distinguished Asian immigrants along racial and citizenship lines, accordingly distancing Asian Americans—even as citizens—from the terrain of national culture. In light of the importance of American national culture in forming subjects as citizens, this distance has created the conditions for the emergence of Asian American culture as an alternative cultural site and the place where the contradictions of immigrant history are read, performed, and critiqued. My discussions consider Asian American cultural forms as alternatives to national cultural forms and as sites for the emergence of subjects and practices that are not exhausted by the narrative of American citizenship. Culture is the terrain through which the individual speaks as a member of the contemporary national collectivity, but culture is also a mediation of history, the site through which the past returns and is remembered, however fragmented, imperfect, or disavowed. Through that remembering, that recomposition, new forms of subjectivity and community are thought and signified. Cultural forms are not inherently "political"—indeed, culture in the modern nation-state has been traditionally burdened to resolve what the political forms of the state cannot—but the contradictions that produce cultural differences are taken up by oppositional practices that are brought to bear on the political institutions that presently exist. Alternative cultural forms and practices do not offer havens of resolution but are often eloquent descriptions of the ways in which the law, labor exploitation, racialization, and gendering work to prohibit alternatives. Some cultural forms succeed in making it possible to live and inhabit alternatives in the encounter with those prohibitions; some permit us to imagine what we have still yet to live.

In this book, I have wished to make connections between Asian American cultural studies and the current range of ethnic cultural studies projects, between discussions of race in the United States and Marxist theories, and between literary study and feminist analyses of racialized women's work. I am not positing an orthodoxy to be followed but connecting these discussions in order to open a space in which others, perhaps finding worthy gaps, errors, or elisions, will make use of and build on the work only begun here.

Over the past decade, I have had the opportunity to work with extraordinary students from whom I have learned much that has affected this book. Our learning together has given me enormous pleasure. My thinking here is dedicated to those students, to thank them for what they have taught me and to contribute to the intellectual and political projects in which they are and will be engaged. My special thanks to Enrique Bonus, Seunghee Cha, Gerardo Colmenar, Kimberly Dillon, Kip Fulbeck, Ramon Garcia, Mahnaz

Ghavnazi, Grace Kyungwon Hong, Claudia Huiza, Eleanor Jaluague, Helen Heran Jun, James Bong-Su Kang, Min-Jung Kim, Leng Loh, Minh-Tram Nguyen, Amie Parry, Nhu-loc Phan, Démian Pritchard, Chandan Reddy, Gigi Sabo, Vanita Sharma, Carol Song, Anupama Taranath, Ramie Tateishi, and Michael Yamamoto.

Without the advice and friendship of Elaine Kim, this book could not have been written; her wisdom, perseverance, and generosity are unmatched. I thank Gary Okihiro for his scholarly example and for offering me detailed queries and comments on the whole manuscript. I wish to acknowledge the attentive comments from Yen Le Espiritu, Michael Omi, and David Palumbo-Liu, each of whom drew from diverse disciplinary training and experience to help me to frame these discussions more adequately. I also respectfully thank L. Ling-chi Wang, who ten years ago encouraged me to begin this work, and whose assistance over the years—whether through bibliography or moral support—has been extremely important. I am grateful to Yong Soon Min for permitting the Press to include her graphic in the cover design.

San Diego has been a fertile community in which to work, and many people have offered sustaining encouragement. George Lipsitz's integrity —his unique sense of justice and steadfast commitment to making our work useful to the largest progressive discussion—has been an inspiration; he is an indefatigable colleague and an invaluable friend, whom I am honored to know. Over the years, Page duBois and Susan Kirkpatrick have given crucial, enduring support to this work as friends and writing partners. I also thank Michael Bernstein, Dana Cuff, Frances Foster, Takashi Fujitani, Rosemary Marangoly George, Judith Halberstam, Stephanie Jed, Masao Miyoshi, Joseph Nebolon, Teresa Odendahl, Vicente Rafael, Rosaura Sanchez, Mary Tong, Winifred Woodhull, and Lisa Yoneyama, whose sympathies and solidarities have sustained me in differently important ways. The laughter of my daughter Juliet has brought me joy throughout.

Colleagues and friends in other locations have inspired and assisted this work at various points, and to them I express my respect and affection: Homi Bhabha, Judith Butler, Oscar Campomanes, James Clifford, Angela Davis, David Eng, Donna Haraway, Barbara Harlow, Cora Kaplan, Laura Hyun Yi Kang, Dorinne Kondo, Chandra Talpade Mohanty, Satya Mohanty,

José David Saldívar, Leti Volpp, and Shelley Sunn Wong. I am indebted
to the accomplishments and loving support of Tani Barlow, Donald Lowe,
Lydia Lowe, and Mei Lee Lowe. Lastly, I am grateful to David Lloyd for rare
intellectual companionship and abiding, faithful love.

   Ken Wissoker has been a superior editor during the process of making
this into a book. Joe Becker and Marc Brodsky were helpful and agreeable
throughout. Grace Hong assisted greatly in the making of the index. The
University of California Humanities Research Institute, and fellows in the
projects on Minority Discourse, Feminism and Discourses of Power, and
Colonialism and Modernity: The Cases of China, Japan, and Korea, provided contexts in which to discuss chapters 2, 6, and 7. Some of the individual chapters, listed below, were published previously in different versions. I thank those publishers for permission to reprint, as well as the
volume editors who offered indispensable editorial advice:

   "Heterogeneity, Hybridity, Multiplicity: Marking Asian American Dif-
ferences," *Diaspora* 1, no. 1 (Spring 1991); "Canon, Institutionalization,
Identity: Contradictions for Asian American Studies," in *The Ethnic Canon:
Histories, Institutions, Interventions,* ed. David Palumbo-Liu (Minneapolis:
University of Minnesota Press, 1994); "Imagining Los Angeles in the
Production of Multiculturalism," in *Mapping Multiculturalism,* ed. Avery
Gordon and Christopher Newfield (Minneapolis: University of Minne-
sota Press, 1996); "Decolonization, Displacement, Disidentification: Asian
American 'Novels' and the Question of History," in *Cultural Institutions
of the Novel,* ed. Deidre Lynch and William Warner (Durham: Duke Uni-
versity Press, 1996); "Unfaithful to the Original: The Subject of *Dictée,*"
in *Writing Self/Writing Nation: Selected Essays on Theresa Hak Kyung Cha's
DICTEE,* ed. Elaine Kim and Norma Alarcón (Berkeley: Third Woman
Press, 1993). Also published in *Gender and Colonialism,* ed. Timothy Foley,
Lionel Pilkington, Sean Ryder, and Elizabeth Tilley (Galway, Ireland: Galway University Press, 1995); and "Work, Immigration, Gender: Asian
'American' Women," in *Making Waves II,* ed. Asian Women United of Cali-
fornia (New York: Beacon, forthcoming 1996).

Immigrant Acts

Immigration, Citizenship,

Racialization: Asian

American Critique

Scene 2

[...]

vi: "Event: Announcement by the Vietnam Veterans' Memorial Fund of winning design of a memorial to be placed on the Mall to honor Vietnam Veterans. . . ."

voice: The material used for constructing this memorial is polished black granite imported from India. Approximately 150 panels were cut into three-inch thick blocks, the shortest panel being eight inches tall, the highest ten and a half feet, the largest panel weighing three thousand pounds.

The memorial was conceived in 1981 and eventually built over the next two years, 1982 to '84. In comparison, the Lincoln Memorial to your right took sixty years to complete. The landscape was leveled, and the apex of the wall reaches a depth of almost eleven feet. Notice the mementos left by those who visit: medals, pictures, flowers, helmets, photos of teenage boys frozen in youth, of babies never seen by their fathers.

This represents an entire war a nation meant to forget.

Scene 7

[...]

maya: It's been mentioned—many times, in fact—the fact that me as the designer of a memorial to an Asian war was upsetting. I'm a young woman, a student. And I'm Chinese American. We're all lumped together, us "gooks."

—Jeannie Barroga, "Walls"

Nothing that has ever happened should be regarded as lost for history.

—Walter Benjamin, "Theses on the Philosophy of History"

I

Citizens inhabit the political space of the nation, a space that is, at once, juridically legislated, territorially situated, and culturally embodied. Although the law is perhaps the discourse that most literally governs citizenship, U.S. national culture—the collectively forged images, histories, and narratives that place, displace, and replace individuals in relation to the national polity—powerfully shapes who the citizenry is, where they dwell, what they remember, and what they forget. Insofar as the legal definition and political concept of the citizen enfranchises the subject who inhabits the national public sphere, the concept of the abstract citizen—each formally equivalent, one to the other—is defined by the negation of the material conditions of work and the inequalities of the property system. In the United States, not only class but also the historically sedimented particularities of race, national origin, locality, and embodiment remain largely invisible within the political sphere. In this sense, the legal and political forms of the nation have required a national culture in the integration of the differentiated people and social spaces that make up "America," a national culture, broadly cast yet singularly engaging, that can inspire diverse individuals to identify with the national project.

It is through the terrain of national culture that the individual subject is politically formed as the American citizen: a terrain introduced by the Statue of Liberty, discovered by the immigrant, dreamed in a common language, and defended in battle by the independent, self-made man. The heroic quest, the triumph over weakness, the promises of salvation, prosperity, and progress: this is the American feeling, the style of life, the ethos and spirit of being. It is in passing by way of this terrain of culture that the subject is immersed in the repertoire of American memories, events, and narratives and comes to articulate itself in the domain of language, social hierarchy, law, and ultimately, political representation. In being represented as citizen within the political sphere, however, the subject is "split off" from the unrepresentable histories of situated embodiment that contradict the abstract form of citizenship. Culture is the medium of the *present*—the imagined equivalences and identifications through which the individual invents lived relationship with the national collective—but it is simultaneously the site that mediates the *past,* through which history is grasped as difference, as fragments, shocks, and flashes of disjunction. It is through culture that the subject becomes, acts, and speaks itself as "American." It is likewise in culture that individuals and collectivities struggle and remember and, in that difficult remembering, imagine and practice both subject and community differently.

In a manner unprecedented in the twentieth century, the Vietnam War (1959–1975) shook the stability and coherence of America's understanding of itself. An "unpopular" war contested by social movements, the press, and the citizenry, a disabling war from which the United States could not emerge "victorious"—there is perhaps no single event in this century that has had such power to disunify the American public, disrupting traditional unities of "community," "nation," and "culture."[1] It radically altered these unities not only because of the traumas of death, loss, and breakdown that the Vietnam War brought and has come to symbolize but also because the national understanding of the war was formed by and formative of the contemporary crises in understandings of racial groupings, class identities, and notions of masculinity and femininity. Jeannie Barroga's play "Walls" portrays the controversy surrounding the Vietnam War Memorial, its aesthetic, the young Chinese American woman architect Maya Ying Lin who designed it, and the veterans—and veterans organizations—who argued that they were not "represented" in the abstract modernist lines of the design. The play revoices fundamental divisions instantiated by the war—between men and women, veterans and antiwar activists, Americans and Asians—by depicting their inevitable resurfacing around the national project of memorializing the war's veterans. The play dramatizes the unspoken racial tension underpinning the artistic and political controversy surrounding the "representative" qualities of an American monument designed by a young Chinese American woman commemorating the U.S. soldiers who fought a war in Vietnam.[2]

Barroga's "Walls" focuses primarily on the veterans' protests against Lin's modernist, nonrepresentational design as a means of objecting to Lin's position as an Asian American woman. Through the performance of these conflicts and struggles, the play suggests that the national project of "re-membering" the Vietnam War—who its heroes were, who must be forgotten, who may mourn—is a crucial site in which the terms of "membership" in the national "body" are contested, policed, and ultimately redefined. In particular, by dramatizing the debate as to whether a national monument designed by an Asian American can represent the American nation, the play makes clear that the question of aesthetic representation is always also a debate about political representation. The veterans demand that a statue with soldiers and an American flag be placed next to the official monument, a black V-shaped stone horizontal to the earth etched with the names of the dead. The central antagonism between the veterans' demand for a representational monument and Lin's insistent commitment to a nonrepresentational aesthetic embodies the conflict between the nationalist desire for resolution through representational forms and the unassimilable conflicts and particularities that cannot be represented by those forms. For the nation defined by victory in U.S. wars in Asia throughout the twentieth century—in the Philippines, Japan, and Korea—and its citizenry specified for so much of the country's history by the exclusion of Asians from naturalization and citizenship, the national monument commemorating veterans of the war "lost" in Vietnam designed by the twenty-one-year-old daughter of Asian immigrants was an unresolved contradiction, a return of the repressed, a "gash that would not heal."[3] Barroga, a Filipina American, has written an "Asian American" play that triangulates Chinese American, Filipina American, and the descendants of the unremembered Vietnamese—all different sites in which the "Asian" interfaces with the "American."[4] I begin my discussion with this example in order to thematize Asian American cultural productions as countersites to U.S. national memory and national culture.[5]

In the last century and a half, the American *citizen* has been defined over against the Asian *immigrant*, legally, economically, and culturally.[6] These definitions have cast Asian immigrants both as persons and populations to be integrated into the national political sphere and as the contradictory, confusing, unintelligible elements to be marginalized and returned to their alien origins. "Asia" has been always a complex site on which the manifold anxieties of the U.S. nation-state have been figured: such anxieties have figured Asian countries as exotic, barbaric, and alien, and Asian laborers immigrating to the United States from the nineteenth century onward as a "yellow peril" threatening to displace white European immigrants.[7] Orientalist racializations of Asians as physically and intellectually different from "whites" predominated especially in periods in which a domestic crisis of capital was coupled with nativist anti-Asian backlash, intersecting significantly with immigration exclusion acts and laws against naturalization of Asians in 1882, 1924, and 1934.[8] Exclusionist rhetoric ranged from nativist agitation, which claimed that "servile coolie" Chinese labor undercut "free white" labor, to declarations about the racial unassimilability of the Japanese, to arguments that Asian social organization threatened the integrity of American political institutions.[9] During the crises of national identity that occurred in periods of U.S. war in Asia—with the Philippines (1898–1910), against Japan (1941–1945), in Korea (1950–1953), and in Vietnam—American orientalism displaced U.S. expansionist interests in Asia onto racialized figurations of Asian workers within the national space. Although predictions of Asian productivity supplanting European economic dominance have gripped the European and American imaginations since the nineteenth century, in the period from World War II onward, "Asia" has emerged as a particularly complicated "double front" of threat and encroachment for the United States: on the one hand, Asian states have become prominent as external rivals in overseas imperial war and in the global economy, and on the other, Asian immigrants are still a necessary racialized labor force within the domestic national economy.[10] Immigration exclusion acts and naturalization laws have thus been not only means of regulating the terms of the citizen and the nation-state but also an intersection of the legal and political terms with an orientalist discourse that defined Asians as culturally and racially "other" in times when the United States was militarily and economically at war with Asia.

Historically and materially, Chinese, Japanese, Korean, Asian Indian, and Filipino immigrants have played absolutely crucial roles in the building and the sustaining of America; and at certain times, these immigrants have been fundamental to the construction of the nation as a simulacrum of inclusiveness. Yet the project of imagining the nation as homogeneous requires the orientalist construction of cultures and geographies from which Asian immigrants come as fundamentally "foreign" origins antipathetic to the modern American society that "discovers," "welcomes," and "domesticates" them. A national memory haunts the conception of the Asian American, persisting beyond the repeal of actual laws prohibiting Asians from citizenship and sustained by the wars in Asia, in which the Asian is always seen as an immigrant, as the "foreigner-within," even when born in the

United States and the descendant of generations born here before. It is this premise that Barroga's play highlights through the veterans' objection that Maya Lin's monument cannot represent the American nation: the American soldier, who has in every way submitted to the nation, is the quintessential citizen and therefore the ideal representative of the nation, yet the American of Asian descent remains the symbolic "alien," the *metonym* for Asia who by definition cannot be imagined as sharing in America.[11] Narratives of immigrant inclusion—stories of the Asian immigrant's journey from foreign strangeness to assimilation and citizenship—may in turn attempt to produce cultural integration and its symbolization on the national political terrain. Yet these same narratives are driven by the repetition and return of episodes in which the Asian American, even as a citizen, continues to be located outside the cultural and racial boundaries of the nation. Rather than attesting to the absorption of cultural difference into the universality of the national political sphere as the "model minority" stereotype would dictate, the Asian immigrant—at odds with the cultural, racial, and linguistic forms of the nation—emerges in a site that defers and displaces the temporality of assimilation.[12] This distance from the national culture constitutes Asian American culture as an alternative formation that produces cultural expressions materially and aesthetically at odds with the resolution of the citizen in the nation. Rather than expressing a "failed" integration of Asians into the American cultural sphere, this distance preserves Asian American culture as an alternative site where the palimpsest of lost memories is reinvented, histories are fractured and retraced, and the unlike varieties of silence emerge into articulacy.[13]

Thus, the immigration of Asians to the United States has been the *locus* of meanings that are simultaneously legal, political, economic, cultural, and aesthetic. In this book I attempt to situate these meanings and to gather them into a coherent, contemporary formation that is both a record of the emergence of Asian American "culture" within a U.S. national and an international context and a comprehension of the dialectical critique generated by that emergence.

My title, *Immigrant Acts*, first invokes the history of Asian immigration to the United States since the mid–nineteenth century. It names the history of immigration exclusion acts that restricted and regulated the possibilities of Asian American settlement and cultural expression—the exclusion of Chinese in 1882, of Asian Indians in 1917, of Koreans and Japanese in 1924, and of Philippine immigrants in 1934.[14] It names the series of Asian exclusion repeal acts passed between 1943 and 1952, which dramatically changed the status of immigrants of all Asian origins, from "aliens ineligible to citizenship," to that of "citizen."[15] It names, as well, the dramatic shifts in Asian immigration to the United States after the Immigration and Nationality Act of 1965 abolished former national-origin quotas and exclusions, since which we have witnessed an enormous widening of the definitions of "Asian American."[16] Because of the many historical and political economic changes of which the act of 1965 is an expression, the majority of Asian Americans are at present Asian-born rather than multiple-generation, and new immigrant groups from South Vietnam, South Korea, Cambodia, Laos, Thailand, the Philippines, Malaysia, India, and Pakistan have diversified the already existing Asian American group of largely Chinese, Japanese, Korean, and Filipino descent. As such, to focus on Asian Americans as "immigrants" is not to obscure the understanding that almost half of Asian Americans are U.S.-born citizens, and of that group, many date the history of their settlement in the United States back four or five generations. It is not to draw attention away from the fact that most Asian Americans are now currently naturalized or native-born citizens and that Asian American struggles for inclusion and equality have significantly advanced American democratic ideals and their extension.[17] It is rather to observe that the life conditions, choices, and expressions of Asian Americans have been significantly determined by the U.S. state through the apparatus of immigration laws and policies, through the enfranchisements denied or extended to immigrant individuals and communities, and through the processes of naturalization and citizenship.[18] It is to underscore that both in the period from 1850 to World War II and in the period after 1965, immigration has been a crucial *locus* through which U.S. interests have recruited and regulated both labor and capital from Asia. It is also to maintain that there has been an important continuity between the considerable distortion of social relations in Asian countries affected by U.S. imperialist war and occupation and the emigration of Asian labor to the United States throughout the last century.

"Immigrant acts," then, attempts to name the *contradictions* of Asian immigration, which at different moments in the last century and a half of Asian entry into the United States have placed Asians "within" the U.S. nation-state, its workplaces, and its markets, yet linguistically, culturally, and racially marked Asians as "foreign" and "outside" the national polity.[19] Under such contradictions, late-nineteenth-century Chinese immigrants labored in mining, agriculture, and railroad construction but were excluded from citizenship and political participation in the state.[20] The contradiction of immigration and citizenship took a different but consistently resonant form during World War II, when U.S.-born Japanese Americans were nominally recognized as citizens and hence recruited into the U.S. military, yet were dispossessed of freedoms and properties explicitly granted to citizens, officially condemned as "racial enemies," and interned in camps throughout the Western United States.[21] Philippine immigration after the period of U.S. colonization animates yet another kind of contradiction. For Filipino immigrants, modes of capitalist incorporation and acculturation into American life begin not at the moment of immigration but rather in the "homeland" already deeply affected by U.S. influences and modes of social organization.[22] The situations of Filipino Americans, or U.S. Filipinos, foreground the ways in which Asian Americans emigrating from previously colonized sites are not exclusively formed as racialized minorities within the United States but are simultaneously determined by colonialism and capital investment in Asia.[23] These different contradictions express distinct yet continuous formations in the genealogy of the racialization of Asian Americans: the Chinese as alien noncitizen, the American citizen of Japanese descent as racial enemy, and the American citizen of Filipino descent as simultaneously immigrant and colonized national.

By insisting on "immigrant acts" as contradictions and therefore as dialectical and critical, I also mean to emphasize that while immigration has been the *locus* of legal and political restriction of Asians as the "other" in America, immigration has simultaneously been the site for the emergence of critical negations of the nation-state for which those legislations are the expression. If the law is the apparatus that binds and seals the universality of the political body of the nation, then the "immigrant," produced by the law as margin and threat to that symbolic whole, is precisely a generative site for the critique of that universality. The national institutionalization of unity becomes the measure of the nation's condition of heterogeneity.[24] If the nation proposes American culture as the key site for the resolution of inequalities and stratifications that cannot be resolved on the political terrain of representative democracy, then that culture performs that reconciliation by naturalizing a universality that exempts the "non-American" from its history of development or admits the "non-American" only through a "multiculturalism" that aestheticizes ethnic differences as if they could be separated from history. In contrast, the cultural productions emerging out of the contradictions of immigrant marginality displace the fiction of reconciliation, disrupt the myth of national identity by revealing its gaps and fissures, and intervene in the narrative of national development that would illegitimately locate the "immigrant" before history or exempt the "immigrant" from history.[25] The universals proposed by the political and cultural forms of the nation precisely generate the critical *acts* that negate those universals. "Immigrant acts" names the *agency* of Asian immigrants and Asian Americans: the *acts* of labor, resistance, memory, and survival, as well as the politicized cultural work that emerges from dislocation and disidentification. Asian immigrants and Asian Americans have not only been "subject to" immigration exclusion and restriction but have also been "subjects of" the immigration process and are agents of political change, cultural expression, and social transformation.

The period from 1850 to World War II was marked by legal exclusions, political disenfranchisement, labor exploitation, and internment for Asian-origin groups in the United States. While some of the legal and political exclusions have been lifted in the period following the McCarran-Walter Act of 1952 and the Immigration and Nationality Act of 1965, the problems of legal definition have continued for Asian origin communities. Indeed, the McCarran-Walter Act, an expression of the cold war era, legislated strict quotas, created an area called the "Asia-Pacific triangle" based on a strategically territorial mapping, and contained language delineating the exclusion of and right to deport "any alien who has engaged or has had purpose to engage in activities 'prejudicial to the public interest' or 'subversive to national security.'"[26] The 1965 act has initiated not fewer but indeed more specifications and regulations for immigrants of Asian origins.[27] Immigration, thus, can be understood as the most important historical and discursive site of Asian American formation through which the national and global economic, the cultural, and the legal spheres are modulated. Whether that determination is expressed through immigration "exclusion" or "inclusion," the U.S. nation-state attempts to "produce" and regulate the Asian as a means of "resolving" economic exigencies, primarily through the *loci* of citizenship and political representation but also in ways that extend to the question of culture.[28] As the state legally transforms the Asian *alien* into the Asian American *citizen*, it institutionalizes the disavowal of the history of racialized labor exploitation and disenfranchisement through the promise of freedom in the political sphere. Yet the historical and continued racialization of the Asian American, as citizen, exacerbates the contradictions of the national project that promises the resolution of material inequalities through the political domain of equal representation.

In the following discussion, I place the legal regulations of the Asian as *alien* noncitizen and the Asian American as *citizen* in terms of the material contradictions that have emerged as the nation has intersected with the global economy during the last century and a half. The economic contradictions of capital and labor on the national level, and the contradictions of the political nation within the global economy, have given rise to the need, over and over again, for the nation to resolve *legally* capitalist contradiction around the definition of the Asian immigrant subject. The history of the legislation of the Asian as *alien* and the administration of the Asian American as *citizen* is at once the genealogy of this attempt at resolution and the genealogy of a distinct "racial formation" for Asian Americans, defined not primarily in terms of biological racialism but in terms of institutionalized, legal definitions of race and national origin.[29] Michael Omi and Howard Winant observe that for most of its history, the U.S. state's racial policy has been one of repression and exclusion, and they read the role of the state in racial formation through a consideration of these state policies and laws. While noting the deep involvement of the state in the organization and interpretation of race, Omi and Winant also note the inadequacy of state institutions to carry out these functions. Therefore, they observe that race is "an unstable and 'decentered' complex of social meanings constantly being transformed by political struggle."[30]

Racialization along the legal axis of definitions of citizenship has also as-cribed "gender" to the Asian American subject. Up until 1870, American citizenship was granted exclusively to white male persons; in 1870, men of African descent could become naturalized, but the bar to citizenship remained for Asian men until the repeal acts of 1943–1952. Whereas the "masculinity" of the citizen was first inseparable from his "whiteness," as the state extended citizenship to nonwhite male persons, it formally desig-nated these subjects as "male," as well.[31] Though the history of citizenship and gender in relation to the enfranchisement of white women is distinct from the history of citizenship and race in relation to enfranchisement of nonwhite males, it is not entirely separate, for the legally defined racial for-mation of Chinese Americans and, later, other Asian Americans has like-wise been a gendered formation. The 1943 enfranchisement of the Chinese American into citizenship, for example, constituted the Chinese immigrant subject as male; in the 1946 modification of the Magnuson Act, the Chinese wives of U.S. citizens were exempted from the permitted annual quota; as the law changed to reclassify "Chinese immigrants" as eligible for natu-ralization and citizenship, female immigrants were not included in this reclassification but were in effect specified only in relation to the changed status of "the Chinese immigrant," who was legally presumed to be male. Thus, the administration of citizenship was simultaneously a "technology" of racialization and gendering.[32] From 1850 until the 1940s, Chinese im-migrant masculinity had been socially and institutionally marked as differ-ent from that of Anglo- and Euro-American "white" citizens owing to the forms of work and community that had been historically available to Chi-nese men as the result of the immigration laws restricting female immi-gration. The Page Law of 1875 and a later ban on Chinese laborers' spouses had effectively halted the immigration of Chinese women, preventing the formation of families and generations among Chinese immigrants; in addi-tion, female U.S. citizens who married an "alien ineligible to citizenship" lost their own citizenship.[33] In conjunction with the relative absence of Chi-nese wives and family among immigrant "bachelor" communities and be-cause of the concentration of Chinese men in "feminized" forms of work—such as laundry, restaurants, and other service-sector jobs—Chinese male immigrants could be said to occupy, before 1940, a "feminized" position in relation to white male citizens and, after 1940, a "masculinity" whose *racialization* is the material trace of the history of this "gendering."

Immigration regulations and the restrictions on naturalization and citizenship have thus racialized and gendered Asian Americans, and this history has situated Asian Americans, even as citizens, in a differential relationship to the political and cultural institutions of the nation-state. The racialization of Asian Americans in relation to the state locates Asian American culture as a site for the emergence of another kind of political subject, one who has a historically "alien-ated" relation to the category of citizenship. That historical alienation situates the Asian American political subject in critical apposition to the category of the citizen, as well as to the political sphere of representative democracy that the concept of the citizen subtends. The differentiation of Asian immigrants from the national citizenry is marked not only politically but culturally as well: refracted through images, memories, and narratives—submerged, fragmented, and sedimented in a historical "unconscious"—it is rearticulated in Asian American culture through the emergence of alternative identities and practices.

The economic and political contradictions that the state seeks to resolve in relation to Asia and Asian immigrants can be discussed generally in terms of two historical phases—the first taking place between 1850 and World War II, and the second, from World War II to the present—and specified by the immigration and citizenship laws that have racialized Asians. Capital deals with its systemic crisis of declining profits by seeking out cheaper factors of production, especially labor. Consequently, throughout the period from 1850 to World War II, the recruitment of Asian immigrant labor was motivated by the imperative to bring cheaper labor into the still developing capitalist economy: Chinese, Japanese, and Filipino laborers were fundamental to the building of the railroads, the agricultural economy, and the textile and service industries. In this first period, the logic of capitalist development contained an economic contradiction that could be nullified by "resolving" the contradiction that existed between capitalism and the state. As Marx observed of the United States in the 1860s, the bulk of the land was still available public property, but labor was in short supply. In this situation in which "every settler on it therefore can turn part of it into his private property and individual means of production," capital needed a cheap, manipulable labor force, yet a surplus of enfranchised workers could run dangerously in excess of the accumulation of capital.[34] Capital in the 1880s utilized racialized divisions among laborers to maximize its profits; it needed the exclusion of further Chinese immigration to prevent a superabundance of cheap labor, and the disenfranchisement of the existing Chinese immigrant labor force, to prevent capital accumulation by these wage laborers.[35] Theoretically, in a racially homogeneous nation, the needs of capital and the needs of the state complement each other. Yet in a racially differentiated nation such as the United States, capital and state imperatives may be contradictory: capital, with its supposed needs for "abstract labor," is said by Marx to be unconcerned by the "origins" of its labor force, whereas the nation-state, with its need for "abstract citizens" formed by a unified culture to participate in the political sphere, is precisely concerned to maintain a national citizenry bound by race, language, and culture.[36] In late-nineteenth-century America, as the state sought to serve capital, this contradiction between the economic and the political spheres was *sublated* through the legal exclusion and disenfranchisement of Chinese immigrant laborers. Capital could increase profit and benefit from the presence of a racialized and tractable labor force up until the point at which the Chinese labor force grew large enough that it threatened capital accumulation by whites. At that point, by excluding and disenfranchising the Chinese in 1882, the state could constitute the "whiteness" of the citizenry and granted political concessions to "white" labor groups who were demanding immigration restrictions.[37] The state reconfirmed bars to citizenship and naturalization that dated back to 1790: the national citizenry and national culture were protected from "foreign" and "racial" corruptions. The state's attempts to "resolve" the economic contradictions of capital and the political contradictions of the nation-state resulted in the successive exclusions of the Chinese in 1882, Asian Indians in 1917, Japanese in 1924, and Filipinos in 1934 and the barring of all these immigrant groups from citizenship and ownership of property. The Alien Land Laws of 1913, 1920, and 1923 prohibited Asian immigrants from owning land and other forms of property through the legal construction of nonwhites as "aliens ineligible to citizenship."[38] The disenfranchisement of Asians was also supported by laws against miscegenation that created an environment extremely hostile to Asian settlement.

Owing to this history in which economic exigencies have been mediated through the legal apparatus that racializes and genders the subject, for Asian immigrants and Asian Americans, class struggles have cut across and been particularized in the various practices of racial and gender exclusion. When the state addressed the economic contradiction between capital and labor—through the legal measures excluding Chinese, Indians, Japanese, Koreans, and Filipinos from rights, property, and citizenship— economic class was mediated by and articulated through race, gender, and national origin. At the same time, organized racial or Asian national solidarity and challenges to legal oppressions almost always articulated protests against injustices that were due to the exploitation of gendered Asian workers under U.S. capitalism, even if such solidarities were not expressed strictly in terms of class identity. For example, in the late nineteenth century, Chinese workers protested ordinances calculated to shut down Chinese laundries, brought litigation to object to unfair taxes, struggled for access to schooling and housing, and brought suits against the state to challenge the exclusions and deportations of Chinese laborers.[39] Thus, the history of the racial formation of Asian immigrants and Asian Americans has always included a "class formation" and a "gender formation" that, mediated through such state apparatuses as the law, articulated a contradiction between capital and racialized, gendered labor.[40] The law, in this sense, must be understood as *both* an ideological and a repressive state apparatus, as both symptomatic and determining of the relations of production. Chinese community challenges to the first anti-Chinese laws; Japanese American objections to the Alien Land Laws; Filipino American agricultural labor organizing; the Asian American social movement of the 1970s with its various efforts to address racism, labor exploitation, and inequality of housing and education; and current projects organizing against the particular exploitation of Asian immigrant women's labor—all significantly disrupted the racial order and addressed the capitalist exploitation of racialized and gendered labor. Because the legal apparatus of racialization and gendering has been so thoroughly imbricated in capitalist relations, these movements organized around racial identities have challenged the injustices of an economic order as well as those of civil society. Oppositional solidarity movements have been organized around racial identities because of social and economic oppressions that have targeted those identities, and these movements have succeeded in transforming racial meanings and the conditions of racialized peoples. Yet the limits of such transformations are reached if the struggle is confined to the question of political rights, precisely since the history of citizenship was underwritten by economic, racial, and gender inequalities. The continued exploitation of Asian and other racialized immigrants throughout and beyond the period of "enfranchisement" after 1965 makes evident that a critical interrogation of both the concept of citizenship and the state's role as the guarantor of citizens' rights has been and is still necessary. These concepts are in contradiction with both the racialist foundations of capitalism in the United States and U.S. development projects elsewhere.

In the period after World War II, as production began to shift to Asia and Latin America where export-oriented economies were emerging, the capital imperative came into greater contradiction with the political imperative of the U.S. nation-state. The one required economic internationalism to expand labor and capital, to secure raw materials and consumer markets, to locate areas in which to invest surplus capital, and to provide a safety valve for domestic tensions; the other required consolidation of a strong, hegemonic nation-state in order to regulate the terms of that postwar economic internationalism.[41] In addition, since the 1970s, as manufacturing moved internationally to make use of low-wage labor markets, the proportion of the U.S. work force engaged in manufacturing has fallen as the proportion working in services has increased; the structural transformations of the economy have produced increased demand for immigrants to fill minimum-wage, unskilled, and part-time jobs, yet these same economic processes have initiated new waves of anti-immigrant nativism and exacerbated the state's need to legislate immigration. Several strategies were employed to meet the capital imperative: U.S. capital moved to Asian and Latin American sites of cheaper labor and production, and the 1965 act "opened" immigration, renewing domestic labor supplies. Since 1965, the profile of Asian immigration has consisted of low-wage, service-sector workers as well as "proletarianized" white-collar professionals, a group which supplies laborers for services and manufacturing and which furnishes a technically trained labor force that serves as one form of "variable capital" investment in the U.S. economy.[42] If the nineteenth-century racialized and gendered formation of Chinese male immigrants as laborers *sublated* the contradictions between the imperatives of capitalism and the state, then these contradictions *reemerge* in the demographic composition of the post-1965 Asian immigrant group, a group still racialized and exploited yet complicated by class and gender stratification. Since the 1980s, the increased proletarianization of Asian immigrant women's labor in the United States is an index of new forms of contradiction and is commensurate with a new gendered international division of labor that makes use of third world and racialized immigrant women as a "flexible" work force in the restructuring of capitalism globally.[43] Transnational industry's use of Asian and Latina immigrant women's labor in the United States is the current site where the contradictions of the national and the international converge in an overdetermination of capitalism, anti-immigrant racism, and patriarchal gender stratification.[44]

Another distinguishing feature of the post-1965 Asian immigration is the predominance of immigrants from South Korea, the Philippines, South Vietnam, and Cambodia, countries deeply affected by U.S. colonialism, war, and neocolonialism. Despite the usual assumption that Asians immigrate from stable, continuous, "traditional" cultures, most of the post-1965 Asian immigrants come from societies already disrupted by colonialism and distorted by the upheavals of neocolonial capitalism and war. The material legacy of the repressed history of U.S. imperialism in Asia is borne out in the "return" of Asian immigrants to the imperial center. In this sense, these Asian Americans are determined by the history of U.S. involvements in Asia *and* the historical racialization of Asians in the United States. The post-1965 Asian immigrant displacement differs from that of the earlier migrations from China and Japan, for it embodies the displacement from Asian societies in the aftermath of war and colonialism to a United States with whose sense of national identity the immigrants are in contradiction precisely because of that history. Once here, the demand that Asian immigrants identify as U.S. national subjects simultaneously produces alienations and disidentifications out of which critical subjectivities emerge. These immigrants retain precisely the memories of imperialism that the U.S. nation seeks to forget.[45]

Insofar as the United States sought to address the imperatives of capital through the expansion of markets and labor supplies, it also sought hegemony internationally through foreign wars in Asia. Following the colonization of the Philippines, the foreign policy of the United States in relation to Asia, its involvements in World War II, and the wars in Korea and Vietnam must be understood in relation to a contradiction between the growing need for economic internationalism and the desire to fortify the political nation-state and cannot be simply described in terms of the containment of Communism. We can trace these two phases of contradiction in terms of American wars in Asia during the twentieth century. In the U.S. colonization of the Philippines in 1898–1946, war and occupation served national capital imperatives through expansion and the interruption of the previous conditions of the agrarian Philippines, which displaced Filipinos from previous forms of work, thus providing an exploitable labor force available for emigration to the United States.[46] The U.S. war against Japan during World War II, in contrast, is explicable less in terms of U.S. domestic labor needs and more in terms of the United States asserting and assuming hegemony in the world system. The United States aimed to succeed Britain and Europe as the heir to the empire that was breaking down under the pressure of anticolonial nationalist and liberation movements throughout the colonized world and, in this effort, sought to curtail Japanese expansion in Asia. The U.S. actions in World War II were directed toward creating the geopolitical basis for the postwar world order that would take place under America's "protective" aegis.

During the period of unprecedented aggregate growth of global capitalism in the 1950s and 1960s, the Western domination of Asia that had been expressed through direct colonialism was transformed into a U.S. imperialist project by way of modernization and development.[47] U.S. foreign policy was characterized by the contradiction between the imperatives of internationalizing the economy and the political necessity of the nation-state as a vehicle for exercizing hegemony. In the struggle for leadership in the postwar global order, the United States sought to achieve the military superiority, economic supremacy, and ideological predominance necessary to determine the terms of the postwar economic internationalism and to establish secure access to raw materials and markets.[48] In this sense, the foreign policy that framed wars in Korea and Vietnam and neocolonial domination of the Philippines was a liberal hybrid that combined economic internationalism and anti-communism, responding equally to the need to take economic supremacy and to contain the Soviet Union diplomatically. Although the U.S. wars in Korea and Vietnam reflected the general desire to incorporate the extractive economies of Asia into the industrial core, the twenty-year period in which the United States vied for power over the rimlands of Northeast Asia, Southeast Asia, and Taiwan also constituted a brutal theater in which the conquest and occupation of Asian countries were the means for the United States to perform its technological modernity and military force in relation to the Asiatic world, a process legitimated by the emergence of the Soviet Union's and China's global influences. Yet the wars in Korea and Vietnam were as much a stage for the ideological lesson that the United States could and should determine how capital could move globally as the wars also secured the material conditions for that movement.[49] The wars of the 1950s to the 1970s laid the groundwork for the U.S. investment and material extraction in Asia that took place only later in the 1980s with global restructuring, displacing Korean and Vietnamese populations, some of which have immigrated to the United States. By the 1990s, the United States had reached a period of "imperial overstretch," marked by the decline of its economic hegemony and the emergence of Japan and Germany; the contradictions of the U.S. capital investment and development in Asia is further expressed in the rapid growth of the newly industrializing countries in Asia—Hong Kong, Singapore, South Korea, and Taiwan.

The emergence of successful capitalist states in Asia has necessitated global restructuring for U.S. capital, reinvigorating American anxiety about Asia, but such anxiety about the Asian is clearly not new. Throughout the twentieth century, the figure of the Asian immigrant has served as a "screen," a phantasmatic site, on which the nation projects a series of condensed, complicated anxieties regarding external and internal threats to the mutable coherence of the national body: the invading multitude, the lascivious seductress, the servile yet treacherous domestic, the automaton whose inhuman efficiency will supersede American ingenuity. Indeed, it is precisely the unfixed liminality of the Asian immigrant—geographically, linguistically, and racially at odds with the context of the "national"—that has given rise to the necessity of endlessly fixing and repeating such stereotypes.[50] Stereotypes that construct Asians as the threatening "yellow peril," or alternatively, that pose Asians as the domesticated "model minority," are each equally indices of these national anxieties. Yet the discursive fixing of the Asian is not exclusively a matter of stereotypical representation in the cultural sphere; as I have been arguing, it has historically been instantiated through the state's classification of racialized Asian immigrant identities. The state announces its need to fix and stabilize the identity of the immigrant through legal exclusions and inclusions, as well as through juridical classifications. "Legal" and "illegal," "citizen" and "noncitizen," and "U.S.-born" and "permanent resident" are contemporary modes through which the liberal state discriminates, surveys, and produces immigrant identities. The presence of Asia and Asian peoples that currently impinges on the national consciousness sustains the figuration of the Asian immigrant as a transgressive and corrupting "foreignness" and continues to make "Asians" an object of the law, the political sphere, as well as national culture.

Though Congress never enacted a law that specifically named "Asians" or "Orientals" as an Asiatic racial category, legal theorist Neil Gotanda has argued that the sequence of laws in 1882, 1917, 1924, and 1934 that excluded immigrants from China, Japan, India, and the Philippines, combined with the series of repeal acts overturning these exclusions, construct a common racial categorization for Asians that depended on consistently racializing each national-origin group as "nonwhite."[51] The classification of individual Asian-origin groups as nonwhites was legally established in case after case related to the question of citizenship. For example, the 1790 naturalization act granted all "free whites" the right to claim citizenship and barred all nonwhites until after the Civil War in 1870, when the statute was enlarged to include freemen of African nativity or descent. Yet even after the enfranchisement of men of African descent, the racial bar to naturalization of Asians was reconfirmed in the early 1920s when the Supreme Court ruled on the constitutionality of the bar in relation to Takeo Ozawa, a U.S.-educated Japanese immigrant, and Baghat Singh Thind, an Indian who was a World War I veteran.[52] The barrier to citizenship continued for immigrants from all parts of Asia until the Magnuson Act of 1943. The Magnuson Act had three significant parts: it repealed the Exclusion Act of 1882; it established a quota for Chinese immigrants; and it made Chinese eligible for citizenship, negating the 1790 racial bar. There were subsequent Asian exclusion repeal acts (1946, for Filipino and East Indian), and the McCarran-Walter Act of 1952 abolished the 1917 "Asia Barred Zone" concept, replacing it with quotas of one hundred persons annually for countries within the Asia-Pacific Triangle. Gotanda observes that in these separate statutes, Chinese, Indians, Filipinos, and Guamanians were allowed to become U.S. citizens as *exceptions* to the whites-only barrier; he argues that the categorization of Asians as diverse, racialized ethnic groups, rather than as a single racialized category, supports and obscures the powerful centrality of the white racial category.[53] In other words, through the legal enfranchisement of specific Asian ethnic groups as *exceptions* to the whites-only classification, the status of Asians as *nonwhite* is legally restated and reestablished. Thus, the historical racialization of Asian-origin immigrants as nonwhite "aliens ineligible to citizenship" is actually rearticulated in the processes of legal enfranchisement and the ostensive lifting of legal discriminations in the 1950s.

The final abolition of Asian quotas came with the 1965 act. As the Immigration Reform and Control Act of 1986 and the Immigration Act of 1990 attest, however, immigration legislation continues to be the site for the resurgence of contradiction between capital and the state, between economic and political imperatives, between the "push-pull" of markets and the maintenance of civil rights and is riddled with conflicts as the state attempts to control through law what is also an economically driven phenomenon. In the 1990s, recent official immigration policies and de facto immigration policies express this contradiction around the "crisis" of illegal immigration, particularly from Mexico and Latin America (though Haitian and Chinese examples have also emerged). Reminiscent of the nineteenth-century laws barring Chinese from naturalization, education, and safe working conditions, California's Proposition 187 passed in 1994, attempts to deny schooling and medical care to illegal immigrants; although the referendum does not specify immigrants from Mexico and Latin America, its execution would certainly be aimed at these groups.[54]

Since the 1950s, undocumented immigrants from Mexico and Latin America have provided much of the low-wage labor in agriculture, construction, hotels, restaurants, and domestic services in the western and southwestern United States. The wages and working conditions of these jobs do not attract U.S. workers: state policy will not legislate the improvement of labor conditions, but neither does it declare officially that the U.S. economy systematically produces jobs that only third world workers find attractive. The result is an officially disavowed and yet unofficially mandated, clandestine movement of illegal immigration, which addresses the economy's need for low-wage labor but whose dehumanization of migrant workers is politically contradictory. In particular, the liberal principles of American democracy are profoundly at odds with a tiered hierarchy of immigrant populations, enforced by the police functions that control and regulate immigrant and refugee flows.[55] Again, as before, the state, and the law as its repressive apparatus, takes up the role of "resolving" the contradictions of capitalism with political democracy. The historical racial formation of Asian immigrants before 1965 has mediated the attempt to resolve the imperatives of capital and the state around the policing of the Asian. In the period since 1965, legal regulations on immigration include Asians among a broad segment of racialized immigrants, while the policing has refocused particularly on "alien" and "illegal" Mexican and Latino workers. Asian Americans, with the history of being constituted as "aliens," have the collective "memory" to be critical of the notion of citizenship and the liberal democracy it upholds; Asian American culture is the site of "remembering," in which the recognition of Asian immigrant history in the present predicament of Mexican and Latino immigrants is possible.

The legal genealogy of the Asian immigrant constitutes what Omi and Winant have called a "racial formation": the shifting construction of racial meanings formed in the dialectic between state categorization and social challenges to those categorizations, and the sociohistorical process by which racial meanings are created, lived, and transformed. They write: "The racial order is equilibrated by the state—encoded in law, organized through policy-making, and enforced by a repressive apparatus. But the equilibrium thus achieved is unstable, for the great variety of conflicting interests encapsulated in racial meanings and identities can be no more than pacified—at best—by the state."[56] Extending Omi and Winant's notion that racial formation is the changing product of the negotiations between social movements and the state, I have been arguing that the material contradictions of the national economy and the political state are expressed in the legal exclusion, disenfranchisement, and restricted enfranchisement of Asian immigrants and that culture is the material site of struggle in which active links are made between signifying practices and social structure.[57] Racism is not a fixed structure; society's notions about race are not static and immutable, nor has the state been built on an unchanging exclusion of all racialized peoples. Rather, legal institutions function as flexible apparatuses of racialization and gendering in response to the material conditions of different historical moments. Instead of understanding the law as merely a part of the "superstructure" that "reflects" social relations, I have posited that legal institutions *reproduce* the capitalist relations of production as *racialized gendered relations* and are therefore symptomatic *and* determining of the relations of production themselves. In other words, immigration law reproduces a racially segmented and stratified labor force for capital's needs, inasmuch as such legal disenfranchisements or restricted enfranchisements seek to resolve such inequalities by deferring them in the promise of equality on the political terrain of representation. The state governs through the political terrain, dictating in that process the forms and sites of contestation. Where the political terrain can neither resolve nor suppress inequality, it erupts in culture. Because culture is the contemporary repository of memory, of history, it is through culture, rather than government, that alternative forms of subjectivity, collectivity, and public life are imagined. This is not to argue that cultural struggle can ever be the exclusive site for practice; it is rather to argue that if the state suppresses dissent by governing subjects through rights, citizenship, and political representation, it is only through culture that we conceive and enact new subjects and practices in antagonism to the regulatory *locus* of the citizen-subject, by way of culture that we can question those modes of government.

The social movements of the 1960s and 1970s brought together Asian American struggles with those of African Americans, Native Americans, and Chicano-Latinos in a concerted demand for racial equality and social justice. These movements challenged institutionalized racial segregation and disenfranchisement through direct action and grassroots mobilization; through incursions into the political terrain (electoral projects from voter registration to community organizing to building alternative institutions); and through the development of "resistance cultures."[58] At that historical juncture, the extended set of social movements had a variety of targets and agendas, from the battle for educational space in universities to protests against the U.S. war in Vietnam, from community controls over housing to the transformation in the conditions of racialized laborers.[59] But precisely because *racialization* had been the site of the contradiction between the promise of political emancipation and the conditions of economic exploitation, the Civil Rights movement emerged as the organizing center for a cross-race mobilization of Asians, Blacks, Native Americans, and Chicanos simultaneously allied with the third world liberation struggles.[60] Because civil rights highlighted racialization as the site of this contradiction, its struggles were met as forcefully by state violence as by state attempts at political co-optation. Yet at the same time, civil rights struggles for racial equality could not but find themselves constrained precisely by the constitutive contradiction of liberal democracy: in a political system constituted by the historical exclusion and labor of racialized groups, the promise of inclusion through citizenship and rights cannot resolve the material inequalities of racialized exploitation. In focusing the struggle in the political domain, the civil rights project extended the opportunities of some segments of minority communities and made substantial gains; by demanding that the state extend its promise of freedom and opportunity to Black auto industry workers, Japanese American internees, and Chicano agricultural laborers, it focused attention on the fundamental condition that the American nation has been built on the exploitation and political exclusion of these populations. The demand for civil rights for racialized people heightened the contradictions inherent in the promise of universal equality; it addressed civil society and the state in terms of that promise, as if it actually embodied those principles of universal distribution of opportunity, property, and livelihood. Yet the civil rights project confronts its limits where the pursuit of enfranchisement coincides with a refortification of the state as the guarantor of rights and precludes the necessary critique of the state as the protector of liberal capitalism, steadily dividing the racialized labor forces it continues to exclude from those rights. The persistence of racial inequality that exists in the United States in our present moment derives not from a failure of strategy or a lack of will on the part of the movements for civil rights but from the continuation of a system of property that profits through racialization. Civil rights struggles deepen the contradiction of liberal democracy and throw into relief the unabated and new forms of racialized subordination, thereby converging with the ongoing struggles calling for radical transformations of U.S. society for the redistribution of resources for all people.

The historical necessity, gains, and limits of the civil rights project offer us an important analysis of citizenship as a site of contradiction for racialized Americans. The formation of Asian Americans, in particular, with a specific genealogy of racialization in relation to citizenship, gives us access to a critique of both the liberal theory of democratic society and the Marxist criticism of that liberal theory. The liberal political understanding of citizenship emerged in the late eighteenth century in the wake of the French and American Revolutions that overturned older feudal arrangements, and the concept of citizenship as political emancipation was established to secure the "rights of man" in civil society. The *Declaration of the Rights of Man and of the Citizen* (1793) enumerates the rights of man to include equality, liberty, security, and property; in this last regard, the Constitution of the United States states: "The right of property is that which belongs to every citizen of enjoying and disposing as he will of his goods and revenues, of the fruits of his work and industry." The state is the political form that protects and secures those rights and freedoms. Article 2 of the *Declaration of the Rights of Man and of the Citizen* of 1791 reads: "The end of every *political association* is the *preservation* of the natural and imprescriptible rights of man." Article 1 of the Declaration of 1793 states: "Government is instituted in order to guarantee man's enjoyment of his natural and imprescriptible rights." As Marx points out in "On the Jewish Question," in liberal capitalist societies, it is the property system that underlies the concept of "rights" in the civil society for which the political state is the abstract guarantor.

The most powerful contradiction of liberal democracy arises from the condition that each individual man's right to property violates the rights of others. Liberal political theory embodied in the Constitution establishes that the right to liberty in civil society ceases to be a right when it conflicts with political life, yet if political life is that which guarantees the rights of the individual man to property, then the political sphere becomes no more than a guarantor of capitalist relations of exploitation. Marx defines *man* as the subject of civil society (which is "the sphere of human needs, labour, private interests and civil law"), whereas the *citizen* is the abstract subject of the political state guaranteeing that civil society and the capitalist relations therein; the abstraction of the *citizen* is always in distinction to the particularity of *man*'s material condition. In this context, for Marx, "political emancipation" of the *citizen* is the process of relegating to the domain of the private all "nonpolitical" particulars of religion, social rank, education, occupation, and so on in exchange for representation on the political terrain of the state where "man is the imaginary member of an imaginary sovereignty, divested of his real, individual life, and infused with an unreal universality."[61] For Marx, "political emancipation" of the *citizen* permits the reproduction of capitalist social relations and the relations of production. Marx's critique unmasks the political state as the apotheosis of the property system in capitalist nations and points to the need for a critique of citizenship and "rights" defined as the right to property or, in effect, the right of the capitalist to exploit.

The specific history of the United States and the crucial role of racialized immigrant labor, however, reveal the limits of Marx's analysis of the state and civil society. To the extent that Marx adopts the abstract and universalist propositions of the economic and political spheres, his classic critique of citizenship cannot account for the particular racialized relations of production on which this nation has been founded. Despite its trenchant indictment of liberal democracy as the protector of capitalist relations, Marx's theory cannot account for the historical conditions through which U.S. capital profited precisely from racializing Chinese, Japanese, and Filipino immigrant labor in distinction to white labor and excluding those racialized laborers from citizenship. Furthermore, it cannot account for the current global restructuring of capitalism in which U.S. capital maximizes its profits through strategies of "mixed production" and "flexible accumulation" that cross national boundaries, erode national political institutions such as citizenship, and make use of racialized female immigrant labor.⁶² Asian immigrant and Asian American communities can be one site for generating such a critique, for rather than exemplifying the assimilation of private "particularities" into the abstract universality of the national political sphere, Asian Americans formed through a history of racialized immigrant labor exploitation remain in contradiction with that universality or, indeed, inhabit the contradictions of that universality. Marx describes the dissolution of economic difference in its displacement onto the political terrain of representation in liberal democratic states; yet the historical exclusion that racializes Asian immigrant labor and the "formation" of the Asian American that rearticulates that racialization, even as citizen, reveal *race* to be that material evidence that cannot be dissolved into political representation. Therefore, it was on racial equality that the Civil Rights movement focused its energies and through race that a coalition of Blacks, Chicanos, and Asians could form. Yet these struggles have revealed that the granting of rights does not abolish the economic system that profits from racism.⁶³ In our present moment, it is an understanding of *race* not as a fixed singular essence, but as the *locus* in which economic, gender, sex, and race contradictions converge, that organizes current struggles for immigrant rights, prisoner's rights, affirmative action, racialized women's labor, and AIDS and HIV patients in communities of color. Both the "successes" and the "failures" of struggles over the last thirty years demonstrate the degree to which *race* remains, after citizenship, the material trace of history and thus the site of struggle through which contradictions are heightened and brought into relief.

According to liberal political theory and the Marxist critique, citizenship requires that the subject deny its particular private interests to become the "abstract citizen" of the political state. Rousseau described the exchange of the insecurities of nature for equal, civil freedom that is protected by the "social contract."⁶⁴ Marx described the negation of "private" individual particulars of the subject who becomes the "abstract citizen" of the political state. But for Asians within the history of the United States—as for African Americans, Native Americans, or Chicanos—"political emancipation" through citizenship is never an operation confined to the negation of individual "private" particulars; it requires the negation of a history of social relations that publicly racialized groups and successively constituted those groups as "nonwhites ineligible for citizenship." For Asian immigrants from Vietnam, Korea, or the Philippines, this negation involves "forgetting" the history of war in Asia and adopting the national historical narrative that disavows the existence of an American imperial project. It requires acceding to a political fiction of equal rights that is generated through the denial of history, a denial that reproduces the omission of history as the ontology of the nation. In contradistinction to liberal theories and Marxist critiques that abstractly propose the universal granting of citizenship to all members as the foundational moment of civil society and the state, the U.S. nation was founded exactly by establishing citizenship as a legal and political category for white male persons that historically excluded nonwhites and women and that guaranteed the rights of those white male citizens over nonwhites and women.[65] While the nation proposes immigrant "naturalization" as a narrative of "political emancipation" that is meant to resolve in American liberal democracy as a terrain to which all citizens have equal access and in which all are equally represented, it is a narrative that denies the establishment of citizenship out of unequal relationships between dominant white citizens and subordinated racialized noncitizens and women.

For Marx, the dissolution of economic inequality into political equality takes place to the extent that it is the tendency of capital to use "abstract labor," or labor as "use value" unencumbered by specific human qualities. In the *Grundrisse*, Marx describes abstract labor "as the use value which confronts money posited as capital, labour is not this or another labour, but *labour pure and simple*, abstract labour; absolutely indifferent to the particular substance of which a given capital consists; but since capital *as such* is indifferent to every particularity of its substance, and exists not only as the totality of the same but also as the abstraction from all its particularities, the labour which confronts it likewise subjectively has the same totality and abstraction itself."[66] According to Marx, abstract labor in the economic sphere underwrites abstract citizenship in the political sphere. Abstract labor, subject to capitalist rationalization and the logic of equivalence through wages, is the adjunct of the formal political equality granted through rights and representation by the state. Yet in the history of the

United States, capital has maximized its profits not through rendering labor "abstract" but precisely through the social productions of "difference," of restrictive particularity and illegitimacy marked by race, nation, geographical origins, and gender. The law of value has operated, instead, by creating, preserving, and reproducing the specifically racialized and gendered character of labor power. These processes of differentiation have provided the means for capital to exploit through the fracturing and segmentation of different sectors of the labor force. In his critical analysis of the economic and political spheres as they have been posited by liberal theory, Marx remains committed to Enlightenment universalisms through which we can neither account for the specificity of racialized Asian immigrant labor within the U.S. economy nor for the role of colonialism and imperialism in the emergence of the political nation. Moreover, the argument that capital accumulates through universal homogenization rather than through differentiation is contradicted, particularly, by the current global restructuring of capitalism in which operations of "flexible" capital accumulation and "mixed production" permit transnational corporations to maximize profit precisely by fragmenting production and moving parts of the assembly and manufacturing to sites in which manipulable, differentiated immigrant or third world labor can be most effectively employed. Asian immigrants and Asian Americans have been neither "abstract labor" nor "abstract citizens," but have been historically formed in contradiction to both the economic and the political spheres. Thus, this contradictory formation locates the Asian American in antagonism to the resolution of the citizen to the nation in a manner which is in contradiction to liberal ideologies and institutions, yet which cannot be fully captured by the Marxist critique: Asian American particularity returns a differently located dialectical critique of the universality proposed by both the economic and the political spheres.

Asian American critique proceeds immanently by inhabiting the historical formation of Asian immigrants and Asian Americans in contradiction with the economic and political spheres. Yet this critique extends to more than rearticulating itself as the negative residue of the nonuniversal. The dialectic of Asian American critique begins in the moment of negation that is the refusal to be the "margin" that speaks itself in the dominant forms of political, historical, or literary representation. This transforms the "minority" position from being the only form of inclusion within the universal postulates of the nation to a critique of liberal pluralism and its multicultural terrain. For, as the consideration of Asian American cultural forms in subsequent chapters demonstrates, the demand that the immigrant subject "develop" into an identification with the dominant forms of the nation gives rise to contradictory articulations that interrupt the demands for identity and identification, that voice antagonisms to the universalizing narratives of both pluralism and development, and that open Asian American culture as an alternative site to the American economic, political, and national cultural spheres. This dialectic not only addresses the dominant culture and the political state it represents but also reaches back into the reservoir of memory out of which the distinct forms and practices of Asian American culture itself emerge. The "past" that is grasped as memory is, however, not a naturalized, factual past, for the relation to that past is always broken by war, occupation, and displacement. Asian American culture "re-members" the past in and through the fragmentation, loss, and dispersal that constitutes that past. Asian American culture is the site of more than critical negation of the U.S. nation; it is a site that shifts and marks alternatives to the national terrain by occupying other spaces, imagining different narratives and critical historiographies, and enacting practices that give rise to new forms of subjectivity and new ways of questioning the government of human life by the national state.

American national culture takes up the role of resolving the history of inequalities left unresolved in the economic and political domains; where the state is unable to accommodate differences, it has fallen to the terrain of national culture to do so. Unlike English and European cultures that have traditionally sought, since the eighteenth century, an identity of culture, language, race, and nation, the material history of immigration and settlement in the U.S. has not allowed such fictions of cultural homogeneity. Owing to this different history, by the early twentieth century the American nation proposed a plurality of cultural origins that "melted" into the uniformity of American culture. By the 1960s, in light of civil rights struggles that forced into visibility the conditions of segregation beneath the promise of assimilation, the liberal vision of the "melting pot" was revised into "multiculturalism," a new "universalism" designed to accommodate the irreducible diversity of American society. This official "multiculturalism" is evidently quite different from the grassroots cross-racial coalitions that have worked for large-scale transformations of society, for the redistribution resources and opportunities, and for the retrieval of lost histories. "Multiculturalism" supplements abstract political citizenship where the unrealizability of the political claims to equality become apparent: it is the national cultural form that seeks to unify the diversity of the United States through the integration of differences as *cultural* equivalents abstracted from the histories of racial inequality unresolved in the economic and political domains. In Chapter 4, "Imagining Los Angeles in the Production of Multiculturalism," I discuss the "multicultural" aestheticization and commodification of racialized ethnic cultures and observe that, in general, aestheticization can take place only through "forgetting" the material histories of racialization, segregation, and economic violence. In the particular instance of Asian Americans, the consequences of such "forgettings" are very specific: Asian immigrants have been incorporated primarily through the economic sphere as labor and, since 1965, as labor and capital; yet, simultaneously, historical exclusion along racial and citizenship lines has explicitly distanced Asians, even as enfranchised Asian Americans, from the terrain of national culture. The contradictions of multicultural inclusion for Asian Americans are acute in ways that emerge from both a history of racial and political exclusion and a history of being "foreign" to the national cultural terrain.

In light of the importance of American national culture and its institutions in the education of subjects as citizens of the nation, the contradictory history of Asian Americans produces cultural forms that are materially and aesthetically at odds with the resolution of the citizen to the nation. This "difference" is not a matter of mere technical innovation that we might find in aestheticist texts that are critical of traditional forms and of mass culture but resides in racial formation as the material trace of history. The aesthetic theories of the Frankfurt school held that within conditions of mass culture, older traditional forms of human activity have been instrumentally reorganized according to capitalist rationality; for Adorno, Horkheimer, and others who theorized the increasingly universalized reification of culture, the last site of "cultural negativity" inhered in "high" modern-ist art.[67] Yet a quite different critique of universality emerges out of Asian American culture, situated differently in the material contradictions of history rather than in the marginalizations of autonomous "high" culture.[68] Contrary to what Adorno would term the "cultural negativity" of "high" art that might lie in the residual resistance of an abstract subject outside instrumentalized culture, Asian American "cultural negativity" inheres in the concrete particulars unassimilable to modern institutions, particulars that refuse both integration into dominant forms and the logic of exchange. The emergence of a racially differentiated U.S. society that cannot be captured adequately by the antinomy of mass and traditional culture obliges us to respecify historically what other sources of contradiction might exist aside from valorized modernist art. Asian American cultural forms neither seek to reconcile constituencies to idealized forms of community or subjectivity, nor propose those forms as "art" that resides in an autonomous domain outside of mass society and popular practices. Unlike either American national culture or "high" art, forms of Asian American culture and other racialized minority cultures emerge differently from those of traditionally conceived aesthetic projects.[69] Literary critic Sau-ling Wong has observed: "Asian American authors are not, as a mechanical analogy with universalistic Western ludic discourse would suggest, promoting a rarefied aestheticism. Instead, they are formulating an 'interested disinterested-ness' appropriate to their condition as minority artists with responsibilities to their community."[70]

Asian American cultural forms emphasize instead that because of the complex history of racialization, sites of minority cultural production are at different distances from the canonical nationalist project of resolution, whether posed in either national modern or postmodern multiculturalist versions. In Chapter 2, "Canon, Institutionalization, Identity," a discussion of the university as a contradictory site for Asian American formation, I consider the ways in which Asian American literature may produce effects of dissonance, fragmentation, and irresolution even and especially when that literature appears to be performing a canonical function.[71] The kind and degree of contradiction that exists between the historical specificities of immigrant displacement and racialization and canonized forms of national culture generates formal deviations whose significances are mis-read if simply assimilated as modernist or postmodernist aesthetic modes. Asian American work is not properly or adequately explained by the notion of postmodernism as an aesthetic critique of high modernism, for Asian American work emerges out of very different contradictions of modernity: out of the specific conditions of racialization in relation to modern insti-tutions of state government, bourgeois society's separate spheres, and the liberal citizen-subject. In Chapter 5, "Decolonization, Displacement, Dis-identification," I differentiate European and American postmodern chal-lenges to representation from the "decolonizing" writing that emerges from third world, diaspora, and racialized U.S. American sites. The effects of these works are more radically grasped in terms of their constant in-terrogation of the discrepancies between national modern forms and what Walter Benjamin would term the material "catastrophes" those forms ob-scure.[72] Just as the previous discussion highlighted the contradiction be-tween racialized Asian immigrant subjectivity and the abstract citizen pro-posed by the political sphere of representation, in the following chapters I argue that the subject that emerges out of Asian American cultural forms is one in excess of and in contradiction with the subjectivities proposed by national modern and postmodern modes of aesthetic representation.[73] The discussion of Asian American culture in the chapters that follow begins as "immanent critique" and considers the cultural dynamics of Asian Ameri-can work as revealing the contradiction between American claims to univer-sality and the particularities erased by those claims, but then dialectically replaces the work in the context of social determinations that generate the work's inner contradictions. Asian American critique proceeds immanently but enacts the shifting position of dialectical criticism; it can neither im-merse itself in the object in the manner of idealizing, redemptive criticism nor take a stand entirely outside culture to criticize the totality as reified.[74]

The contradictions that produce these particulars demand a different notion of the aesthetics of Asian immigrant work, which I elaborate in Chapter 5 and Chapter 6, "Unfaithful to the Original," as an aesthetic of "disidentification" and "infidelity." This aesthetic is as critical of representa-tional modes such as realism or naturalism as it is critical of a conception of autonomous art separated from material conditions. With regard to the discussion of aesthetics, the notion of "immigrant acts" attempts to locate in the works the "performativity" of immigration, that is, the aesthetics of disidentification and the practices of resignification that the "outsider-within" condition of Asians in America enables.[75] For example, in Chapter 6, I discuss the Korean immigrant's disidentification with the U.S. nation as being legible in Theresa Hak Kyung Cha's critique of the core values of aesthetic realism—correspondence, mimesis, and equivalence—which her text *Dictée* treats as contradictions. Through an aesthetic of fragmented recitation and episodic nonidentity, repetition is taken to its parodic extreme and disengaged as the privileged mode of imitation and realism. This aesthetic characterizes works that are the sites for the emergence of a new subject.

The contemporary social formation emerges out of a mode of production that conjoins distinct national economies with transnational forms of industry that rely on mixed production, flexible accumulation, and the mobility of capital. Hence, at the present moment, forms of the "modern" U.S. state—citizenship, law, police, military—conjoin with the "postmodern" movements and forces of the global economy, and the political subject that emerges out of this conjunction cannot be strictly captured by the terms of the national political sphere. Thus, "becoming a national citizen" cannot be the exclusive narrative of emancipation for the Asian American subject. Rather, the current social formation entails a subject less narrated by the modern discourse of citizenship and more narrated by the histories of wars in Asia, immigration, and the dynamics of the current global economy.[76] These new conditions displace a former conception of culture and the formation of the citizen it upheld, generating the need for an alternative understanding of cultural production. These discussions consider Asian American culture as one terrain on which the subject formerly narrated by the discourse of citizenship is superseded by a differently located political subject. I argue in Chapter 7, "Work, Immigration, Gender," that this subject comes into a political formation that is not that of an Asian American claim to citizenship within the nation but one that inhabits a new conjunction and its contradictions, radically challenging nationalist institutions and the simultaneous global economic exploitation of immigrant and third world labor, particularly women.

In keeping with the thesis that a new political subject allegorized by the "immigrant" is articulated simultaneously within both U.S. national and global frameworks, I move from a discussion of Asian American cultural production within a U.S. national context (Chapters 2–4) to one that places the question of Asian American and Asian immigrant culture within an international context (Chapters 5–7). The contradictions of the "nation" are never exclusively bounded in the "local"; rather, local particularisms implicate and are implicated in global movements and forces. This imbrication of the national formation of racialized groups within the global political economy is as relevant for Chicano/Latino culture and Anglo-American Black cultures as it is for Asian American culture. As José David Saldívar has argued in *The Dialectics of Our America*, "Local metanarratives never tell the whole story . . . and perhaps we are condemned to oscillate between two metanarratives—one of totalization, the other of emergence." [77] Likewise, in *The Black Atlantic*, Paul Gilroy described the Black "countercultures of modernity" that emerge in the space between nationalistic thinking and "the rhizomorphic, fractal structure of the transcultural, international formation" that is nationalism's antithesis. [78]

In Chapter 3, "Heterogeneity, Hybridity, Multiplicity," the material heterogeneities of Asian Americans, of class, gender, and national origin, are discussed in relation to both the modern U.S. nationalist and the oppositional Asian American "cultural nationalist" impulses toward identity. The argument I advance in the move from the contradictions of "the national" to the those of "the national-within-the-international" is that the "cultural nationalist" formation of some Asian American work is motivated by a desire to represent, to make visible the erased and evacuated histories in realist and naturalist modes, and to regard representation of the racialized ethnic group through the aesthetic work as the political function of culture within both an Asian American cultural nationalist and a U.S. national framework. In contrast, contemporaneous work that dialectically engages with the national formation of Asian Americans from the perspective of an international history and location is critical of the representational project and is antagonistic to the "modern" in both aesthetic and political senses. These cultural projects offer alternatives to realist narratives of resolution to the nation, working against the notion of the subject as representative of the nation or group in order to generate conceptions of collectivity that are neither regulated by notions of identity nor prescribed by aesthetic, psychoanalytic, and political modes of identification.

In the former project, the immigrant is fixed and taken as the *symbol* of Asian Americans; as a figure, the immigrant conveys an "ideal type" who represents the generalized condition of the group. In such symbolic figurations, there is a persistent belief in a knowable social totality of which the representative figure is a reflection and in terms of which that figure can be recognized. In the latter project, however, the immigrant is at once both *symbol* and *allegory* for Asian Americans. The immigrant is located in social relations and dialectically placed within historical process and struggle, but the concept of allegory presumes that social and historical processes are not transparent, taking place through what Benjamin calls "correspondences" rather than through figures that represent or reflect a given totality.[79] Such correspondences are neither resemblances nor analogies, but displaced, mediated connections in which the "seizing" of the relation depends not only on a formal analysis of the social and historical conditions but also on the simultaneous comprehension of a displacement, a break, or even an absence—all signaling the impossibility of totality.

The latter project proposes immigration as the *locus* for the encounter of the national border and its "outsides" as the site of both the law and the "crossing of the borders" that is its negative critique. Immigration as both *symbol* and *allegory* does not metaphorize the experiences of "real" immigrants but finds in the located contradictions of immigration both the critical intervention in the national paradigm at the point of its conjunction with the international and the theoretical nexus that challenges the global economic from the standpoint of the locality. In addition, the allegory of immigration does not isolate a singular instance of one immigrant formation, but cuts across individualized racial formations and widens the possibility of thinking and practice across racial and national distinctions. The specific history of Asian immigration in relation to U.S. citizenship is different from the histories of other migrant or racialized groups, such as African Americans, Native Americans, and Chicanos/Latinos, yet the Asian American critique of citizenship generated by its specific history opens the space for such cross-race and cross-national possibilities. One of the important *acts* that the immigrant performs is breaking the dyadic, vertical determination that situates the subject in relation to the state, building instead horizontal community with and between others who are in different locations subject to and subject of the state. Asian American culture is thus situated to generate what Dipesh Chakrabarty has termed "other narratives of self and community that do not look to the state/citizen bind as the ultimate construction of sociality."[80]

Canon, Institutionalization,

Identity: Asian American Studies

In our headlong rush to educate everybody, we are . . . destroying our ancient
edifices to make ready the ground upon which the barbarian nomads of the
future will encamp in their mechanised caravans.
           —T. S. Eliot, *Notes Towards a Definition of Culture* (1949)

Mrs. Hammerick . . . Boiling Spring Elementary School . . . I was scared of
her like no dark corners could ever scare me. You have to know that all the
while she was teaching us history . . . she was telling all the boys in our class
that I was Pearl and my last name was Harbor. They understood her like she
was speaking French and their names were all Claude and Pierre. I felt it in
the lower half of my stomach, and it throbbed and throbbed.
           —Monique Thuy-Dung Truong, "Kelly" (1991)

In the previous chapter, I argued that the modern nation-state forms abstract citizens for the political sphere, disavowing the racialization and gendering of noncitizen labor in the economic sphere through the reproduction of an exclusive notion of national culture in the cultural sphere. Here,
I extend this argument to focus on the liberal educational apparatus of the
university as an important site in which these processes come into contradiction. Approaching the question of Asian American Studies in the university as one location of visible struggles over culture, education, and citizenship, I pose T. S. Eliot's 1949 lament that democratized education puts
Western culture at risk from the encroachments of both non-Western cultures and mass culture against Monique Thuy-Dung Truong's 1991 short

37

story "Kelly" in order to ground my discussion in two fundamental relationships. First, the juxtaposition of Eliot's nostalgia for the "ancient edifice"
of Western culture and Truong's story of a Vietnamese immigrant girl in a
North Carolina classroom renders explicit a relationship between the culturalist narrative that valorizes Western culture as a separate sphere and the
materially, racially, and sexually differentiated society against which that
notion of autonomous culture is constructed and whose contradictions it
works to conceal. Second, I hope my discussion may reinscribe a connection between the developmental narrative that privileges the elite subject
of a "prior" Western civilization and the voiceless invisibility imposed on
students of color in the classroom produced by that narrative. In this chapter, I explore the institutionalization of Asian American literary study as
a medium for the contradictions implied by these two relationships and
consider the importance of Asian American Studies as an oppositional site
from which to contest the educational apparatus that reproduces and continues to be organized by Western culturalist, as well as developmental,
narratives. Considering the contemporary university as an "ideological state
apparatus," in which intellectual and pedagogical labors make and remake
alternative spaces by exploiting the contradictions of that state apparatus,
I locate the critical engagement with Asian American cultural identity in
the university as a *locus* of struggle by focusing especially on questions of
literary canon and the formation of the subject. In the following chapter, I
will turn to a discussion of popular culture in order to continue this critical interrogation of the production of Asian American cultural identity by
dominant institutions and within the discourse of Asian American cultural
politics itself. In both discussions, I suggest that while Asian American
cultural identity emerges in the context of the racialized exclusion of Asian
immigrants from enfranchisement in the political and cultural spheres of
the United States, important contradictions exist between an exclusively
Asian American cultural nationalist construction of identity and the material heterogeneity of the Asian American constituency, particularly class,
gender, and national-origin differences among peoples of Asian descent in
the United States.

We need not look far to find residues of Eliot's distress over Western
cultural "disintegration" within contemporary American discourse about

education; William Bennett, Lynne Cheney, Allan Bloom, Dinesh D'Souza, and others have contributed their share to this concerted lament. Yet, it is evident that these attempts to maintain a fixed, autonomous notion of Western culture belie precisely the material strata and social differentiations for which this notion has traditionally functioned as a resolution. As Mas'ud Zavarzadeh and Donald Morton have pointed out, the rise of modern humanities in the eighteenth century and their institutionalization in the nineteenth century were themselves directly related to the rise of the Western bourgeoisie, who won their battle with the old aristocracy by redefining the liberal subject in the context of competition by free agents in the marketplace.[1] In the last half of the twentieth century in the United States, society's need for a trained, yet stratified labor force; the Civil Rights movement that exposed the realities of race beneath the promise of democracy; as well as post-1965 increases in racialized immigrant populations: each have made it all the more difficult for contemporary discourse about education, both liberal and neoconservative, to ignore, as Eliot's nostalgia for "a more articulated society" did, the mandate for the democratization and diversification of the modern educational apparatus. In this sense, the neoconservative educational agenda, as Henry Giroux and Peter McClaren have observed, operates through two platforms: on the one hand, through the advocacy of "cultural unification" and a demand for a recanonization of Western classics; and on the other, through an expansion (at the expense of humanities or social science research) of a technicist or vocationalist curriculum that blames the demise of U.S. economic hegemony on the failure of education to train competitive professional and technical classes adequately.[2] The liberal discourse on education has challenged this reformulation of a unified Western culture by advocating a diversification of the humanities curriculum and urging an integration of the university through student and faculty affirmative action. Yet to the degree that liberal challenges have remained wedded to a culturalist paradigm, however "multiculturalist," that still tends to isolate culture from material relations, they have yet to disrupt adequately the neoconservative management of the function of university education. The university continues to be organized by means of a bifurcated conception that at once protects Western cultural study as a largely autonomous domain and "democratizes" the institution

only to the extent that it addresses the needs of an increasingly heterogeneous student population through the development of business, engineer-
ing, technical, and other professionalizing programs. The result is a contradiction in which "culture" remains canonical in the traditional Western
European sense, while the educational system (claiming a "multicultural"
conscience) serves to socialize and incorporate students from other backgrounds into the capitalist market economy. In Martin Carnoy's analysis,
the contradiction which brings new social groups into the educational system for vocationalization but which continues to universalize a closed, autonomous notion of culture precisely implies "an exploitable political space
for those that are willing to engage in the struggle for change."[3]

In contemporary universities, (this contradiction is visibly animated in
the emergence of interdisciplinary fields, such as Ethnic Studies, Women's
Studies, Third World Studies, and Cultural Studies. Interdisciplinary
studies express contradiction—or in Carnoy's terms, "exploitable political
space"—to the degree that they provide the sites from which to reevaluate
disciplinary methods that assume Western cultural autonomy and the universality of the Western subject. Interdisciplinary studies disrupt the narratives of traditional disciplines that have historically subordinated the concerns of non-Western, racial and ethnic minority peoples, and women,
insofar as they hold the potential to transform disciplinary divisions that
guarantee the self-evidence of these narratives. In women's studies, for
example, work by and about women of color—for example, the very different theoretical work of Chela Sandoval, Kimberlé Crenshaw, or Evelyn
Nakano Glenn—illustrates this interdisciplinarity to the degree that this
work makes use of a varied constellation of critical apparatuses that refuses
univocality, totalization, and scholarly indifference.[4] This work redefines
the traditional separations of the scholar-subject and the object of study;
it persistently argues for the inseparability of the nonequivalent determinations of race, class, and gender. To the extent that the university and its
institutionalized divisions of knowledge production often pressures interdisciplinary studies to formalize and legitimate themselves in terms of
established criteria, however, interdisciplinary programs and departments
have always needed to be vigilant in relation to institutionalization. In this
sense, Ethnic Studies scholars do not reproduce the methods of literary,

historical, or sociological studies merely to celebrate "ethnic culture" as an object separated from the material conditions of production and reception; they theorize, in a critical, dialectical manner, the relationship between cultural artifacts and the social groupings by which they are produced and which they, in turn, help to produce.⁵ At the same time, (institutionalizing such fields as Ethnic Studies still contains an inevitable paradox: institutionalization provides a material base within the university for a transformative critique of traditional disciplines and their traditional separations, and yet the institutionalization of any field or curriculum that establishes orthodox objects and methods submits in part to the demands of the university and its educative function of socializing subjects into the state.)While institutionalizing interdisciplinary study risks integrating it into a system that threatens to appropriate what is most critical and oppositional about that study, the logic through which the university incorporates areas of interdisciplinarity provides for the possibility that these sites will remain oppositional forums, productively antagonistic to notions of autonomous culture and disciplinary regulation and to the interpellation of students as univocal subjects. In terms of Asian American Studies, the approach to questions of reading texts, constituting objects of study, and teaching students can determine the extent to which Ethnic Studies serves the traditional function of the university and the extent to which it provides for a continuing and persistent site from which to educate students to be actively critical of that traditional function.

One manner by which Asian American Studies' interdisciplinarity and self-determination can be incorporated into the university is through a particular deployment of a brand of "multiculturalism," which must be clearly distinguished from panethnic or cross-racial coalitions of students and faculty which ally with other groups around the demand for more radical transformations of the university.⁶ Exploiting the notion of "multiculturalism," the university can refer to the study of ethnic cultures in its claim to be an institution to which all racial and ethnic minority groups have equal access and in which all are represented, while masking the degree to which the larger institution still fails to address the needs of populations of color. For example, though many universities have begun to reappraise their curricula in the humanities, adding texts by non-Western or female

authors to Western civilization courses, there are fewer Black students attending college today than in 1975. A multiculturalist agenda may thematize the pressures that demographic increases of immigrant, racial, and
ethnic populations bring to the educational sphere. But these pressures are
registered only partially and inadequately when the studies of ethnic traditions are, on an intellectual level, assimilated as analogues of Western
European traditions or exoticized as primitive and less "developed" and,
on an institutional level, tokenized as examples of the university's commitment to "diversity," while being marginalized through underfunding. Such
pluralist multiculturalism may be, for the contemporary period, a central
arena for what Antonio Gramsci called "hegemony," the process by which a
ruling group gains "consent" of its constituents to determine the cultural,
ideological, and political character of a state. The terrain of multiculturalism is then marked by the incorporative process by which a ruling group
elicits the "consent" of racial, ethnic, or class minority groups through the
promise of equal participation and representation; but to the extent that
multiculturalism—as a discourse designed to recuperate conflict and difference through inclusion—is itself the index of crisis in a specific dominant formation, the terrain of multiculturalism also provides for the activities of racial, class, and sexual minority groups who organize and contest
that domination. Within this context, we can appreciate the evident importance of self-determined interventions by groups that both distinguish
themselves from liberal multiculturalism and do not exclusively reproduce
pluralist arguments of inclusion and rights.

The establishment of a canon of Asian American literature is one part of a
project of institutional change within which racialized Americans as social
subjects articulate an educational space within the university and constitute literary objects as expressions of a distinct, self-determining group and
through which the notion of the "subject" interpellated by the university is
altered and revised in light of the heterogeneous social formations of racialized immigrant subjects. Yet, paradoxically, according to the contradiction
that I have just outlined, the definition of an "ethnic literature," figured
by an "ethnic canon," may compromise the *critical* project of institutional
change if it is forced to subscribe to criteria defined by the majority canon

in order to establish the formal unity of a literary tradition; for it is precisely the standard of a literary canon that the Eurocentric and professionalizing university demands of Asian Americans and other racial and ethnic minority cultures so as to formalize those cultures as "developed" traditions. In drawing a distinction between "major" and "minor" literatures, David Lloyd has argued that the Anglo-European function of canonization is to unify aesthetic culture as a domain in which material stratifications and differences are reconciled. A "major" literary canon traditionally performs that reconciliation by means of a selection of works that uphold a narrative of ethical formation in which the individual relinquishes particular differences through an identification with a universalized form of subjectivity; a "minor" literature may conform to the criteria of the "major" canon, or it may interrupt the function of reconciliation by challenging the concepts of identity and identification and by voicing antagonisms to the universalizing narrative of development.[7] In response to the demand that the Asian American canon function as a supplement or corollary to the "major" tradition of Anglo-American literature, Asian American literary texts often reveal heterogeneity rather than reproducing regulating ideas of cultural identity or integration. On one level, this heterogeneity is expressed in the unfixed, unclosed field of texts written by authors at different distances and generations from cultures as different as Chinese, Japanese, Korean, Philippine, Indian, Vietnamese, and Lao—or, as in the case of Hawaiian and Pacific Islander cultures, not *immigrants* at all but colonized, dispossessed, and deracinated.[8] The Asian American constituency is composed of men and women of exclusively Asian parents and of mixed race, of refugees and nonrefugees, of the English speaking and the non-English speaking, of people of urban, rural, and different class backgrounds, and of heterosexuals as well as gays and lesbians. For this reason, even when anthologies have offered selected literary works to represent the tradition, such as in *Aiiieeeee!: An Anthology of Asian-American Writers* (1975) or the more recent *Forbidden Stitch: An Asian American Women's Anthology* (1989) and *Unbroken Thread: An Anthology of Plays by Asian American Women* (1993), their editors have clearly historicized their definitions as products of particular moments of Asian American cultural definition and, to thematize the possibility of shifts, revisions, and different formations, to account for the heterogeneous and uneven development of the various groups that make up the Asian American community.[9] Mayumi Tsutakawa writes of *Forbidden Stitch*, for example, that "no one should think of this book as the single definitive text. . . . This is not a book with a shelf life of forever" (14).

On another level, the literature expresses heterogeneity not merely in the constituency it is construed to "represent" but also in the manners through which it puts into relief the material conditions of production. Indeed, the study of Asian American literature has been historically an endeavor that has been committed to a consideration of the work in terms of its material contexts of production and reception. For this reason, Elaine Kim's immeasurably important first critical study, *Asian American Literature: An Introduction to the Writings and Their Social Context* (1982), emphasizes "how the literature elucidates the social history of Asians in the United States" rather than focusing exclusively on "the formal literary merit" of those works.[10] Kim makes clear that her decision to interrogate Asian American literature as an expression of social context is due not to the literature's lack of stylistic or rhetorical complexity but to the way in which the literature itself captures a "movement between social history and literature." Asian American literature, by virtue of its distance from the historical formation of American national literature, resists the formal abstraction of aestheticization and canonization. We have understood that the moment of "cultural negativity" in Asian American literature resides not in its status as autonomous "high" art but in material contradictions of history that generate concrete particulars unassimilable to dominant forms. If Asian American literary expression is evaluated in exclusively canonical terms, it reveals itself as an aesthetic product that cannot repress the material inequalities of its conditions of production; its aesthetic is defined by contradiction, not sublimation, such that discontent, nonequivalence, and irresolution call into question the project of abstracting the aesthetic as a separate domain of unification and reconciliation. It is a literature that, if subjected to a canonical function, dialectically returns a critique of that function.

In this sense, just as the conception of an Asian American canon animates a contradiction between an institutional demand for assimilation to major criteria and the unassimilable alterity of racialized cultural difference, so too do Asian American works themselves precisely underscore

the tension between unifying American cultural narratives and the heterogeneous, intersecting formations of racialized immigrant subjects that are
antagonistic to those narratives. Considering one of the core works of Asian
American literature—Carlos Bulosan's *America Is in the Heart* (1943)—we
observe that on one level the novel may be read as an Asian American version of the form of the bildungsroman, or novel of formation, to the degree
that it narrates the protagonist's development from the uncertainty, locality,
and impotence of "youth" to the definition, mobility, and potency of "maturity." At the same time, to the degree that the narrative captures the complex, unsynthetic constitution of the immigrant subject between an already
twice-colonized Philippine culture, on the one hand, and the pressure to
conform to Anglo-American society, on the other, it troubles the closure
and reconciliation of the bildungsroman form. Whether the novel is read
as a narrative of immigrant assimilation or even as a narrative of successful
self-definition (the hero leaves the poverty and lack of opportunity of the
Philippines to become a laborer in the United States; he achieves a state of
self-consciousness that allows him to become a journalist and to author his
autobiography), both characterizations privilege a telos of development that
closes off the most interesting conflicts and indeterminacies in the text. In
addition, reading the novel as an analogue of the European novel subordinates Asian American culture in several significant ways: not only does the
form itself structurally imply an integration and submission of individual
particularity to a universalized social norm (which, in the case of the Asian
American novel, is racial or ethnic difference coded as anterior to, less than,
Western civilization), but in privileging a nineteenth-century European
genre as the model to be approximated, Asian American literature is cast
as imitation, mimicry, the underdeveloped other. For these reasons, we can
attend instead to the ways in which a novel such as *America Is in the Heart*
does not comply with the notion of a unified aesthetic form and how the
concepts of development, synthesis, and identity are themselves challenged
in the text. Taught as an ethnic bildungsroman, as a tale of the subject's
journey from foreign estrangement to integrated citizenship, the novel responds to the reconciliatory and universalizing functions of canonization;
taught with attention to social and historical, as well as formal and the-
matic, contradictions, the novel may eloquently thematize how the demand

for canonization simultaneously produces a critique of canonization itself.

Bulosan's novel portrays its hero as highly seduced by the notion of individual freedom through education. The narrative that begins in the Philippines, where the hero's family sacrifices greatly to send their oldest son, Macario, to school, figures both English literacy and American education as paths to freedom and self-development, particularly in the myths of Robinson Crusoe and Abraham Lincoln. Once in the United States, however, the hero does not have access to formal schooling and is forced to teach himself; that he creates his own curriculum out of the fragments of books and resources available to him reveals the disjunction between the promise of education and the unequal access of different racial and economic groups to that education. From the outset, the protagonist's literary education is a disrupted, partial, and fragmentary one. Moreover, his "education" is equally informed by his observations of the exploitation, violence, marginality, and incarcerations suffered by Philippine immigrants to the United States, which further challenge his belief in the promise of American democracy. This contradiction is explicitly foregrounded when the narrator ponders the paradox of America: "Why was America so kind and yet so cruel? Was there no way to simplifying things in this continent so that suffering would be minimized? Was there no common denominator on which we could all meet? I was angry and confused and wondered if I would ever understand this paradox." [11] When he suggests that there is a "common denominator on which we could all meet," the narrator poses his questions within the adopted language of democratic pluralism, a language that pronounces a faith in the promise of equal opportunity and inclusion. Yet it is precisely this notion of "common denominator" that the narrator comes to understand as contradictory and riddled with exceptions, strata, and exclusions, when he later quotes his brother Macario at length:

> America is a prophecy of a new society of men: of a system that knows no sorrow or strife or suffering. . . .
> America is also the nameless foreigner, the homeless refugee, the hungry boy begging for a job and the black body dangling on a tree. America is the illiterate immigrant who is ashamed that the world of books and intellectual opportunities is closed to him. We are all that nameless foreigner, that homeless refugee, that hungry boy, that illit-

erate immigrant and that lynched black body. All of us, from the first
Adams to the last Filipino, native born or alien, educated or illiterate—
We are America! (188–89)

In this later meditation, two starkly different visions of "America" are posed
against each other: the national fiction of democratic nation-state without
sorrow or suffering, and a nation whose members barely survive owing
to exclusion from that nation-state. The "America" that is "in the heart"
is a stratified, contradictory figure divided between the named promise
of democracy and the unnamed refugees, immigrants, and victims of violence who live beneath that promise. In this sense, the proclamation "We
are America!" does not represent an identification of the immigrant subject with the national fiction of inclusion so much as it contests that identification by inserting a heterogeneous "we"—"that nameless foreigner,
that homeless refugee, that hungry boy, that illiterate immigrant and that
lynched black body"—into the concept of polity. This insertion introduces
antinomy into the promise of synthesis, displaces unity with antagonism,
and renders visible the political differentiation and disenfranchisement
prematurely resolved by a fiction of reconciliation; through the insertion
of these *allegories* of immigration, the figure of "the immigrant" is unfixed
as *symbol* and *bildung* and dialectically placed within the shifting formation
of history. The narrative of *America Is in the Heart* is punctuated throughout by the continual migration of Filipino work crews that move from job
to job up and down the western United States, and the novel closes with a
description of the narrator departing again with another crew en route to
Portland. He observes, from the window of the bus, a group of workers in
the fields: "I wanted to shout good-by to the Filipino pea pickers. . . . How
many times in the past had I done just that?" (326). The novel ends with the
repetition of yet another departure and relocation, framed as symptomatic
of a continuing inequality between powerful agribusiness capital and immigrant labor, rather than with settlement, permanence, or resolution. It is an
uneven, divided notion of America that concludes the novel, rather than a
naturalized unification of those unevennesses and divisions. Thus, *America
Is in the Heart* does not "develop" the narrating subject's identification with
a uniform American nation: the achievement of narrative voice is precisely
the effect of the subject's critical estrangement from and dissymmetrical

relationship to American culturalist, economic, and nationalist formations.

The manner in which Asian American literature refuses the premature reconciliation of Asian immigrant particularity is also illustrated by three novels that portray the internment and relocation of first- and second-generation Japanese in the United States and Canada during World War II. Monica Sone's *Nisei Daughter* (1953), John Okada's *No-No Boy* (1957), and Joy Kogawa's *Obasan* (1981) each represent different narrative treatments of Japanese North Americans during and following the internment, men and women who were forced either to identify with the Japanese state and be named enemies of the United States, or Canada, or to assimilate unquestioningly to American or Canadian culture and to repudiate any Japanese cultural affiliation. This impossibly binary demand, encountered in different ways by the protagonists of all three novels, is not dissimilar to the predicament of many racialized minority peoples who face disenfranchisement unless they abandon their particular cultures to become citizens assimilated by way of a common culture. Yet for Japanese American and Japanese Canadian men and women, this process was coercively enforced through physical detention in the camps and for nisei men through the demand that they prove their patriotism by enlisting in the armed services to fight against Japan. In portraying the effects of the internment on Japanese North Americans, none of the novels delivers an undivided, assimilated subject who comes to identify with the American or Canadian citizenry; all three narratives refuse, in different manners, to develop, reconcile, and resolve.

Of the three novels, Sone's *Nisei Daughter* is formally the most conventional—a semiautobiographical first-person narrative that proceeds linearly from a girlhood in the Seattle Japanese community, moves through and beyond the events of the internment, and ends by pronouncing that "the Japanese and American parts of me were now blended into one."[12] But because of *Nisei Daughter*'s depiction of anti-Japanese racism, employment segregations, immigration restrictions, and ultimately the internment, the blending of "Japanese" and "American" is conceived only in terms of the larger structure of unequal power within which Japanese Americans are subordinated by the U.S. government. Throughout the novel, many scenes dramatize the nonequivalent force of Japanese and American cultures on the nisei, and this nonequivalence contextualizes the final statement of "blending" as a rhetorical response to the demand that the nisei resolve their identity issues by assimilating as American citizens. Considering the larger narrative, we can read for the "false ring" of the ending, can call its premature resolution into question. While the nisei child rebels against the normalizing expectations of both Japanese and American socializations, the Japanese customs are encouraged by parents and family friends, whereas the representative agents of American ways are armed policemen who, in one episode, storm into the Itoi home to arrest Kazuko's father on false charges of which he is later cleared. Thus, midway through the novel when the Itoi family is interned, this nonequivalence becomes even more explicit, and the narrative turns into a concerted critique of the suppression of Japanese and Japanese Americans by the U.S. government. After a family friend has been abducted by the FBI, the Itois are warned that they must destroy everything and anything Japanese that could incriminate them, yet Kazuko cannot bring herself to destroy all the Japanese items in their home: "I gathered together my well-worn Japanese language schoolbooks which I had been saving over a period of ten years with the thought that they might come in handy when I wanted to teach Japanese to my own children. I threw them into the fire and watched them flame and shrivel into black ashes. But when I came face to face with my Japanese doll which Grandmother Nagashima had sent me from Japan, I rebelled" (155). The destruction of Japanese-language books described in this passage emblematizes the ways in which Japanese Americans were forced to internalize the negation of Japanese culture and to assimilate to Anglo-American majority culture during World War II. Kazuko's refusal to destroy all Japanese items is reiterated at other moments in the novel in which she expresses defiant anger at the treatment of the Japanese—for example, in the rage she feels while looking at the barrel of the soldier's gun pointed toward internees boarding a bus (170). These moments, which underscore the attempted destruction of Japanese American cultural forms by the U.S. state and its repressive military and police apparatuses, render the final "blending" of two equal parts a provisional response to both social and canonical demands for resolution. Rather than a final synthesis which denies the damage of the internment or which reconciles the Japanese American subject divided by the "enemy/not enemy" logic of the state, we can read the declaration of Japanese and American "blending" as a manner of naming a continuing project of suspicion and survival as the nisei subject narrates the violence of a system that demands assimilation through internment, obligatory patriotism, and military service.

The suspicion beneath the premature reconciliation of Nisei Daughter is thrown even further into relief when Sone's text is considered in conjunction with Okada's No-No Boy, a novel of discontent in which the Japanese American protagonist angrily refuses adjustment to his postinternment and postimprisonment circumstances, and Kogawa's Obasan, a weave of personal, familial, and historical memory whose formal modernism suggests the recomposition of fragments, rather than a unified development, as the narrative expression of the relocated Japanese Canadian subject.[13] Virtually ignored when it was published in 1957 and rejected by the reading public for its uncompromisingly unconventional style, No-No Boy was reissued in 1976 by the University of Washington Press after an excerpt of it was featured in the anthology Aiiieeeee! No-No Boy may be characterized as a realist narrative to the extent that its action proceeds chronologically. But it is antidevelopmental in the sense that its condensed, almost static portrait takes place within the small period of several weeks, and it repeatedly undermines uniperspectivalism by alternating inconsistently between a third-person omniscient narration and despairing, angry, or confused interior monologues. The narrative shifts back and forth between different voices within long, run-on sentences, conveying the confusion and entropy of the protagonist Ichiro on his return to Seattle after two years of internment and two subsequent years in prison for refusing to serve in the U.S. Army, and documenting his bitter confusion, isolation, and shame as he confronts nisei soldiers and veterans, nisei women, white Americans, his parents, and other Japanese issei. Ichiro is a deeply divided subject, antagonistic both to the American government that interned and imprisoned Japanese Americans and to Japanese patriots like his mother who feverishly deny Japan's defeat in the war; in effect, the "no-no boy" not only refuses loyalty to either Japan or the United States but also refuses the "enemy/not-enemy" logic of the choice itself. Just as Ichiro's "no" dramatizes the Asian American subject's refusal to accept the dividing, subordinating terms of assimilation, so the novel's stasis, fragmentation, and discontent refuse the development, synthesis, and reconciliation required by traditional canonical criteria.

Formally more complex than either *Nisei Daughter* or *No-No Boy*, Kogawa's *Obasan* makes use of different narrative and dramatic techniques to portray the splitting, silencing, and irresolution of Japanese Canadian subjects. The novel's opening places the narrator in 1972, three decades after the internment and relocation of the Japanese Canadians; the text moves back and forth between different time periods, making use of private memory, dreams, diaries, letters, and documented history to dramatize the narrator's project of reconstructing the events which led to the loss of her mother, father, and grandparents and to the fragmented dispersal of other family and community during the relocation and internment years. Yet the task of recomposing history out of silence and fragmentation requires the narrator first to recount her childhood sexual abuse by a neighbor, which has become conflated with the confiscation of property and the dislocation of internment, as well as the separation from her mother who left for Japan the same year. Throughout the course of the novel, she must reach back to confront and bear the deaths of her uncle, father, grandfather, and grandmother and, ultimately, to piece together the details of her mother's anguished suffering in the atomic bombing of Nagasaki. The violences to the narrator and her family, figured throughout *Obasan* in metaphors of abuse, silence, darkness, and disease, cannot be lightened or healed; they can only be revealed, narrated, and reconfigured.[14] Out of the fragmentations of subject, family, and community, there emerges nothing like a direct retrieval of unified wholeness. Rather, the narrator retraces and recomposes an alternative "history" out of flashes of memory, tattered photographs, recollections of the mother's silence, and an aunt's notes and correspondence: dreams, loss, and mourning. In this sense, all three novels are antagonistic to the reconciliation of Asian American particularity within a narrative of development, as much as the formal differences between the three works further signify the discontinuous, heterogeneous range of Asian American alternative narratives.

There are other Asian American texts that even more dramatically disrupt the narrative that incorporates the immigrant subject into a national or cultural uniformity. For example, Theresa Hak Kyung Cha's *Dictée* (1982), which I discuss at greater length in Chapter 6, is a Korean American text that refuses to provide either a linear, unified development of the writing subject or an aesthetic synthesis or ethical resolution at the text's conclusion.[15] In combining autobiographical and biographical fragments, photographs, historical narrative, calligraphy, and lyric and prose poems in a complex multilingual piece, *Dictée* blurs conventions of genre and narrative authority, troubling the formal categories on which canonization depends. Furthermore, *Dictée* challenges the notion of a discrete typology of "Asian American experience," for it evokes a Korean American subject who not only is the product of multiple determinations—gender, language, religion—but bears the traces of differentiated layers of colonial and imperial dominations as well. The text juxtaposes a series of disparate episodes that alternately depict subjects incompletely formed within specific linguistic and historical circumstances: for example, the first section thematizes the use of dictation and recitation in the conversion of the student into a faithful French Catholic subject; the section "Clio" alludes to the disciplining of the Korean as colonial subject during the period of Japanese occupation (1910–1945); in "Melpomene" the narrator describes the incorporation of the individual into South Korean nationalism during the Korean War (1950–1953); and in "Calliope," written from the standpoint of a Korean American returning to South Korea, the narrator recalls her naturalization as an immigrant into American citizenship. The series of unfinished subject formations—illustrating the female student's antagonism to the educational and religious apparatuses, the colonized subject's disloyalty to the empire, and the Korean immigrant's incomplete incorporation into the U.S. state—suggests not only that subjectivity is multiply determined but also that each determination is uneven and historically differentiated, with no single one continuously or monolithically defining the subject. *Dictée* thus dramatizes that each interpellation organizes the female/colonized/postcolonial/racialized subject irregularly and incompletely, leaving a variety of residues that remain uncontained by and antagonistic to the educational, religious, colonial, and imperial modes of domination and assimilation. If one function of canonization is the resolution of material contradiction through a narrative of formation in which differences—of gender, race, nationality, or sexuality—are subsumed through the individual's identification with a universalized form, *Dictée* is a text that continually disrupts such identifications. *Dictée*, instead, "voices" the traces of colonial and imperial damage and dislocation on the Korean immigrant subject. In rearticulating the immigrant subject's displacement from the various national fictions of identity and development, it "performs" and imagines a new subject, for whom the "disidentification" from national forms of identity is crucial to the construction of new forms of solidarity.

Another important manner in which Asian American literature defies canonization is that it is a literature that is still being written—an unclosed, unfixed body of work whose centers and orthodoxies shift as the makeup of the Asian-origin constituency shifts and within which new voices are continually being articulated.[16] The diversity of contemporary interventions is evident in, for example, a 1991 collection of writing by younger Asian/Pacific authors, *Burning Cane,* a special issue of the *Amerasia Journal* that includes writings by Asian American gays and lesbians, by mixed-race Asian Americans, and by a variety of Southeast Asian American writers.[17] While *Burning Cane* is unified by a common project of articulating cultural resistance, the heterogenous selection of pieces suggests that given the increasingly various Asian American constituency, the profile of traits that characterize Asian American "identity" is as much in flux as the orthodoxy of which constituencies make up and define Asian American "culture." First-generation, post-1975 Southeast Asian writing introduces new themes to and emphasizes concerns different from those in the existing body of multigenerational Asian American literature—for example, some of the pieces in *Burning Cane* by newer immigrants focus on deracination and displacement, rather than on struggles against incorporation or assimilation. In T. C. Huo's short fiction "The Song Sent across the Mekong," the narrator meditates on the image of a man singing to a woman left behind on the riverbank as a paradigmatic figure for leaving, separation from family, and loss of homeland. While the narrator identifies with the man who has left, his mourning consists of different attempts at narrating the woman's position, reconstructing her thoughts and actions, and imagining her dead and alive. Huynh-Nhu Le's poem "Hearts & Minds" expresses a similar grief through a simple yet poignant chiasmus in which Vietnam, the poet's birthplace, is alien and unknown, whereas the new land of the United States is overly familiar, yet unwelcoming: "Vietnam: / A land I know not much, / A water I did not swim, / A mountain I did not climb / . . . / America: / A land I know quite well, / A river I might have drowned, / A mountain I have fallen." (98) The suppression of prepositions in Le's poem—not "A water I did not swim *through*, / A mountain I did not climb *up*," but "A water I did not swim, / A mountain I did not climb"—underscores the sense of displacement. Other stories in this collection broaden the spectrum of Asian American writing by depicting Asian American subjects as formed by a multiplicity of intersecting and conflicting determinations—gender, generation, sexuality, national origin, and economic class, as well as race and ethnicity; some explore the tensions and connections between subjects of different racial and ethnic backgrounds. The narrator of Patrick Leong's story "Graveyard Picnics" is a Chinese/Mexican American who, attending the gravesite of his Chinese grandfather, ponders whether he ought to worship the dead in the traditional Chinese ceremony led by his father or pray for them in church according to the Catholic traditions of his maternal family. Inheriting aspects of different cultural systems, yet belonging wholly to neither, the narrator finds himself located as a "hinge" between two separate but interlocking ethnic cultures. Wynn Young's "Poor Butterfly!" is narrated by a bitterly ironic, young Asian American gay, as he considers the fetishism of white gays who prefer Asian men and as he worries about being endangered by his partner's uncurbed sexual activity. Such a collection as *Burning Cane* opens up the definitions of what constitutes Asian American writing by drawing attention to recent immigrant writing and by featuring pieces that explore the intersecting, complex determinations that characterize the Asian American subject.

By way of conclusion, I return to the story by Monique Thuy-Dung Truong with which this discussion began, which appears in *Burning Cane*. The narrator is a Vietnamese American woman who recalls her elementary school education in a predominantly white town in North Carolina during the 1970s: "Mrs. Hammerick . . . I was scared of her like no dark corners could ever scare me. You have to know that all the while she was teaching us history . . . she was telling all the boys in our class that I was Pearl and my last name was Harbor. They understood her like she was speaking French and their names were all Claude and Pierre. I felt it in the lower half of my stomach, and it throbbed and throbbed. . . . It would be so many years . . . before I would understand that Pearl Harbor was not just in 1941 but in 1975."[18] Truong's story portrays the simultaneous indictment and silencing of the young Asian immigrant student within the classroom regulated by an American nationalist projection of the Asian as *enemy*. A binary logic of patriot and enemy invigorates American nationalism during the Vietnam War period, gathering more force through a conflation of the Viet Cong and the Japanese that naturalizes American neocolonialism in Vietnam through the appeal to a nationalist historical narrative about World War II. The narrator's observation that the teacher's history lesson addresses "all the boys" further instantiates how the American nationalist narrative recognizes, recruits, and incorporates male subjects, while "feminizing" and silencing the students who do not conform to that notion of patriotic subjectivity. But at the same time, Truong's story is an epistolary fiction addressed to one of the narrator's few friends within that classroom, a white female student named Kelly. Although the classroom is remembered as a site of pain, the retrospective renarration of that pain, not as individually suffered, but as a shared topos between writer and addressee, is in contrast a source of new pleasure and a differently discovered sense of community. The narrator writes: "I guess it was Mrs. Hammerick's books that brought you and me together. I think you and I would have had to find each other anyway, but I like to tell our story this way, you know, like it was destiny and not necessity. . . . You and I were library kids, do you remember that?" (43). The repetition of "you and me," "you and I," and "you and I" sutures, on the narrative level, the intersubjective relationality between the narrator and Kelly. As the story proceeds, it delicately portrays relationships that cross boundaries of race, class, and constructions of femininity; girls are thrown into tentative but sympathetic intimacies based on their quite different exclusions—the narrator is ostracized as a Vietnamese immigrant, her friend Kelly because she is overweight, and another girl Michelle because of her family's poverty. The girls' friendships are marked by distinct, yet overlapping dynamics of power and powerlessness, but in response they form courageous bridges across distinct lines of opportunity and restriction.

Truong's story yields several points with which I wish to end this chapter on Asian American literary canon and the university. First, by focusing on the classroom as the place where the narrator's difference is most sharply delineated, the story emphasizes that education is a primary site through which the narratives of national group identity are established and reproduced, dramatizing that the construction of others—as *enemies*—is a fundamental logic in the constitution of national identity. Second, it is suggestive about the process through which the students' conformity to those narratives is demanded and regulated: the historical narrative about victors and enemies elicits an identification of the male student with that victorious national body, and in that process of identification, the student consents to his incorporation as a subject of the American state. I refer to this subject of ideology in the classroom as a "he," for just as the history lesson in Truong's story is addressed to "all the boys," I would argue that the subject position of the American student/citizen is coded, narrated, and historically embodied as a masculine position. We might say that the American nationalist narrative of citizenship incorporates the subject as male citizen according to a relationship that is not dissimilar to the family's oedipalization, or socialization, of the son. In terms of the racialized subject, he becomes a citizen when he identifies with the paternal state and accepts the terms of this identification by subordinating his racial difference and denying his ties with the feminized and racialized "motherland."

Third, by representing this classroom from the perspective of the immigrant female student, the story underscores how this identification requires the painful suppression of differences. In terms of group formation, it calls attention to how curricula that universalize the values and norms of a "common" national culture are in contradiction with a society that is materially divided and stratified in terms of race, class, gender, sexuality, and national origin. In terms of individual subject formation, it suggests that the interpellation of the individual splits the subject off from itself, suppressing those material, racial, and sexual aspects that contradict and are in excess of that generic subject formation.[19] But this interpellation, or oedipalization, is not univocal or total, for even though aspects may be conditionally split off, the subject may be insufficiently captured by the nationalist subject formation such that antagonisms arise against that formation out of the contradiction of interpellation itself. In using the term "contradiction" to conceive of both group and individual identities, I mean to take up the sense in which contradiction describes the condition within which a system produces, in the course of providing for its effective hegemony, the conflicts that will bring about its own expiration and undoing. The contradiction of nationalist identity formation is that it is precisely the demand for national cultural uniformity that inflects differences with oppositional significance in antagonism to the apparatuses whose function it is to dictate that uniformity. In other words, the dominant construction of American nationalist identity logically provides for the negative critiques of that identity from the standpoints of groups racialized, sexualized, or classed as *other*. Another condition of contradiction is of course that none of these valences of otherness is independently articulated; throughout lived social relations, race is class-inflected, sexuality is racialized, and labor is gendered. There is no contradiction that is not articulated with other contradictions, and society is increasingly characterized by intersections, in which racial, gendered, and economic contradictions are inseparable and mobilized by means of and through one another.

In this regard, the final point I would like to draw out of Truong's story is that by focusing on the friendships among three differently marginalized female students, the story ultimately allegorizes a network of alliance across lines of race, class, and gender, a network that is not only a means of surviving the classroom but also the basis of contesting the historically differentiated but intersecting determinations of racist colonialism, patriarchy, and capitalism, for which that classroom is a primary locus of reproduction. Sites that express overdetermination or the convergence of a complex of contradictions may move in the direction of either an inhibition and neutralization of contradictory possibility or a rupture, a mobilization of contradictions within which the coincidence of racial, gender, and class determinations would bring forward a disruption of the multiply articulated structure of domination. The concerted articulation of converged contradiction "fuses" what Louis Althusser calls a "ruptural unity" that makes possible the emergence of different subjects and constituencies in a "grouped assault" on a specific hegemony or a specific dominant formation.[20] We may recall from Chapter 2 that Gramsci writes of hegemony as not simply a political rule but also a process within which any specific dominant configuration exists always within the context of contesting pressures from other sites, classes, and groups in different conditions of self-identification and formation.[21] Put otherwise, the overdetermination of class, race, and gender contradictions in the construction of American nationalist identity makes possible the continuation of painful silences and exclusions in the American classroom, but this convergence of contradictions may also constitute precisely the ground from which antiracist, feminist, and class struggles against those nationalist dominations necessarily emerge.

I want to cast the project of securing the conditions for teaching U.S. racialized minority, postcolonial, and women's literatures in the contemporary university as something like the network of alliances described in Truong's story, as a collection of linked alternative pedagogies central to contesting both the traditional function of the educational apparatus to incorporate students as subjects of the state, and the narratives through which that socialization takes place. Like the affinities in Truong's story, it is a set of links that is not predicated on notions of similarity or identity but is a project built out of material, historical, and topical differentiation. Let us observe, too, that Truong's story is a U.S. racialized minority, postcolonial, *and* woman's text; it is an object that dissolves the notion that these three areas can be conceived as discrete or discontinuous. Through concerted pedagogical and curricular changes taking place in different institutional sites, we can locate and displace the powerful ideological narratives that traditionally structure the current university (that is, the two with which we began: the culturalist one that projects Euro-American culture as an autonomous domain, and the developmental narrative that abstracts and privileges the subject of that "prior" Western civilization, defining that subject against others who are identified with less autonomous, less developed, and disintegrated and disintegrating contemporary cultures). The teaching of an immigrant female and postcolonial text, like Truong's, decenters the autonomous notion of Western culture by recentering the complexities of racialized female and postcolonial collectivities and unmasks the developmental narrative as a fiction designed to justify the histories of colonialism, neocolonialism, and forced labor and to erase the dislocations and hybridities that are the resulting conditions of those histories. Through such pedagogical and curricular shifts, we may also be able to alter the ways in which students are interpellated as subjects by the educational apparatus, opening the possibility that the university will ultimately offer to students more than a universalized subject formation, more than an incorporation into a dehistoricized national or cultural identity, and more sites and practices than those permitted by one generic subject position.

Heterogeneity, Hybridity,

Multiplicity: Asian

American Differences

In a poem by Janice Mirikitani, a Japanese American nisei woman describes her sansei daughter's rebellion. The daughter's denial of Japanese American culture and its particular notions of femininity reminds the nisei speaker that she, too, has denied her antecedents, rebelling against her own more traditional issei mother:[1]

> I want to break tradition—unlock this room
>   where women dress in the dark.
>   Discover the lies my mother told me.
>   The lies that we are small and powerless
>   that our possibilities must be compressed
>   to the size of pearls, displayed only as
>   passive chokers, charms around our neck.
> Break Tradition.
>   I want to tell my daughter of this room
>   of myself
>   filled with tears of shakuhatchi,
>
>   . . . .
>
>   poems about madness,
>   sounds shaken from barbed wire and
>   goodbyes and miracles of survival.
>   This room of open window where daring ones escape.
> My daughter denies she is like me . . .
>   her pouting ruby lips, her skirts

> swaying to salsa, teena marie and the stones,
> her thighs displayed in carnivals of color.
> I do not know the contents of her room.
>   She mirrors my aging.
>   She is breaking tradition.²

The nisei speaker repudiates the repressive confinements of her issei mother: the disciplining of the female body, the tedious practice of diminution, the silences of obedience. In turn, the crises that have shaped the nisei speaker—internment camps, sounds of threatening madness—are unknown to and unheard by her sansei teenage daughter. The three generations of women of Japanese descent in this poem are separated by their different histories and by different conceptions of what it means to be female and Japanese. The poet who writes "I do not know the contents of her room" registers these separations as "breaking tradition."

In another poem, by Lydia Lowe, Chinese women workers are also divided by generation but, even more powerfully, by class and language. The speaker is a young Chinese American who supervises an older Chinese woman in a textile factory.

> The long bell blared,
> and then the *lo-ban*
> made me search all your bags
> before you could leave.
>
> Inside he sighed
> about slow work, fast hands,
> missing spools of thread—
> and I said nothing.
>
> I remember that day
> you came in to show me
> I added your tickets six zippers short.
> It was just a mistake.
>
> You squinted down
> at the check in your hands

like an old village woman peers
at some magician's trick.

That afternoon
when you thrust me your bags
I couldn't look or raise my face.
Doi m-jyu.

Eyes on the ground,   .
I could only see
one shoe kicking against the other.[3]

This poem, too, invokes the breaking of tradition, although it thematizes another sort of stratification among Asian women: the structure of the factory places the English-speaking younger woman above the Cantonese-speaking older one. Economic relations in capitalist society force the young supervisor to discipline her elders, and she is acutely ashamed that her required behavior does not demonstrate the respect traditionally owed to parents and elders. Thus, both poems foreground commonly thematized topoi of immigrant cultures: the disruption and distortion of traditional cultural practices—like the practice of parental sacrifice and filial duty or the practice of respecting hierarchies of age—not only as a consequence of displacement to the United States but also as a part of entering a society with different class stratifications and different constructions of gender roles. Some Asian American discussions cast the disruption of tradition as loss, representing the loss in terms of regret and shame, as in the latter poem. Alternatively, the traditional practices of family continuity and hierarchy may be figured as oppressively confining, as in Mirikitani's poem, in which the two generations of daughters contest the more restrictive female roles of the former generations. In either case, many Asian American discussions portray immigration and relocation to the United States in terms of a loss of the "original" culture in exchange for the new "American" culture.

In many Asian American novels, the question of the loss or transmission of the "original" culture is frequently represented in a family narrative, figured as generational conflict between the Chinese-born first generation and the American-born second generation.[4] Louis Chu's 1961 novel *Eat a Bowl of Tea*, for example, allegorizes the differences between "native" Chinese values and the new "westernized" culture of Chinese Americans in the conflicted relationship between father and son. Other novels have taken up this generational theme; one way to read the popular texts Maxine Hong Kingston's *The Woman Warrior* (1975) or Amy Tan's *The Joy Luck Club* (1989) would be to understand them as versions of this generational model of culture, refigured in feminine terms, between mothers and daughters. In this chapter, however, I argue that interpreting Asian American culture exclusively in terms of the master narratives of generational conflict and filial relation essentializes Asian American culture, obscuring the particularities and incommensurabilities of class, gender, and national diversities among Asians. The reduction of the cultural politics of racialized ethnic groups, like Asian Americans, to first-generation/second-generation struggles displaces social differences into a privatized familial opposition. Such reductions contribute to the aestheticizing commodification of Asian American *cultural* differences, while denying the immigrant histories of material exclusion and differentiation of the kind discussed in Chapter 1.

To avoid this homogenizing of Asian Americans as exclusively hierarchical and familial, I would contextualize the "vertical" generational model of culture with the more "horizontal" relationship represented in Diana Chang's "The Oriental Contingent."[5] In Chang's short story, two young women avoid the discussion of their Chinese backgrounds because each desperately fears that the other is "more Chinese," more "authentically" tied to the original culture. The narrator, Connie, is certain that her friend Lisa "never referred to her own background because it was more Chinese than Connie's, and therefore of a higher order. She was tact incarnate. All along, she had been going out of her way not to embarrass Connie. Yes, yes. Her assurance was definitely uppercrust (perhaps her father had been in the diplomatic service), and her offhand didacticness, her lack of self-doubt, was indeed characteristically Chinese-Chinese" (173). Connie feels ashamed because she assumes herself to be "a failed Chinese"; she fantasizes that Lisa was born in China, visits there frequently, and privately disdains Chinese Americans. Her assumptions about Lisa prove to be quite wrong, however; Lisa is even more critical of herself for "not being genuine." For Lisa, as Connie eventually discovers, was born in Buffalo and was adopted by American parents; lacking an immediate connection to Chinese culture, Lisa projects on all Chinese the authority of being "more Chinese." Lisa confesses to Connie at the end of the story: "The only time I feel Chinese is when I'm embarrassed I'm not more Chinese—which is a totally Chinese reflex I'd give anything to be rid of!" (176). Chang's story portrays two women polarized by the degree to which they have each internalized a cultural definition of "Chineseness" as pure and fixed, in which any deviation is constructed as less, lower, and shameful. Rather than confirming a traditional anthropological model of "culture" in which "ethnicity" is passed from generation to generation, Chang's story explores the relationship between women of the same generation. Lisa and Connie are ultimately able to reduce each other's guilt at not being "Chinese enough"; in each other they are able to find a common frame of reference. The story suggests that the making of Chinese American culture—the ways in which it is imagined, practiced, and continued—is worked out as much "horizontally" among communities as it is transmitted "vertically" in unchanging forms from one generation to the next. Rather than considering "Asian American identity" as a fixed, established "given," perhaps we can consider instead "Asian American cultural practices" that produce identity; the processes that produce such identity are never complete and are always constituted in relation to historical and material differences. Stuart Hall has written that cultural identity "is a matter of 'becoming' as well as of 'being.' It belongs to the future as much as to the past. It is not something which already exists, transcending place, time, history and culture. Cultural identities come from somewhere, have histories. But, like everything which is historical, they undergo constant transformation. Far from being eternally fixed in some essentialized past, they are subject to the continuous 'play' of history, culture and power."[6]

Asian American discussions of ethnic culture and racial group formation are far from uniform or consistent. Rather, these discussions contain a spectrum of positions that includes, at one end, the desire for a cultural identity represented by a fixed profile of traits and, at the other, challenges to the notion of singularity and conceptions of *race* as the material *locus* of differences, intersections, and incommensurabilities. These latter efforts attempt to define Asian American identity in a manner that not only accounts for the critical inheritance of cultural definitions and traditions but also accounts for the *racial formation* that is produced in the negotiations between the state's regulation of racial groups and those groups' active contestation and construction of racial meanings.[7] In other words, these latter efforts suggest that the making of Asian American culture may be a much less stable process than unmediated vertical transmission of culture from one generation to another. The making of Asian American culture includes practices that are partly inherited, partly modified, as well as partly invented; Asian American culture also includes the practices that emerge in relation to the dominant representations that deny or subordinate Asian and Asian American cultures as "other."[8] As the narrator of *The Woman Warrior* suggests, perhaps one of the more important stories of Asian American experience is about the process of critically receiving and rearticulating cultural traditions in the face of a dominant national culture that exoticizes and "orientalizes" Asians. She asks: "Chinese-Americans, when you try to understand what things in you are Chinese, how do you separate what is peculiar to childhood, to poverty, insanities, one family, your mother who marked your growing with stories, from what is Chinese? What is Chinese tradition and what is the movies?"[9] Or the dilemma of cultural syncretism might be posed in an interrogative version of the uncle's impromptu proverb in Wayne Wang's film *Dim Sum:* "You can take the girl out of Chinatown, but can you take the Chinatown out of the girl?"[10] For rather than representing a fixed, discrete culture, "Chinatown" is itself the very emblem of shifting demographics, languages, and populations. The residents of the urban "bachelor society" Chinatowns of New York and San Francisco from the mid–nineteenth century to the 1950s, for example, were mostly male laborers—laundrymen, seamen, restaurant workers—from southern China, whereas today, immigrants from Taiwan, mainland China, and Hong Kong have dramatically reconfigured contemporary suburban Chinese settlements such as the one in Monterey Park, California.[11]

I begin with these particular examples drawn from Asian American cultural texts in order to observe that what is referred to as "Asian America" is clearly a heterogeneous entity. As I have argued in Chapter 1, in relation to the state and the American national culture implied by that state, Asian Americans have certainly been constructed as different, and as other than, white Americans of European origin. But from the perspectives of Asian Americans, we are extremely different and diverse among ourselves: as men and women at different distances and generations from our "original" Asian cultures—cultures as different as Chinese, Japanese, Korean, Filipino, Indian, Vietnamese, Thai, or Cambodian—Asian Americans are born in the United States and born in Asia, of exclusively Asian parents and of mixed race, urban and rural, refugee and nonrefugee, fluent in English and non-English-speaking, professionally trained and working-class. As with other immigrant groups in the United States, the Asian-origin collectivity is unstable and changeable, with its cohesion complicated by intergenerationality, by various degrees of identification with and relation to a "homeland," and by different extents of assimilation to and distinction from "majority culture" in the United States. Further, the historical contexts of particular waves of immigration within single groups contrast one another; Japanese Americans who were interned during World War II encountered social and economic barriers quite different from those faced by individuals who arrive from Japan to southern California today. And the composition of different waves of immigrants varies in gender, class, and region. For example, in the case of the Chinese, the first groups of immigrants to the United States in the 1850's were from Canton Province, male by a ratio of ten to one, and largely of peasant backgrounds, whereas the more recent Chinese immigrants are from Hong Kong, Taiwan, or the People's Republic (themselves quite heterogeneous and of discontinuous "origins") or from the Chinese diaspora in other parts of Asia, such as Malaysia or Singapore, and they have a heterogeneous profile that includes male and female assembly and service-sector workers as well as "middle-class" professionals and business elites.[12] Further, once arriving in the United States, very few Asian immigrant cultures remain discrete, impenetrable communities; the more recent groups mix, in varying degrees, with segments of the existing groups; Asian Americans may intermarry with other racialized ethnic groups, live in neighborhoods adjacent to them, or work in the same businesses and on the same factory assembly lines. The boundaries and definitions of Asian American culture are continually shifting and being contested from pressures both "inside" and "outside" the Asian-origin community.

I stress heterogeneity, hybridity, and multiplicity in the characterization of Asian American culture as part of a twofold argument about cultural politics, the ultimate aim of which is to disrupt the current hegemonic relationship between "dominant" and "minority" positions. Heterogeneity, hybridity, and multiplicity are not used here as rhetorical or literary terms but are attempts at naming the material contradictions that characterize Asian American groups. Although these concepts appear to be synonymous in their relationship to that of "identity," they can be precisely distinguished. By "heterogeneity," I mean to indicate the existence of differences and differential relationships within a bounded category—that is, among Asian Americans, there are differences of Asian national origin, of generational relation to immigrant exclusion laws, of class backgrounds in Asia and economic conditions within the United States, and of gender. By "hybridity," I refer to the formation of cultural objects and practices that are produced by the histories of uneven and unsynthetic power relations; for example, the racial and linguistic mixings in the Philippines and among Filipinos in the United States are the material trace of the history of Spanish colonialism, U.S. colonization, and U.S. neocolonialism. Hybridity, in this sense, does not suggest the assimilation of Asian or immigrant practices to dominant forms but instead marks the history of survival within relationships of unequal power and domination. Finally, we might understand "multiplicity" as designating the ways in which subjects located within social relations are determined by several different axes of power, are multiply determined by the contradictions of capitalism, patriarchy, and race relations, with, as Hall explains, particular contradictions surfacing in relation to the material conditions of a specific historical moment.[13] Thus, heterogeneity, hybridity, and multiplicity are concepts that assist us in critically understanding the material conditions of Asians in the United States, conditions in excess of the dominant, "orientalist" construction of Asian Americans. Although orientalism seeks to consolidate the coherence of the West as subject precisely through the representation of "oriental" objects as homogenous, fixed, and stable, contradictions in the production of Asians and in the noncorrespondence between the orientalist object and the Asian American subject ultimately express the limits of such fictions.

On the one hand, the observation that Asian Americans are heterogenous is part of a strategy to destabilize the dominant discursive construction and determination of Asian Americans as a homogeneous group. As we have seen in Chapter 1, throughout the late nineteenth and early twentieth centuries, Asian populations in the United States were managed by exclusion acts, bars from citizenship, quotas, and internment, all of which made use of racialist constructions of Asian-origin groups as homogeneous. The "model minority" myth that constructs Asians as the most successfully assimilated minority group is a contemporary version of this homogenization of Asians. On the other hand, it is equally important to underscore Asian American heterogeneities—particularly class, gender, and national differences among Asians—to contribute to a dialogue within Asian American discourse, to point to the limitations inherent in a politics based on cultural, racial, or ethnic identity. In this sense, I argue for the Asian American necessity to organize, resist, and theorize *as* Asian Americans, but at the same time, I inscribe this necessity within a discussion of the risks of a cultural politics that relies on the construction of sameness and the exclusion of differences.

The first reason to emphasize the dynamic fluctuation and heterogeneity of Asian American culture is to release our understandings of either the "dominant" or the emergent "minority" cultures as discrete, fixed, or homogeneous and to arrive at a different conception of the terrain of culture. In California, for example, it has become commonplace for residents to consider themselves as part of a "multicultural" state, as embodying a new phenomenon of cultural adjacency and admixture; this "multiculturalism" is at once an index of the changing demographics and differences of community in California and a pluralist attempt at containment of those differences.[14] For if racialized minority immigrant cultures are perpetually changing—in their composition, configuration, and signifying practices, as well as in their relations to one another—it follows that the "majority" or "dominant" culture, with which minority cultures are in continual relation, is also unstable and unclosed. The understanding that the general cultural terrain is one social site in which "hegemony" is continually being both established and contested permits us to theorize about the roles that racialized immigrant groups play in the making and unmaking of culture and to explore the ways that cross-race and cross-national projects may work to change the existing structure of power, the current hegemony. We remember that

Antonio Gramsci writes about hegemony as not simply political or economic forms of rule but as the entire process of dissent and compromise
through which a particular group is able to determine the political, cultural,
and ideological character of a state.[15] Hegemony does not refer exclusively
to the process by which a dominant group exercises its influence but refers
equally to the process through which emergent groups organize and contest any specific hegemony.[16] The reality of any specific hegemony is that,
although it may be for the moment dominant, it is never absolute or con-
clusive. Hegemony, in Gramsci's thought, is a concept that describes both
the social processes through which a particular dominance is maintained,
as well as the processes through which that dominance is challenged and
new forces are articulated. When a hegemony representing the interests of
a dominant group exists, it is always within the context of resistances from
emerging groups.[17] We might say that hegemony is not only the political
process by which a particular group constitutes itself as "the one" or "the
majority" in relation to which "minorities" are defined and know themselves to be "other," but is equally the process by which various and incommensurable positions of otherness may ally and constitute a new majority,
a "counterhegemony."[18]

Gramsci writes of "subaltern," prehegemonic, not unified groups "un-
realized" by the State, whose histories are fragmented, episodic, and iden-
tifiable only from a point of historical hindsight. They may go through different phases when they are subject to the activity of ruling groups, may
articulate their demands through existing parties, and then may themselves
produce new parties. In "History of the Subaltern Classes" in *The Prison
Notebooks,* Gramsci describes a final phase at which the "formations [of the
subaltern classes] assert integral autonomy" (52). The definition of the subaltern groups includes some noteworthy observations for our understanding of the roles of racialized immigrant groups in the United States who
have the histories of being "aliens ineligible to citizenship." The assertion
that the significant practices of the subaltern groups may not be understood as hegemonic until they are viewed with historical hindsight is interesting, for it suggests that some of the most powerful practices may not
always be the explicitly oppositional ones, may not be understood by con-
temporaries, and may be less overt and recognizable than others. That the
subaltern classes are by definition "not unified" is provocative, too—that

is, these groups are not a fixed, unified force of a single character. Rather, the assertion of "integral autonomy" by "not unified" classes suggests a coordination of distinct, yet allied, positions, practices, and movements — class-identified and not class-identified, in parties and not, race-based and gender-based — each in its own, not necessarily equivalent manner transforming, disrupting, and destructuring the apparatuses of a specific hegemony. The independent forms and locations of challenge — cultural, as well as economic and political — constitute what Gramsci calls a "new historical bloc," a new set of relationships that together embody a different hegemony and a different balance of power. In this sense, we have in the instance of the growing and shifting racialized immigrant populations in California an active example of this new historical bloc described by Gramsci; and in the negotiations between these groups and the existing "majority" over what interests constitute the "majority," we have an illustration of the concept of hegemony, not in the more commonly accepted sense of "hegemony maintenance," but in the often ignored sense of "hegemony creation."[19] The observation that the Asian American community and other racialized and immigrant communities are both incommensurate and heterogeneous lays the foundation for several political operations. First, by reconceiving "the social" so as to centralize the emergent racialized and immigrant groups who are constantly redefining social relations in ways that move beyond static oppositions such as "majority" and "minority," or the binary axis "black" and "white," we recast cultural politics so as to account for a multiplicity of various, nonequivalent racialized groups, one of which is Asian Americans. Second, the conception of racialized group formation as heterogeneous provides a position for Asian Americans that is both historically specific and yet simultaneously uneven and unclosed. Asian Americans can articulate distinct challenges and demands based on particular histories of exclusion and racialization, but the redefined lack of closure — which reveals rather than conceals differences — opens political lines of affiliation with other groups in the challenge to specific forms of domination insofar as they share common features.

The articulation of an "Asian American identity" as an organizing tool has provided a concept of political unity that enables diverse Asian groups to understand unequal circumstances and histories as being related. The building of "Asian American culture" is crucial to this effort, for it articulates and empowers the diverse Asian-origin community vis-à-vis the institutions and apparatuses that exclude and marginalize it. Yet to the extent that Asian American culture fixes Asian American identity and suppresses differences—of national origin, generation, gender, sexuality, class —it risks particular dangers: not only does it underestimate the differences and hybridities among Asians, but it may also inadvertently support the racist discourse that constructs Asians as a homogeneous group, that implies Asians are "all alike" and conform to "types." To the extent that Asian American culture dynamically expands to include both internal critical dialogues about difference and the interrogation of dominant interpellations, however, Asian American culture can likewise be a site in which the "horizontal" affiliations with other groups can be imagined and realized. In this respect, a politics based exclusively on racial or ethnic identity willingly accepts the terms of the dominant logic that organizes the heterogeneous picture of differences into a binary schema of "the one" and "the other." The essentializing of Asian American identity also reproduces oppositions that subsume other nondominant groups in the same way that Asians and other groups are marginalized by the dominant culture: to the degree that the discourse generalizes Asian American identity as male, women are rendered invisible; or to the extent that Chinese are presumed to be exemplary of all Asians, the importance of other Asian groups is ignored. In this sense, a politics based on racial, cultural, or ethnic identity facilitates the displacement of intercommunity differences—between men and women or between workers and managers—into a false opposition of "nationalism" and "assimilation." We have an example of this in recent debates where Asian American feminists who challenge Asian American sexism are cast as "assimilationist," as betraying Asian American "nationalism."

To the extent that Asian American discourse articulates an identity in reaction to the dominant culture's stereotype, even if to refute it, the discourse may remain bound to and overly determined by the logic of the dominant culture. In accepting the binary terms ("white" and "nonwhite" or "majority" and "minority") that structure institutional policies about race, we forget that these binary schemas are not neutral descriptions. Binary constructions of difference utilize a logic that prioritizes the first term and subordinates the second; whether the pair "difference" and "sameness" is figured as a binary synthesis that considers "difference" as always contained within the "same" or that conceives of the pair as an opposition in which "difference" structurally implies "sameness" as its complement, it is important to see each of these figurations as versions of the same binary logic. The materialist argument for heterogeneity seeks to challenge the conception of difference as exclusively structured by a binary opposition between two terms, by proposing instead another notion of "difference" that takes seriously the historically produced conditions of heterogeneity, multiplicity, and nonequivalence. The most exclusive construction of Asian American identity—one that presumes masculinity, American birth, and the speaking of English—is at odds with the formation of important political alliances and affiliations with other groups across racial and ethnic, gender, sexuality, and class lines. An exclusive "cultural identity" is an obstacle to Asian American women allying with other women of color, and it can discourage laboring Asian Americans from joining with workers of other colors, conjunctions that are explored in Chapter 7. It can short-circuit potential alliances against the dominant structures of power in the name of subordinating "divisive" issues to *the* national question.

Some of the limits of "identity politics" are discussed most pointedly by Frantz Fanon in his books about the Algerian resistance to French colonialism. Before turning to some Asian American cultural texts to trace the ways in which the dialogues about identity and difference are represented within the discourse, I would like to consider one of Fanon's most important texts, *The Wretched of the Earth* (*Les damnés de la terre*, 1961). Although Fanon's treatise was cited in the 1960s as the manifesto for a nationalist politics of identity, rereading it in the 1990s, we ironically find his text to be the source of a serious critique of nationalism. Fanon argues that the challenge facing any movement that is dismantling colonialism (or a system in which one culture dominates another) is to provide for a new order that does not reproduce the social structure of the old system. This new order must avoid, he argues, the simple assimilation to the dominant culture's roles and positions by the emergent group, which would merely caricature the old colonialism, and it should be equally suspicious of an uncritical nativism or racialism that would appeal to essentialized notions of precolonial identity. Fanon suggests that another alternative is necessary, a new order, neither assimilationist nor nativist inversion, that breaks with the structures and practices of cultural domination, that continually and collectively criticizes the institutions of rule. One of the more remarkable turns in Fanon's argument occurs when he identifies both bourgeois assimilation and bourgeois nationalism as conforming to the same logic, as being responses to colonialism and reproducing the same structure of domination. It is in this sense that Fanon warns against the nationalism practiced by bourgeois postcolonial governments: the national bourgeoisie replaces the colonizer, yet the social and economic structure remains the same. Ironically, he points out, these separatisms, or "micronationalisms," are themselves legacies of colonialism: "By its very structure, colonialism is regionalist and separatist. Colonialism does not simply state the existence of tribes; it also reinforces and separates them."[20] That is, a politics of bourgeois cultural nationalism may be congruent with the divide-and-conquer logics of colonial domination. Fanon links the practices of the national bourgeoisie that has "assimilated" colonialist thought and practice with "nativist" practices that privilege one group or ethnicity over others; for Fanon, nativism and assimilationism are not opposites—they are similar logics that both enunciate the old order.

Fanon's analysis implies that an essentialized bourgeois construction of "nation" is a classification that excludes subaltern groups that could bring about substantive change in the social and economic relations, particularly those whose social marginalities are due to class: peasants, immigrant workers, transient populations. We can add to Fanon's criticism of nationalism that the category of "nation" often erases a consideration of women: the fact of difference between men and women and the conditions under which they live and work in situations of economic domination. This is why the concentration of women of color in domestic service or reproductive labor (child care, home care, nursing) in the contemporary United States is not adequately explained by a nation-based model of analysis.[21] It is also why the position of Asian and Latina immigrant female workers in the current global economy, discussed in Chapter 7, exceeds the terms offered by racial or national analyses. We can make more explicit—in light of feminist theory that has gone perhaps the furthest in theorizing multiple determinations and the importance of positionalities—that it may be difficult to act exclusively in terms of a single valence or political interest—such as race, ethnicity, or nation—because social subjects are the sites of a variety of differences. Trinh T. Minh-ha, Chela Sandoval, Angela Davis, and others have described the subject-positions of women of color as constructed across a multiplicity of social relations. Trinh writes:

> Many women of color feel obliged [to choose] between ethnicity and womanhood: how can they? You never have/are one without the other. The idea of two illusorily separated identities, one ethnic, the other woman (or more precisely female), partakes in the Euro-American system of dualistic reasoning and its age-old divide-and-conquer tactics. . . . The pitting of anti-racist and anti-sexist struggles against one another allows some vocal fighters to dismiss blatantly the existence of either racism or sexism within their lines of action, as if oppression only comes in separate, monolithic forms.[22]

In other words, the conceptualization of racism and sexism as if they were distinctly opposed discourses is a construction that serves the dominant formations; we cannot isolate "race" from "gender" without reproducing the logic of domination. To appreciate this interconnection of different, nonequivalent discourses of social stratification is not to argue against the strategic importance of Asian American identity or against the building of Asian American culture. Rather, it is to suggest that acknowledging class and gender differences among Asian Americans does not weaken the group. To the contrary, these differences represent greater opportunity to affiliate with other groups whose cohesions may be based on other valences of oppression rather than "identity." Angela Davis argues, for example, that we might conceive of "U.S. women of color" not as a "coalition" made up of separate groups organized around racial identities but as a *political formation* that decides to work together on a particular issue or agenda. She states: "A woman of color formation might decide to work around immigration issues. This political commitment is not based on the specific histories of racialized communities or its constituent members, but rather constructs an agenda agreed upon by all who are a part of it. In my opinion, the most exciting potential of women of color formations resides in the possibility of politicizing this identity—basing the identity on politics rather than the politics on identity."[23]

As we have already seen, within Asian American discourse there is a varied spectrum of discussion about the concepts of racialized group identity and culture. At one end are discussions in which cultural identity is essentialized as the cornerstone of a cultural nationalist politics. In these discussions the positions of "cultural nationalism" and of assimilation are represented in polar opposition: cultural nationalism's affirmation of the separate purity of its culture opposes assimilation of the standards of dominant society. Stories about the loss of a "native" Asian culture tend to express some form of this opposition. At the same time, there are criticisms of this cultural nationalist position, most often articulated by feminists who charge that Asian American nationalism prioritizes masculinity and does not account for women. Finally, at the other end, interventions exist that refuse static or binary conceptions of culture, replacing notions of "identity" with multiplicity and shifting the emphasis from cultural "essence" to material hybridity. Settling for neither nativism nor assimilation, these interventions expose the apparent opposition between the two as a constructed figure (as Fanon does when he observes that bourgeois assimilation and bourgeois nationalism often conform to the same colonialist logic). In tracing these different types of discussions about identity through Asian American cultural debates, literature, and film, I have chosen several texts because they are accessible, "popular," and commonly held. But I do not intend to limit "discourse" to only these particular forms. By "discourse" I intend a rather extended meaning—a network that includes not only texts and cultural documents but also social practices, formal and informal laws, policies of inclusion and exclusion, institutional forms of organization, and so forth, all of which constitute and regulate knowledge about its object, Asian America.

The terms of the debate about "nationalism" and "assimilation" become clearer if we look first at the discussion of Asian American identity in certain debates about the representation of culture. Readers of Asian American literature will be familiar with the attacks by Frank Chin, Ben

Tong, and others on author Maxine Hong Kingston, attacks that have been cast as nationalist criticisms of Kingston's "assimilationist" works. Her novel/autobiography *The Woman Warrior* is the target of such criticism because it was virtually the first "canonized" piece of Asian American literature. In this sense, a critique of how and why this text became fetishized as the exemplary representation of Asian American culture is necessary and important. But Chin's critique reveals other kinds of notable tensions in Asian American culture: he does more than accuse Kingston of having exoticized Chinese American culture, arguing that she has "feminized" Asian American literature and undermined the power of Asian American men to combat the racist stereotypes of the dominant white culture. Kingston and other women novelists such as Amy Tan, Chin charges, misrepresent Chinese history to exaggerate its patriarchal structure; as a result, Chinese society is portrayed as being even more misogynistic than European society. While Chin and others have cast this conflict in terms of nationalism and assimilationism, perhaps it may be more productive to see this debate, as Elaine Kim does, as a symptom of the tensions between nationalist and feminist concerns in Asian American discourse.[24] I would add to Kim's analysis that the dialogue between nationalist and feminist concerns animates a debate about identity and difference, or identity and heterogeneity, rather than between nationalism and assimilationism. It is a debate in which Chin and others insist on a fixed masculinist identity, whereas Kingston, Tan, or such feminist literary critics as Shirley Lim or Amy Ling, with their representations of female differences and their critiques of sexism in Chinese culture, throw this notion of identity repeatedly into question. Just as Fanon points out that some forms of nationalism can obscure class, Asian American feminists point out that Asian American cultural nationalism—or the construction of a fixed, "native" Asian American subject—obscures gender. In other words, the struggle that is framed as a conflict between the apparent opposites of nativism and assimilation can mask what is more properly characterized as a struggle between the desire to essentialize ethnic identity and the condition of heterogeneous differences against which such a desire is spoken. The trope that opposes nativism and assimilationism can be itself a "colonialist" figure used to displace the challenges of heterogeneity, or subalternity, by casting them as assimilationist or anti-cultural nationalist.

The trope that opposes nativism and assimilation does not only orga-nize the cultural debates of Asian American discourse but figures *in* Asian American literature as well. More often than not, however, this symbolic conflict between nativism and assimilation is figured in the topos with which I began, that of generational conflict. There are many versions of this topos; I will mention only a few so as to elucidate some of the most relevant cultural tensions. In one model, a conflict between generations is cast in strictly masculinist terms, between father and son; in this model, mothers are absent or unimportant, and female figures exist merely as peripheral objects to the side of the central drama of male conflict. Louis Chu's *Eat a Bowl of Tea* exemplifies this masculinist generational symbolism, in which a conflict between nativism and assimilation is allegorized in the relation-ship between the father Wah Gay and the son Ben Loy in the period when the predominantly Cantonese New York Chinatown community changes from a "bachelor society" to a "family society."[25] Wah Gay wishes Ben Loy to follow "Chinese" tradition and to submit to the father's authority, whereas the son balks at his fathers "old ways" and wants to make his own choices. When Wah Gay arranges a marriage for Ben Loy, the son is forced to obey. Although the son had had no trouble leading an active sexual life before his marriage, once married, he finds himself to be impotent. In other words, Chu's novel figures the conflict of nativism and assimilation in terms of Ben Loy's sexuality: submitting to the father's authority, marrying the "nice Chi-nese girl" Mei Oi and having sons, is the so-called traditional Chinese male behavior; this path represents the nativist option. By contrast, Ben Loy's former behaviors—carrying on with American prostitutes, gambling, and the like—are coded as the American path of assimilation. At the "nativist" Chinese extreme, Ben Loy is impotent and is denied access to erotic plea-sure, and at the "assimilationist" American extreme, he has great access and sexual freedom. Rather than naming the U.S. state as the "father," whose immigration laws determined the restricted conditions of the "bachelor" society for the first Chinese immigrants, and the repeal of which permitted the gradual establishment of a "family" society for the later generations, Chu's novel allegorizes Ben Loy's cultural options in the "oedipal" story of the son's sexuality. The novel suggests that a third "Chinese American" alternative becomes available, in which Ben Loy is able to experience erotic pleasure with his Chinese wife, when the couple moves away to another state, away from his father Wah Gay; Ben Loy's relocation to San Francisco Chinatown and the priority of pleasure with Mei Oi over the begetting of a son (which, they ultimately do have) both imply important breaks from his father's authority and the father's representation of "Chinese" tradition. Following Fanon's observations about the affinities between nativism and assimilation, we can consider Chu's 1961 novel as an early masculinist rendering of culture as conflict between the apparent opposites of nativism and assimilation, with an oedipal resolution in a Chinese American male "identity." Only with hindsight can we propose that the opposition may itself be a construction that allegorizes the dialectic between an articulation of a fixed symbolic cultural identity and the context of heterogeneous differences.

Amy Tan's more recent *Joy Luck Club* refigures this topos of generational conflict in a different social context, among first- and second-generation Mandarin Chinese in San Francisco. Tan's book rearticulates the generational themes of *Eat a Bowl of Tea* but deviates from the figuration of Asian American identity in a masculine oedipal dilemma by refiguring it in terms of mothers and daughters. This shift to the relationship between women alludes to the important changes after the repeal acts of 1943–1952, which permitted Chinese women to immigrate to the United States and eventually shifted the "bachelor" society depicted in Chu's novel to a "family" society. Yet to an even greater degree than *Eat a Bowl of Tea*, *Joy Luck Club* risks being appropriated as a text that privatizes social conflicts and contradictions, precisely by confining them to the "feminized" domestic sphere of family relations. In *Joy Luck Club*, both privatized generational conflict and the "feminized" relations between mothers and daughters are made to figure the broader social shifts of Chinese immigrant formation.[26]

Joy Luck Club represents the first-person narratives of four sets of Chinese-born mothers and their American-born daughters; the daughters attempt to come to terms with their mothers' demands, while the mothers try to interpret their daughters' deeds, the novel thus expressing a tension between the "Chinese" expectation of filial respect and the "American" inability to fulfill that expectation. Although it was heralded and marketed as a novel about mother-daughter relations in the Chinese American family (one cover review characterized it as a "story that shows us China, Chinese American women and their families, and the mystery of the mother-daughter bond in ways that we have not experienced before"), *Joy Luck Club* also betrays antagonisms that are not exclusively generational but due as well to different conceptions of class and gender among Chinese Americans. Toward the end of the novel, for example, Lindo and Waverly Jong reach a climax of misunderstanding, in a scene that takes place in a central site for the production of American femininity: the beauty parlor. After telling the stylist to give her mother a "soft wave," Waverly asks her mother, Lindo, if she is in agreement. The mother narrates: "I smile. I use my American face. That's the face Americans think is Chinese, the one they cannot understand. But inside I am becoming ashamed. I am ashamed she is ashamed. Because she is my daughter and I am proud of her, and I am her mother but she is not proud of me."[27] The American-born daughter believes she is treating her mother, rather magnanimously, to a day of pampering at a chic salon; the Chinese-born mother receives this gesture as an insult, clear evidence of a daughter ashamed of her mother's looks. The scene not only marks the separation of mother and daughter by generation but, perhaps more important, their separation by class and cultural differences that lead to divergent interpretations of how "femininity" is understood and signified. On the one hand, the Chinese-born Lindo and American-born Waverly have different class values and opportunities; the daughter's belief in the pleasure of a visit to an expensive San Francisco beauty parlor seems senselessly extravagant to the mother whose rural family had escaped poverty only by marrying her to the son of a less humble family in their village. On the other hand, the mother and daughter also conflict over definitions of proper female behavior. Lindo assumes female identity is constituted in the practice of a daughter's deference to her elders, whereas for Waverly, this identity is determined by a woman's financial independence from her parents and her financial equality with men, by her ability to speak her desires, and is cultivated and signified in the styles and shapes that represent middle-class feminine beauty. In this sense, it is possible to read *Joy Luck Club* not as a novel that exclusively depicts "the mystery of the mother-daughter bond" among generations of Chinese American women but rather as a text that thematizes how the trope of the mother-daughter relationship comes to symbolize Asian American culture. That is, we can read the novel as commenting on the national public's aestheticizing of mother-daughter relationships in its discourse about Asian Americans, by placing this construction within the context of the differences—of class and culturally specific definitions of gender—that are rendered invisible by the privileging of this trope.

Before concluding, I turn to a final text that not only restates the narrative that opposes nativism and assimilation but also articulates a critique of that narrative, calling the nativist/assimilationist dyad into question. If *Joy Luck Club* can be said to pose the dichotomy of nativism and assimilation by multiplying the figure of generational conflict and thematizing the privatized trope of the mother-daughter relationship, then Peter Wang's film *A Great Wall* (1985)—both in its emplotment and in its medium of representation—offers yet another alternative.[28] Wang's film unsettles both poles of the antinomy of nativist essentialism and assimilation by performing a continual geographical juxtaposition and exchange between the national spaces of the People's Republic of China and the United States. *A Great Wall* portrays the visit of Leo Fang's Chinese American family to China and their month-long stay with Leo's sister's family, the Chaos, in Beijing. The film concentrates on the primary contrast between the habits, customs, and assumptions of the Chinese in China and the Chinese Americans in California by going back and forth between shots of Beijing and northern California, in a type of continual filmic "migration" between the two, as if to thematize in its very form the travel between cultural spaces. From the first scene, however, in the opposition between "native" and "assimilated" spaces, the film foregrounds that neither space begins as a pure, uncontaminated site or origin; and as the camera eye shuttles back and forth, both poles of the constructed opposition shift and are altered. (Indeed, the Great Wall of China, from which the film takes its title, is a monument to the historical condition that not even ancient China was "pure" but coexisted with "foreign barbarians" against which the Middle Kingdom erected such barriers.) In this regard, the film contains a number of emblematic images that call attention to the syncretic, composite quality of many cultural spaces, particularly in the era of transnational capital: the young Chinese Liu is given a Coca-Cola by his scholar-father when he finishes the college entrance exam; children crowd around the single village television to watch a Chinese opera singer imitate Pavarotti singing Italian opera; the Chinese student learning English recites the Gettysburg Address. Although the film concentrates on both illustrating and dissolving the apparent opposition between Chinese Chinese and American Chinese, a number of other contrasts are likewise explored: the differences between generations within both the Chao and the Fang families; differences between men and women (accentuated by two scenes, one in which Grace Fang and Mrs. Chao talk about their husbands and children, the other in which Chao and Leo get drunk together); and finally, the differences between capitalist and Communist societies (highlighted in a scene in which the Chaos and Fangs talk about their different attitudes toward "work"). The representations of these other contrasts complicate and diversify the ostensible focus on cultural differences between Chinese and Chinese Americans, as if to testify to the condition that there is never only one exclusive valence of difference but rather that cultural difference is always simultaneously bound up with gender, economics, age, and other distinctions. In other words, when Leo says to his wife that the Great Wall makes the city "just as difficult to leave as to get in," the wall at once signifies the construction of a variety of barriers— not only between Chinese and Americans but also between generations, men and women, capitalism and Communism—as well as the impossibility of ever remaining bounded and impenetrable, of resisting change, recomposition, and reinvention.

The film continues with a series of contrasts: the differences in their bodily comportments when the Chinese American Paul and the Chinese Liu play table tennis, between Leo's jogging and Mr. Chao's tai chi, between Grace Fang's and Mrs. Chao's ideas of what is fitting and fashionable for the female body. The two families have different senses of space and of the relation between family members. Ultimately, just as the Chaos are marked by the visit from their American relatives, by the time the Fang family returns home to California, each brings back a memento or practice from their Chinese trip, and they, too, are altered. In other words, rather than privileging either a nativist or assimilationist view or even espousing a "Chinese American" resolution of differences, A Great Wall performs a filmic "migration" by shuttling between the two national cultural spaces. We are left, by the end of the film, with the sense of culture as dynamic and open material site.

In keeping with the example of *A Great Wall*, we might consider as a possible model for the ongoing construction of "identity" the migratory process suggested by Wang's filmic technique and emplotment, conceiving of the making and practice of Asian American culture as contested and unsettled, as taking place in the movement between sites and in the strategic occupation of heterogeneous and conflicting positions. This is not to suggest that "hybrid" cultural identities are occasioned only by voluntary mobility and literally by the privileges that guarantee such mobility; as Sauling Cynthia Wong has pointed out in *Reading Asian American Literature*, the American nation is founded on myths of mobility that disavow the histories of both the immobility of ghettoization and the forced dislocations of Asian Americans.[29] Rather, the materialist concept of hybridity conveys that the histories of forced labor migrations, racial segregation, economic displacement, and internment are left in the material traces of "hybrid" cultural identities; these hybridities are always in the process of, on the one hand, being appropriated and commodified by commercial culture and, on the other, of being rearticulated for the creation of oppositional "resistance cultures." Hybridization is not the "free" oscillation between or among chosen identities. It is the uneven process through which immigrant communities encounter the violences of the U.S. state, and the capital imperatives served by the United States and by the Asian states from which they come, and the process through which they survive those violences by living, inventing, and reproducing different cultural alternatives.

The grouping "Asian American" is not a natural or static category; it is a socially constructed unity, a situationally specific position, assumed for political reasons. It is "strategic" in Gayatri Chakravorty Spivak's sense of a "strategic use of a positive essentialism in a scrupulously visible political interest."[30] The concept of "strategic essentialism" suggests that it is possible to utilize specific signifiers of racialized ethnic identity, such as "Asian American," for the purpose of contesting and disrupting the discourses that exclude Asian Americans, while simultaneously revealing the internal contradictions and slippages of "Asian American" so as to insure that such essentialisms will not be reproduced and proliferated by the very apparatuses we seek to disempower. This is not to suggest that we can or should do away with the notion of Asian American identity, for to stress only differences would jeopardize the hard-earned unity that has been achieved in the last thirty years of Asian American politics. Just as the articulation of identity depends on the existence of a horizon of differences, the articulation of differences dialectically depends on a socially constructed and practiced notion of identity. As Stuart Hall suggests, cultural identity is "not an essence but a *positioning*. Hence, there is always a politics of identity, a politics of position, which has no absolute guarantee in an unproblematic, transcendental 'law of origin.'"[31] In the 1990s, we can afford to rethink the notion of racialized ethnic identity in terms of differences of national origin, class, gender, and sexuality rather than presuming similarities and making the erasure of particularity the basis of unity. In the 1990s, we can diversify our practices to include a more heterogeneous group and to enable crucial alliances—with other groups of color, class-based struggles, feminist coalitions, and sexuality-based efforts—in the ongoing work of transforming hegemony.

Imagining Los Angeles

in the Production

of Multiculturalism

Ridley Scott's science fiction thriller film *Blade Runner* (1982) portrays Los Angeles in the year 2019 as a ruined, deteriorating city in postindustrial decay, a grand slum plagued by decaying garbage, dirt, ethnic ghettos, and radioactive rain. In composing this dystopic setting, Scott represents Los Angeles as a pastiche of third world—and particularly Asiatic—settlements: the storefronts are marked by neon Chinese ideograms, and the streets are filled with Chinese, Latino, Egyptian, and Cambodian faces. Everyone is talking "city-speak," which the blade runner Deckard's voice-over narration describes as "a mish-mash of Japanese, Spanish, German, French what-have-you. . . . I knew the lingo." Overlooking the city is a "Japanese simulacrum," a huge advertisement that alternates the image of a seductive Japanese woman's face and a Coca-Cola sign, a portentous emblem of future Japanese economic hegemony in the City of Angels.[1] The portrait of Los Angeles as a metropolis congested with poor Asian, Latino, African, and Arab immigrants projects the future of the first world *as* the third world. In *Blade Runner*'s version of the twenty-first century, it is no longer necessary to travel out to see "the world": "the world" has come and now inhabits, indeed possesses, Los Angeles. At the same time, the film's main intrigue—a narrative in which Deckard serves the law by hunting down replicants but ultimately, in fleeing with his replicant-lover Rachel, subverts the law that would maintain the dominance of humans over androids—performs many of the orientalist displacements and strategies we have already observed. "Asia" is both constructed as the "foreign" threat to U.S. capital and, in the representation of Los Angeles as a ghetto for "hordes" of Asian immigrants involved in service-sector labor, as the occulted horizon for the visible emergence of the free, white liberal subject. In other words, *Blade Runner*'s representation of a third world, largely Asian, invasion of Los Angeles rearticulates orientalist typographies in order to construct the white citizen against the background of a multicultural dystopia.

Against *Blade Runner*'s gloomy threat of multiculturalism, I wish to pose a more celebratory, but no less problematic, vision of Los Angeles as multicultural metropolis: the city represented in the September 1990 Los Angeles Festival of the Arts. For sixteen days, the L.A. festival represented the city as benevolent host to 550 events by artists and performers from twenty-one countries of Asia, the Pacific, and Latin America. Because of the sheer plenitude of performances, the uniqueness of the geography, and the impossibility of being at all sites, in all neighborhoods, and at all times, it is impossible to constitute the festival as a univocal object. My comments about the multiplicity of the festival-object, however, are directed more at the types of competing narratives that structured the presentation of events. Among the different narratives vying for authority in the festival, I briefly address four, which I term, for convenience, the narratives of authenticity, lineage, variety, and opposition. These narratives overlap and conflict, and in the project of understanding the ways in which the terrain of multiculturalism is both a mode of pluralist containment and a vehicle for intervention in that containment, it does not serve our inquiry to attempt to reconcile the narratives or to determine one as dominant. Rather, it is in identifying the sites of conflict and antagonism between these different narratives that we reveal the crises and the opportunities to which the production of multiculturalism responds.

Although such a film as *Blade Runner* and events like the festival register the increase of immigrant, racial, and ethnic populations in Los Angeles, both "productions" of multiculturalism are problematic. Neither representation reckons with the material differentiations of heterogeneous and unequal racial, ethnic, and immigrant communities in Los Angeles (or, to extend the scope, in the state of California where demographers declare that we are nearing a time in which more than 50 percent of the population will be Asian, Latino, African American, and other "minority" populations). To the degree that multiculturalism claims to register the increasing diversity of populations, it precisely obscures the ways in which that aesthetic representation is not an analogue for the material positions, means, or resources of those populations. This is not so much a question of posing the figural against the literal or the metaphorical against an essentialized notion of the "real" as it is a revelation of an undialectical confusion of historically differentiated spheres.[2] Although the concept of multiculturalism registers the pressures that increases of immigrant, racial, and ethnic populations bring to all spheres, these pressures are expressed only partially and inadequately in aesthetic representations; the production of multiculturalism instead diffuses the demands of material differentiation through the homogenization, aestheticization, and incorporation of signifiers of ethnic differences. Multiculturalism levels the important differences and contradictions within and among racial and ethnic minority groups according to the discourse of pluralism, which asserts that American culture is a democratic terrain to which every variety of constituency has equal access and in which all are represented, while simultaneously masking the existence of exclusions by recuperating dissent, conflict, and otherness through the promise of inclusion.[3] Multiculturalism is central to the maintenance of a consensus that permits the present hegemony, a hegemony that relies on a premature reconciliation of contradiction and persistent distractions away from the historically established incommensurability of the economic, political, and cultural spheres analyzed in Chapter 1.[4] In this sense, the production of multiculturalism at once "forgets" history and, in this forgetting, exacerbates a contradiction between the concentration of capital within a dominant class group and the unattended conditions of a working class increasingly made up of heterogeneous immigrant, racial, and ethnic groups.[5]

   Both *Blade Runner's* and the festival's images of multiculturalism are, in a sense, driven by the increased presence of third world people in Los Angeles—yet whereas *Blade Runner* produces a dystopic image of a decaying city engulfed and taken over by Asians, Africans, and Latinos, the festival presented the city as an aestheticized utopia of third world artists. Multiculturalism in the L.A. festival is represented as a polyvocal symphony of cultures; it is as if the festival's importing of selected "world" artists serves to "inoculate" Los Angeles against unmanaged "alien" invasions of the sort imagined by Scott in *Blade Runner*. A narrative of "authenticity" stressed the role of the city as "curator," whose task was the salvaging and protection of pure cultural objects threatened with extinction in their native lands. This narrative identified originary places and moments of authentic culture (such as the Mayan, Chinese, or Aboriginal), located outside of the city, both temporally and geographically "other" to the contemporary "fallen" milieu of Los Angeles. The narrative of authenticity surrounded, for example, the presentation of the Kun Opera, exiled from Communist China and pro-tected by the city; or the court performers from the Yogyakarta Palace of Java, whose performance was described as "the first time a Javanese court ensemble . . . , and this range of repertoire, has been seen outside Indo-nesia"; or the Balinese gamelan players, Maori haka war dancers, and Ecua-doran folk musicians, which the festival program described as "resisting the disintegration of their culture in the face of rapidly accelerating west-ernization of their Pacific homelands." In this sense, "Los Angeles" was constructed as the Western curator/ethnographer who no longer needed to venture out to meet the exotic tribes, because these cultures could now all be brought to Los Angeles. The production of multiculturalism, following the logic of commodification, is concerned with "importation," not "immi-gration." Museums, exhibits, and festivals may "import" cultural difference separated out from the material conflicts of immigrant community, settle-ment, and survival.

While these authentic cultures were constituted as distant and beyond the local sites of Los Angeles, a concomitant "lineage" narrative of "roots" tied Los Angeles to the ancient Chinese, Mayans, and Aborigines. The pro-gram stated, for example: "Seen side by side, a new reality comes clear— that many of the ideas, traditions, and practices of our colleagues are shared by the artists living and working in Los Angeles today. . . . The Festival celebrates humanity and the cycles of life: the remembrance of *our* ances-tors, *our* hopes for the future." Yet, in conflating third world artists and the general population of the city, the precise relationship between Okinawan dance and black gospel music, for example, was "fudged," glossed over. The festival's staging of theater, dance, and music performances from Thai-land, China, Japan, Australia, the Philippines, Indonesia, Mexico, Central

America, Chile, and Panama—adjacent to work by artists from within the city of Los Angeles itself—also enunciated to some extent this lineage narrative and its pronouncement of a dehistoricized identity and continuity of "global" and "local" cultures. The festival program read:

> 1990. We've arrived at the last decade of our century and it's a new world out there. With 85 languages spoken in the L.A. school system, it turns out that most of that new world is alive and living right here in this city. . . . We are living on the verge of the "Pacific Century." . . . This is a festival of new stories for a new America existing in a new world. . . . It's a delightful opportunity for Los Angelenos to travel to places where they don't usually go, to feel the presence of the multiple cultures that co-exist in our sprawling city. . . . After all, who owns culture?

Built on the notion of connecting traditional non-Western cultural performance with the contemporary residents of Los Angeles, the city became a living museum; the Chicano/Latino, Chinese, Japanese, African American, Thai, and Korean neighborhoods were opened up as locations for the performances by artists from Mexico, China, Japan, Africa, Thailand, and Korea. These connections foregrounded new contrasts, invented new hierarchies, and suggested new cultural mixtures and constellations. And as the final question, "After all, who owns culture?" implies, the juxtapositions were aimed at thematizing the shift in the hegemonic rule of Western art and culture toward a newly invented syncretism of "Pacific culture." The production of multiculturalism as a *representation* of a changing cultural hegemony must, however, be distinguished from shifts in the existing hegemony itself. The synthetic production of multiculturalism unravels and its crises are best seized and contested at the moments when the contradiction between the representational economy of ethnic signifiers, on the one hand, and the material economy of resources and means, on the other, becomes unavoidably clear. That is, what the claim to "new stories for a new America" made dangerously invisible is that to most African Americans, Asians, or Latinos living and working in Los Angeles today, for the other 349 days of the year, it may be very clear indeed *who* "owns" culture. It is pronounced in the official language all must learn to speak, is declared if you can't afford to buy the garments that you are employed to sew, and is evident if your call to 911 fails to bring emergency assistance to your neighborhood.

Antagonistic to the narratives of authenticity and lineage—both of which we could characterize as developmental narratives that depend on notions of continuity, progression, and conversion—was a concurrent narrative of "variety," whose formal mode was juxtaposition, pronounced in apparently random contrasts between the ancient and the postmodern, the arts of the street and the arts of the theater, "high" and "low," the Latin and the Asian, the developing worlds and the overdeveloped worlds. A collection of events at Griffith Park one weekend, for example, featured twenty different acts on five stage locations in the park: Cambodian singers, flamenco dancers, Japanese puppet theater, mariachi bands, and a Balinese children's choir all performed at once. In relying on the organizing modes of variety and juxtaposition, this "narrative" tended to erase the history of each performance by leveling the nonequivalent statuses of each particular form, genre, and cultural location. Afro-Brazilian dancers, zydeco bands, performances of Aboriginal myths and legends, and Hawaiian hula were all accorded the same relative importance. "Los Angeles" was represented as a postmodern multicultural cornucopia, an international patchwork quilt, a global department store; although the "signifiers" were the very uneven, irreducible differences between these diverse acts, the important "signified" was a notion of Los Angeles as multicultural spectacle. In the process, each performance tradition was equated with every other, and its meaning was reduced and generalized to a common denominator whose significance was the exotic, colorful advertisement of Los Angeles. Despite tensions between the narratives of authenticity, lineage and variety, all these narratives effect, in different ways, the erasure and occlusion of the "material" geographies of Los Angeles. None of the productions of multiculturalism reckons with the practical relationships between heterogeneous and economically unequal racial, ethnic, and immigrant communities in Los Angeles, a city that is already the home to more people of Mexican descent than any other city outside Mexico, more Koreans than any other city outside Asia, and more Filipinos than any city outside the Philippines. All depend on "forgetting" the historically produced spatial discipline and geographical separations and ghettoizations of Black Americans and the poorest of these immigrant groups.⁶ The important distinctions and contradictions within and among racial and ethnic minority groups are leveled according to a pluralism that effectively continues to privilege the centrality of dominant culture. As Hal Foster argues, pluralism promotes a form of tolerance that leaves the status quo unthreatened; the margins are absorbed into the center, and the heterogeneous is domesticated into the homogeneous.⁷ Pluralism's leveling of the material, and not simply aesthetic, unevennesses of racial, ethnic, and immigrant cultures, as well as its erasure of exclusions, effects the *depoliticization* of multiculturalism. In this sense, it is the productive conflict and irresolution between pluralist and antipluralist narratives that mark the most interesting moments of the festival.

Thus, although the production of multiculturalism manifests the drive toward aestheticist and pluralist containment, none of the multicultural narratives monolithically "colonizes" the radically nonequivalent populations and locales each seeks to include and represent. In this sense, the "fetishized" rendering of Asian, Latino, and African American "difference" (each itself a contradictory grouping, crossed by differences of language, generation, class, national origin, gender, and religion) is also challenged at moments by important pressures from oppositional narratives that emerged from the festival's placement of performances within those particular communities of Los Angeles. Oppositional narratives and practices reappropriated parts of the festival, exploiting its contradictions. They made use of the juxtapositions employed by the festival but inflected the disjunctions differently, drawing attention to the inequalities between cultural objects by reattaching the objects to contexts of production and reception. In this way, the histories of immigration, racialization, and commodification—through which objects are separated from their material contexts—were rendered more explicit. For example, the contradictions of multiculturalism were exploited by oppositional practices in the staging of the Thai Likay performers at the Wat Thai Temple in North Hollywood and in the placement of the African Marketplace near West Central Los Angeles. That is, according to official multicultural narratives of authenticity and lineage that underlay the organization of the festival, these stagings dictated identifications between cultural performance and local communities: a Thai

temple was connected to Thai performers, and a Black American community was attached to African cultural forms. Yet, at the same time, these
stagings actually threw into relief the histories that disrupted and have rendered discontinuous the relationships between Thai immigrants and Thai
artists and between Black Americans and Africans. Oppositional narratives
did not concede a simple construction of "identity" between the imported
art forms and the situated Los Angeles communities of color but articulated the displacement and disidentification that are the historical products of racialization, immigration, and capitalist exploitation. Likewise, in
the process of these stagings of multiculturalism, disparate communities
were introduced to one another—for example, the performance at the Wat
Thai Temple was the occasion for new and existing relationships between
the Thai and the gay communities in North Hollywood. Where the festival's production of multiculturalism staged a Korean shaman arriving
in a Korean American strip mall, implying a relationship of identity between the Korean shaman and Korean Americans, an oppositional narrative emerged out of the contradiction between the history of shamanism in
precolonial Korea and the fact that many Korean Americans in Los Angeles
are Christian; this contradiction erupted despite multiculturalism's insistence on continuity and the occlusion of the displacement of colonialism
and immigration. Whereas the logic of multiculturalism dictates "identification," oppositional practices exploit the contradictions of identity and
rearticulate practices of "disidentification."

The 1992 riots in Los Angeles following the verdict that freed four white
policemen accused of beating a Black man, Rodney King, are the most vivid
eruption of the contradiction between multiculturalism as the representation of the liberal state and the material poverty and disenfranchisement
that are the conditions of those represented. Though the U.S. media consistently attempted to construct the crisis as a racial conflict between Blacks
and Koreans, the looters enraged by the King verdict were not only Blacks
but also Chicanos, Latinos, and working-class whites; all violently objected
to the denial of brutally racialized economic stratification. In concluding,
I wish to locate a radical critique of multiculturalism in the recent 1993
documentary video *Sa-I-Gu*, by Christine Choy, Elaine Kim, and Dai Sil
Kim-Gibson.[8] The video powerfully disrupts a linear, developmental nar-

rative that seeks to assimilate ethnic immigrants into the capitalist economy. The very different articulations of the Korean immigrant and Korean
American speakers contradict a notion of the homogeneous authenticity
of immigrant groups. Finally, *Sa-I-Gu* radically challenges the liberal myth
of pluralist inclusion, both on the level of the speakers' testimonies and in
terms of the interrupted, particularist form of the video itself.

   Sa-I-Gu collects heterogeneous interviews with Korean immigrant and
Korean American women speaking about the Los Angeles crisis in the
aftermath of the King verdict. Not a narrative, *Sa-I-Gu* offers a series of
clips of Korean immigrant workers, shopkeepers, and owners of grocery,
liquor and convenience stores and laundries—women who speak about
their losses and their disillusionments. Their testimonies are contradictory,
unsynthetic, and unhomogeneous. They speak about the lack of support
from the Los Angeles Police Department and the National Guard during
the uprisings. They speak about the fatigue of working long hours to eke
out a living. They speak about losing sons, husbands, livelihood, and opportunity. The film opens with an interview with the mother of Edward
Jae Song Lee, who was shot and died during the crisis when he was mis-
taken by a store owner for a looter. Her testimony focuses on mourning
the loss of her son, as well as her disillusionment with the promises of
capitalism, democratic inclusion, and protection by police or government.
She says: "At the time, I thought it was one man who shot my son. But
if I think broadly, it is not just an individual matter. Something is drasti-
cally wrong." Another woman interviewed states: "I would like to express
my feeling about this after this riot. Right now I'm angry at everybody. Or
on contrary, I'm angry at myself. Because I don't know to whom to where
I should be angry at them. I am totally confused, totally confused." The
statements of both women articulate the desire to grasp an explanation
of the convergence of racism and capitalism from their location as immigrant women, as much as their "confusion" attests to the unavailability of
this convergence. Indeed, the Los Angeles crisis, in which Korean Americans became the recipients of violent anger that might have been "better"
directed at white capital in other parts of the intensely spatially segre-
gated city, illustrates precisely how a society, "structured in dominance" as
Althusser would say, can mask the interlocking functions of racism, patri-

archy, and capitalism not only by ideologically constructing multicultural inclusion but also by separating and dividing the objects of capitalist exploitation—as black youth, as Korean shopkeeper, as Chicana single mother.[9] It is this isolation of objects that contributes to the fragmentation of racialized life in advanced capitalist society. This isolation likewise contributes to the fragmentation of political organization against the interlocking functions through which domination is effected. The statement of "confusion" at not knowing where to focus blame implies a desire for an explanation for the convergence of dominations; at the same time, it articulates the difficulty of apprehending or seizing more than what appears to be a fragment of that convergence. If the society structured-in-dominance and its oppositional responses remain unavailable to the groups and individuals constrained by those structures, then domination functions and persists precisely through the unavailability of this structure. Multiculturalism is one ideological representation of the liberal state that enacts that unavailability.

The Korean immigrant woman's despair does not signify a powerless lack of knowing but rather the failure of the promise of citizenship proposed by liberal society to answer to the injustice that precipitated and was exemplified in the L.A. crisis. The stated "confusion" articulates the need for new narrative modes of explanation that can address the convergence of determinations which situate racialized workingwomen in Los Angeles and which can be adequate to the kind of political subjectivity they inhabit. This notion of confusion should not suggest that the convergence of determinations can be conceived as contained within anything like an absolute "totality." Indeed, like that of the liberal citizen-subject, emancipatory narratives of consciousness privileging a singular subject's perspective from which totalization becomes possible contribute to just such an illusory idea of "totality." In contrast, the Korean immigrant women speaking in *Sa-I-Gu* voice their situations within multiple, nonequivalent, but linked determinations without assuming their containment within the horizon of an absolute totality and its presumption of a singular subject. The dominant U.S. media construction of the Korean Americans in the L.A. crisis has generally reduced and obscured them as "middle men" within U.S. race and class relations, situating them in an intermediary position within capitalist development and suggesting they are more threatened by Blacks than by corporate capitalism. *Sa-I-Gu* makes clear that Korean Americans understand themselves within a very different history and memory that includes the emergence of Korean nationalism during the Japanese occupation and colonization of Korea (1910–1945), during the period of partition and the Korean War, and through the period of military rule in South Korea.

"Sa-I-Gu" means "4.29," or April 29 (the date of the Rodney King verdicts). By using a Korean convention for naming key moments in the long history of Korean nationalism, the struggles against the 1992 attack on the Korean immigrant community are placed within the context of other Korean nationalist struggles. Elaine Kim wrote of Korean Americans after the Los Angeles uprising:

> Situated as we are on the border between those who have and those who have not, between predominantly Anglo and mostly African American and Latino communities, from our current interstitial position in the American discourse of race, many Korean Americans have trouble calling what happened in Los Angeles an "uprising." At the same time, we cannot quite say it was a "riot." So some of us have taken to calling it *sa-i-ku*, April 29, after the manner of naming other events in Korean history—3.1 (*sam-il*) for March 1, 1919, when massive protests against Japanese colonial rule began in Korea; 6.25 (*yook-i-o*), or June 25, 1950, when the Korean War began; and 4.19 (sa-il-ku), or April 19, 1960, when the first student movement in the world to overthrow a government began in South Korea. The ironic similarity between 4.19 and 4.29 does not escape most Korean Americans.[10]

In light of the naming of the L.A. crisis as "sa-i-ku," we can understand Korean American nationalism in the aftermath of the L.A. crisis not as a direct transference of the meanings of Korean nationalism but as rearticulation of them, one that includes both the history of Koreans as colonized subjects displaced through immigration to the United States and a consideration of the racialization of Korean immigrants in Los Angeles as a community of color.

In *Sa-I-Gu*, a powerful particularism—particular griefs, losses, and anger—demystifies multiculturalist inclusion and moves us toward an interrogation of the converged structure-in-dominance of which multiculturalism is the ideological expression and resolution. *Sa-I-Gu* is a radical objection to multiculturalism and a forceful testimony and critique of the conjunction of global capitalism with racism and patriarchy in Los Angeles. As oppositional narrative and practice, *Sa-I-Gu* conflicts with the multiculturalist narratives of authenticity, lineage, and variety, building pressure against the pluralist tendencies of a produced multiculturalism. If we do not stress these oppositions, the geographies and histories of racialized community and immigrant settlement in Los Angeles are dangerously obscured. Segregation of neighborhoods is masked as spatial contiguity, and racial and class violence between groups is aestheticized in a multicultural juxtaposition of ethnic images. Without these tensions, multiculturalism fails to come to grips with the material inequalities and strata of a city like Los Angeles: the separations, unevennesses of opportunity because of different groups' histories of labor, racism, and poverty.[11] For instance, in an essay on the representation of racial struggles in rap and popular music after the L.A. crisis, Jeff Chang discusses rap artist Ice Cube's "Black Korea" as a pointed expression of interracial conflict between what he calls the "differently disempowered" racialized groups of Blacks and Asians. On the one hand, "Black Korea" is a cultural articulation of Black antagonism to white-dominated society, but Chang argues persuasively that the interpretation of Black anger in terms of a white-black racial axis erases Korean American community. He connects ideology and representation in the media to "the hierarchy of socio-political power in the U.S. that places whites on top, African Americans far below, and Asian Americans still below them," also describing the economic "middle man" position of many Korean Americans in South Central Los Angeles that exacerbates the conflict between Blacks and Asians. Chang actively urges against a "zero-sum game of racial struggle" that would have different groups of color blaming one another and proposes that understanding "differential forms of disempowerment" could help us grapple with different histories of exploitation so that solidarity could be built in terms other than claims to individual group empowerment. In its contribution to the conversation, Chang's interpretation is an intervention that then becomes part of the cultural production itself, and his analysis contributes to the process through which racial identities and political subjectivities are made, remade, and enacted.[12]

Narratives of multiculturalism which do not make these connections between historically differentiated forms of disempowerment or which do not make space for oppositional critiques risk denuding racial and ethnic groups of their specificity. Subject to the leveling operations of both postmodern pastiche and pluralism, African, Asian, and Latino cultures all become equally "other," are metaphorized as equally different and whole without contradiction. The narratives that suppress tension and opposition suggest that we have already achieved multiculturalism, that we know what it is, and that it is defined simply by the coexistence and juxtaposition of greater numbers of diverse groups; these narratives allow us to ignore the profound and urgent gaps, the inequalities and conflicts, among racial, ethnic, and immigrant groups. The suggestion that multicultural discourses might ultimately emphasize, rather than domesticate, the productive irresolution, opposition, and conflict of these various narratives is neither a call for chaos nor a return to traditional Western notions of art and high culture. It is instead to assert that it may be through contradiction that we begin to address the systemic inequalities built into cultural institutions, economies, and geographies and through conflict that we call attention to the process through which these inequalities are obscured by pluralist multiculturalism. We need to think through the ways in which culture may be rearticulated not in terms of identity, equivalence, or pluralism but out of contradiction, as a site for alternative histories and memories that provide the grounds to imagine subject, community, and practice in new ways.

Decolonization, Displacement,

Disidentification: Writing and

the Question of History

> To articulate the past historically does not mean to recognize it "the way it really was" (Ranke). It means to seize hold of a memory as it flashes up at a moment of danger.
> —Walter Benjamin, "Theses on the Philosophy of History"

Frantz Fanon directs our attention, in *Black Skin, White Masks* (1967), to the importance of language as the medium through which a colonizing culture forms the colonized subject: "To speak means to be in a position to use a certain syntax, to grasp the morphology of this or that language, but it means above all to assume a culture, to support the weight of a civilization."[1] In alluding to the paradoxical fluency of the colonized subject in the colonial language and culture, Fanon astutely names the twofold character of colonial formation. The imposition of the colonial language and its cultural institutions, among them the novel, demands the subject's internalization of the "superiority" of the colonizer and the "inferiority" of the colonized, even as it attempts to evacuate the subject of "native" language, traditions, and practices. Yet the colonized subject produced within such an encounter does not merely bear the marks of the coercive encounter between the dominant language and culture, constructed as whole, autonomous, and disinterested, and the specificities of the colonized group's existence. Such encounters produce contradictory subjects, in whom the demands for fluency in imperial languages and empire's cultural institutions simultaneously provide the grounds for antagonism to those demands.

97

In this chapter, Fanon's analysis of the role of colonial narratives is extended to modes of cultural imperialism that cross national boundaries, are in excess of a single nation-state formation, and are complicated further by displacement and immigration. I first examine the function of "official" narratives of integration, such as the novel and the historical narrative, as "cultural institutions" of subject formation, in order to consider alternative forms of subjectivity and history whose emergences are obscured by these dominant forms. Through discussions of "novels" written in English by Asian immigrants and Asian Americans, this chapter considers the novel as a cultural institution that regulates formations of citizenship and the nation, genders the domains of "public" and "private" activities, prescribes the spatialization of race relations, and, most of all, determines possible contours and terrains for the narration of "history." In other words, the cultural institution of the novel legitimates particular forms and subjects of history and subjugates or erases others. In this regard, I explore the institutional and formal continuities between the novel and historical narrative.

With the emergence of print culture as an institution of modernity in the "West," the Anglo-American novel has held a position of primary importance in the interpellation of readers as subjects for the nation, in the gendering of these subjects, and in the racializing of spheres of activity and work. In both England and the United States, the novel as a form of print culture has constituted a privileged site for the unification of the citizen with the "imagined community" of the nation, while the national literary canon functioned to unify aesthetic culture as a domain in which material differences and localities were resolved and reconciled. The bildungsroman emerged as the primary form for narrating the development of the individual from youthful innocence to civilized maturity, the telos of which is the reconciliation of the individual with the social order. The novel of formation has a special status among the works selected for a canon, for it elicits the reader's identification with the bildung narrative of ethical formation, itself a narrative of the individual's relinquishing of particularity and difference through identification with an idealized "national" form of subjectivity.[2]

We can view Jane Austen's *Pride and Prejudice* (1813), for example, as an important artifact and producer of nineteenth-century English discourses

on middle-class morality and propriety, of women's domestic role within
the ideology of separate "public" and "private" spheres, and of the reconciliation of bourgeois individualism and the social order through the
marriage contract. Yet as a result of the institutionalization of the novel
in England as well as in the British Empire's systems of colonial education, the powerfully determining divisions and narrative resolutions of
Austen's novel extend well beyond her nineteenth-century English public
to the globalized readers and recipients of popular culture in the late twentieth century. In reckoning with that legacy, we might think of the ways
in which the orthodoxy of domestic womanhood emerges as a ruling category and terrain of contestation in postcolonial Anglophone novels. Buchi
Emecheta's novel *The Joys of Motherhood*, for example, portrays a Nigerian
woman in the 1930s and 1940s who is poignantly caught between "traditional" Ibo definitions of motherhood within the extended family and
the "modern" capitalist gender relations prescribing female domesticity
within the nuclear family that were imposed by the colonial British state.[3]
The description of colonial education in Jamaica in Michelle Cliff's *Abeng*
also offers an apt allegory for the widespread communication of English
"civility."[4] Just as the Jamaican schoolgirls of *Abeng* are required to recite
William Wordsworth's poem "Daffodils," so they are disciplined to conform
to received notions of proper middle-class English "femininity": "No doubt
the same manuals were shipped to villages in Nigeria, schools in Hong
Kong. . . . Probably there were a million children who could recite 'Daffodils,' and a million who had never actually seen the flower, only the drawing, and so did not know why the poet had been stunned" (85). Though
the resolutions narrated in Austen's bildungsroman were by no means uniform and complete in her own time—there were growing contradictions
between the notion of separate spheres and nineteenth-century social practices, between her narrative of class reconciliation through sentimental
marriage and the turmoil of the period that E. P. Thompson described in
the *Making of the English Working Class*—I would argue that in the institutionalization of the English novel in the British colonies, there was an even
greater contradiction between the values and norms of the colonizing culture and the bifurcated, unequal colonial society that the colonial education
functioned to sustain and reproduce.[5] And the cultural and political identifi-

cations of the United States with Britain insured that the bourgeois English formation detailed in Austen's novels has been disseminated with a scope almost equivalent to that of television reception. Just as the English novel was a central cultural institution in British colonial education and contributed to the formation of subjects in the British colonies of India, Nigeria, and Jamaica, so can we observe this legacy of cultural authority in the relationship between the American novel from *The Scarlet Letter* to *The Sound and the Fury* and the literary and cultural traditions of African Americans, Native Americans, Chicanos/Latinos, and Asian Americans in the United States. I do not intend to imply an always oppositional relationship between an imperial metropolitan culture and its subordinated others, nor am I claiming that the Anglophone writing by colonized or minoritized groups in every case transgresses the imperatives of the English or American novel. Let us emphasize instead that owing to complex, uneven material histories of colonization and the oppression of racialized groups within the United States, the sites of minority or colonized literary production are at different distances from the canonical nationalist project of reconciling constituencies to idealized forms of community and subjectivity. As I argue in Chapter 2, the structural location of U.S. minority literature may produce effects of dissonance, fragmentation, and irresolution even and especially when that literature appears to be performing a canonical function. Even those novels that can be said to conform more closely to the formal criteria of the bildungsroman express a contradiction between the demand for a univocal developmental narrative and the historical specificities of racialization, ghettoization, violence, and labor exploitation. The kind and degree of contradiction between those historical specificities and the national narrative served by the cultural institution of the novel generates formal deviations whose significances are misread if simply assimilated as modernist or postmodernist aesthetic modes. The effects of these works are more radically grasped in terms of their constant interrogation of the discrepancies between canonical historical narratives and what Walter Benjamin would term the material "catastrophes" that those histories obscure.

In the larger part of this chapter I examine three contemporary Asian American/Asian immigrant texts which interrupt the traditional forms for narrating the development of the individual subject and its reconciliation to the national social order and which explore alternative forms of memory, history, and collectivity. These texts challenge the concepts of identity and identification within a universalized narrative of development. They radically skew the relationship of the citizen-subject to the nation by challenging the constructions of both "Asian" and "American." I begin by suggesting the rhetorical and institutional congruence between U.S. historical narratives of Asia and Asian Americans, on the one hand, and the institution of the Anglophone novel, on the other, arguing that the orientalist histories take up the realist aesthetic that governs representation in the novel and that they borrow the formal devices of the novel as a means of situating Asia and narrating the incorporation of Asian immigrants into the U.S. nation. In meditating on the notion of blood as ground and figure of representation in Theresa Hak Kyung Cha's *Dictée* (1982), on gossip as an antifiguration of narrative in Jessica Hagedorn's *Dogeaters* (1990), and on the excavation of urban space as a disruption of overdeveloped temporalization in Fae Myenne Ng's *Bone* (1993), I trace how these Asian American works displace the representational regimes of the institutionalized novel and official historical narrative by writing out of the limits and breakdowns of those regimes. In their writing, these Asian immigrant and Asian American women explore other modes of retrieving and spatializing history. They offer other modes for imagining and narrating immigrant subjectivity and community—emerging out of conditions of decolonization, displacement, and disidentification—and refuse assimilation to the dominant narratives of integration, development, and identification.

■

The concept of the historical progress of mankind cannot be sundered from the concept of its progression through a homogeneous, empty time. A critique of the concept of such a progression must be the basis of any criticism of the concept of progress itself. —Benjamin, "Theses"

Throughout the twentieth century, U.S. orientalism has been determined by several differentiated but interconnected apparatuses of rule. Orientalism was deployed to justify the use of brutal military force in the colonization of the Philippines; the war against Japan, culminating in the nuclear bombing of Hiroshima and Nagasaki; the war in and partition of Korea, and the war in Vietnam. Orientalism also bears a crucial relationship to the history of Asian immigration, exclusion, and naturalization. As I argue in Chapter 1, immigration and naturalization laws have been not only means of policing the terms of the "citizen" and the nation-state but also part of an orientalist discourse that defines Asians as "foreign" in times when the United States has constructed itself as ideologically at war with Asia.

The crisis of U.S. national identity during the period of war in Asia, coupled with the imperatives of racializing and proletarianizing the Asian populations immigrating to the United States from a variety of national origins, has necessitated a complex and variegated discourse for managing "oriental otherness." A racialized and gendered anti-Asian discourse produces and manages a "double front" of Asian threat and encroachment: on the one hand, as external rivals in overseas imperial war and global economy and, on the other, as a needed labor force for the domestic economy. The "blood-will-tell" anti-Japanese racial discourse during World War II, propaganda about the traitorous Asian as subhuman, and the extensive conflation of Asian women with accessible "foreign" territories to be conquered and subdued are all parts of a midcentury U.S. orientalism tailored to homogenize and subordinate both internal and external Asian populations.[6] World War II inaugurated an acute figuration of the Asian as racial enemy. And throughout the postwar period until 1970, war films, popular novels, as well as "official" historical narratives deployed this discourse for the purpose of unifying national identity, justifying the cold war, and assisting the expansion of the domestic American market.[7]

In the post–cold war period, though the traditional anti-Asian figurations persist, the emergence in Asia of formidable capitalist rivals has also given rise to a discourse of economic penetration and trade with those overseas nations that the United States had previously caricatured as enemies. In the meantime, the abolition of national-origin quotas since 1965, allowing for 170,000 immigrants annually from the Eastern Hemisphere, has changed the profile of "Asian Americans" enormously, rendering the majority of the constituency Asian-born, rather than multiple-generation: the new immigrants from South Vietnam, South Korea, Cambodia, Laos, the Philippines, India, and Pakistan have diversified the already existing Asian American group of Chinese, Japanese, and Filipino descent. "Multiculturalism," leveling the important differences and contradictions within and among racial and ethnic minority groups, has since emerged as a discourse that seeks to integrate Asian immigrant workers into the domestic capitalist economy. And, finally, as U.S. capitalism shifts production to the third world, making use, in low-cost export assembly and manufacturing zones, of Southeast Asian and Latin American female labor in particular, the proletarianization of nonwhite women has led to a breakdown and a reformulation of the categories and the relations of national, racial, and gender difference that were characteristic of the earlier, more nationalist-inspired orientalism.

This contemporary shift toward the transnationalization of capital is not exclusively manifested in the "denationalization" of corporate power but, more important, is also expressed in the reorganization of oppositional movements and constituencies against capital that articulate themselves in terms and relations other than the "national"—notably, movements of U.S. women of color and third world women.[8] As I have been suggesting, post-1965 Asian immigrants are a contemporary group emerging out of colonialism in Asia as well as immigrant displacement to the United States, a group at once determined by the histories of Western expansionism in Asia and the racialization of working populations of color in the United States. Especially in light of post-1965 Asian immigrations to the United States, Asian American subjectivity is a complex site of different displacements, particularly the displacement from a decolonizing or neocolonized Asian society to a United States with whose sense of national identity the immigrants are often in contradiction. Once in the United States, the demands that Asians narrate themselves in liberal discourses of development, assimilation, and citizenship provide the grounds for antagonism to such demands. The imperatives that the subject identify—as a national, classed, and gendered subject—take place within the materially differentiated conditions of racialized workers of color that simultaneously produce *disidentification* out of which critical subjectivities may emerge. Disidentification expresses a space in which alienations, in the cultural, political, and economic senses, can be rearticulated in oppositional forms. But disidentification does not entail merely the formation of oppositional identities against the call to identification with the national state. On the contrary, it allows for the exploration of alternative political and cultural subjectivities that emerge within the continuing effects of displacement. In the discussions that follow I attach these important disidentifications and incommensurabilities to the writing of Asian American "novels" as alternative "histories," suggesting that displacement, decolonization, and disidentification are crucial grounds for the emergence of Asian American critique.

Western theorists of modernity and postmodernity, as well as postcolonial intellectuals, subaltern studies historians, and feminist critics of colonialism have articulated critiques of the realist aesthetic as a regime for the production of history. In studies of the rhetoric and tropology of nineteenth-century historical narratives, Hayden White and Dominick LaCapra target verisimilitude, development, and teleology as fundamental to European history's truth effects; for Jean-François Lyotard, notably, the postmodern moment is one that is witnessing the breakdown of such master narratives of dominant culture and aesthetics.[9] That Western historiography itself establishes the congruence of historical narratives with a realist representational project suggests that this aesthetic constitutes not only the historiographical means through which empires narrated their own progress and the aesthetic that imperial subjects used to represent colonies as peripheral objects but also the aesthetic they imposed on their colonies and within which they demanded those colonies narrate themselves. Accordingly, critiques of orientalism have linked the aesthetic interrogation of the project of representation to the historiographical critique of narrative as an apparatus of European colonial rule.[10] Postcolonial theorists have written about the way that colonial powers imposed modes of historical representation on the colonized and have analyzed the violence to, but failed containment of, the colonized within the modes of literary representation.[11] Radical historians of India and the Philippines have argued that official colonialist histories, as well as the elite nationalist histories they have informed and engendered, have favored the narrative structure of progressive, stage-bound development of a unified subject and people, a structure that has subjugated the fragmented, decentralized activities of mass uprisings, peasant revolts, and laborer rebellions.[12] Feminist theorists have further challenged orientalist historiography by interrogating narrative histories as technologies of patriarchal rule: their insistence that all aspects of colonial society are gendered has provided a basis for moving the critique

of orientalism beyond a privileging or universalizing of the colonized subject—male or female—as a means of decentering orientalist history.[13]

In this sense, the authority of orientalist narrative falters on a number of frontiers, yet the documentations of its failure quite evidently take
place differently, depending on the locations and contexts of their productions. While U.S. orientalism makes use of the representational and
narrative regimes of an earlier orientalism that expressed the European
empires' desire to institutionalize colonialism elsewhere, it has also been
transformed by a different state formation and by the global and national
contexts of U.S. expansion in Asia. Keeping this in mind, it is useful to
consider how U.S. historical accounts of Asia take up the formal features
of the aesthetic governing the novel.

In *The Crucial Decade—and After: America, 1945–1960,* Eric Goldman
writes that the commencement of the Korean War lies in a conversation
between Truman and the State Department:

> The American government had long known that Korea was a trouble
> spot. . . . In the spring of 1950, the American Central Intelligence
> Agency was reporting that the North Koreans were continuing to build
> up their military machine with Soviet assistance and might launch a
> full-scale offensive. . . .
>
> . . . Harry Truman had heard enough. He told Acheson that he would
> order his plane, the *Independence,* readied immediately and asked the
> Secretary of State to get together with the military chiefs and prepare
> recommendations. . . . Bess Truman waved good-by to her husband
> with a look very much like the one she had on that eerie evening when
> Vice-President Truman suddenly became President Truman. Margaret
> stood a bit apart from the airport crowd, staring at the plane with her
> hands clasped under her chin as if in silent prayer.

Goldman continues:

> The very nature of the Presidential decisions disarmed critics of the
> Truman-Acheson foreign policy. . . . They put their faith, above all, in
> General Douglas MacArthur. It was at the General's recommendation
> —and this fact was generally known—that full intervention had been
> decided upon, and Douglas MacArthur was in command in Korea. . . .

. . . For one moment, suspended weirdly in the bitter debates . . . the reckless plunge of the North Korean Communists and the bold response of Harry Truman had united America.[14]

In Goldman's narrative, "history" is developmental. A succession of events leads up to a crisis and is then resolved. History is made by elite heroes (the president and secretary of state) whose foes are U.S. public opinion and intragovernmental relations, and the drama is played out before Bess and Margaret, a loyal feminine spectatorship. The narrative structure implies that Korean leaders and mass groups are merely a passive, perhaps colorful, backdrop for the drama of the central noble protagonist, President Truman. The dynamics of Korean nationalism in its relationship to the Japanese occupation, the generational and political schisms within Korean nationalism that were expressed in the partition of Korea, as well as the larger scope of U.S. involvement in Asia before 1950—all are erased or obscured by the central drama of the U.S. government's decision to send General MacArthur into South Korea.

The account of Korea offered by James Thomson, Peter Stanley, and John Curtis Perry in *Sentimental Imperialists: The American Experience in East Asia* (1981) also elucidates features of U.S. orientalist narrative. "Korea's tragedy has been that the nation is alone, precariously situated between the major cultures of China and Japan, with no neighbors comparably small or weak. . . . With one language, one ethnic group, and one society, Korea is one of the world's oldest and most homogeneous nation-states, stubbornly retaining its distinct cultural identity despite periodic invasions and recurring waves of foreign influence. Perhaps this cultural tenacity is in part due to the challenge posed by the outside world."[15] "Korea" is here posited as a fixed, static victim, without differentiation from itself. Unlike the West, which possesses self-consciousness and can know itself through the universal reason of its own histories, "Korea" is fundamentally unphilosophical and atavistic. Thomson, Stanley, and Perry narrate the history of Korea as tragic; their narrative exemplifies the paternalism that figures the West as the father and Asian nations as backward children in need of emancipation. It positions Korea with reference to a West-Other axis, obscuring the relations between Korea and other Asian peoples and suppressing any recognition of Korea as internally complex: as a country of differently classed and propertied populations, men and women, many religions, official and unofficial nationalisms.

The larger project of *Sentimental Imperialists* reiterates the narrative form and function of the bildungsroman. It documents the history of imperialist war in Asia as a story of the progress of the United States from youthful "innocence and grandiosity," through the "dashing of hopes," to the maturity of a nation seasoned by the trials of war in Asia. It narrates the reconciliation of a nation made wiser by the errors of having entered into difficult and not always victorious wars, "educated" by the lessons of anti-Communism and imperialism. Fundamentally, it exemplifies a narrative of nationalist unification—the triumph of liberal tolerance and the magnanimous state that protects and incorporates immigrants.

We have observed that this link between historical narratives of the U.S. nation and novelistic narratives of the individual is mediated by adherence to a realist aesthetic, a fetishized concept of development, and the narration of a single unified subject. Having already mentioned the Euro-American poststructuralist or "postmodern" critique of the congruence of historical narrative and the novel, we must differentiate such "Western" challenges to representation from the "decolonizing" writing that emerges from third world, diaspora, and racialized U.S. sites. In *The Wretched of the Earth*, Fanon defines decolonization as a process of thorough social transformation that disorganizes the stratified social hierarchy beyond the nationalist party's capture of the state from the colonizer. Decolonization, in Fanon's sense, does not prematurely signify the end of colonialism but refers to the multifaceted, ongoing project of resistance struggles that can persist for decades in the midst of simultaneous neocolonial exploitation. Associating bourgeois nationalism and the colonial state's structures of domination, Fanon designates decolonization as a third alternative to colonialism and nationalism, exhausted by neither the political narrative of constitutional representation by the state nor the notion of a nationalist aesthetic that posits national culture and the representative work as sites of resolution.[16] Decolonization can therefore be defined as necessarily antagonistic to existing institutions of representation, aesthetic and literary as well as constitutional or political. We can read Asian American writing as emerging out of decolonization, in this sense. Euro-American postmodernism dissolves the notion of a homogeneous "West" as it has been constructed within Enlightenment literary and philosophical categories; like poststructuralism, it contests the "modern" within European terms and reveals the difference internal to the making of the West.[17] In contradistinction, "decolonizing" writing, which may include features associated with postmodernism (such as nonlinear, antirepresentational aesthetics), emerges not from a terrain of philosophical or poetic otherness within the West but out of the contradictions of what Bipan Chandra has called the "colonial mode of production."[18] Whereas the relations of production of nineteenth-century industrial capitalism were characterized by the management of the urban workers by the urban bourgeoisie, colonialism was built on the split between colonial metropolis and agrarian colony, organizing the agrarian society into a social formation in which a foreign class functioned as the capitalist class. In order to maximize the extraction of surplus value, the necessary reproduction of the relations of production in the colonial mode was not limited to class relations but emphasized the reconstruction of hierarchical relations of region, culture, language, and especially race.

"Decolonization," then, is the social formation that encompasses a multi-leveled and multicentered assault on those specific forms of colonial rule; that project of decolonization is carried forth in the "postcolonial" site but may equally be deployed by immigrant and diasporic populations. In Chapter 4, for example, we observed in the discussion of the Korean American video documentary *Sa-I-Gu* how vocabularies from the decolonizing struggle in Korea became available for rearticulation by Korean immigrant communities in the United States. In other words, if we understand "decolonization" as an ongoing disruption of the colonial mode of production, then Asian American writing performs that displacement from a social formation marked by the uneven and unsynthetic encounters of colonial, neocolonial, and mass and elite indigenous cultures that characterize decolonization. These material pressures produce texts that resist the formal abstraction of aestheticization that is a legacy of European modernism and a continuing feature of European postmodernism. In this sense, the writing of the "decolonizing novel" takes place necessarily by way of a detour into the excavation of "history," as we will see in Theresa Hak Kyung Cha's *Dictée*.[19]

■

. . . the angel of history. His face is turned toward the past. Where we perceived a chain of events, he sees one single catastrophe which keeps piling wreckage upon wreckage and hurls it in front of his feet. — Benjamin, "Theses"

In Theresa Hak Kyung Cha's *Dictée* (1982), there is no full narrative account of the Japanese occupation of Korea from 1910 to 1945 and no linear history of the brutal suppressions of a resistant Korean nationalist movement that originated in the Tonghak Rebellion of 1884–1895 and flowered in the March First Movement of 1919.[20] There are no emancipationist narratives of the Korean War of 1950 and the partition of Korea in 1953. Nor is there a narrative of the exodus of Koreans and their dislocations in the United States, on the one hand, or an explicit narrative history of the U.S. neocolonial role in the military dictatorship and the development of state capitalism in South Korea, on the other. Rather, *Dictée* juxtaposes a series of episodes, scenes, and evocative fragments, including a period of Korean nationalism during the Japanese colonial occupation, a description of the adult narrator's displaced situation as a Korean American immigrant, and a memory of the narrator's return to a military-ruled South Korea after the Korean War.

Images of blood—spilling from the open wound, staining the pavement as a crowd is assaulted by troops, seeping from students caught and beaten—punctuate the episodes in *Dictée*. Descriptions of blood hemorrhaging, emptying, and flowing, erupt in a text that refuses continuous narration of the wars, insurgencies, containments, and violences that are central to both U.S. neocolonial and South Korean nationalist accounts of the Korean people during this century. Allusions to splitting, breaking, and dividing—of tongue, body, family, and nation—pervade *Dictée*. In particular, one scene, depicting the splitting and severing of the body in relation to representation and narrative technique, alludes to the military suppression of the April 19 students' revolt of 1960 (*sa-il-ku*), and in this scene, blood becomes the ground of representation as well as the figure of erasure.

I feel the tightening of the crowd body to body. . . . The air is made visible with smoke it grows spreads without control we are hidden inside the whiteness the greyness reduced to parts, reduced to separation. Inside an arm lifts above the head in deliberate gesture and disappears into the thick white from which slowly the legs of another bent at the knee hit the ground the entire body on its left side. *The stinging, it slices the air it enters* thus I lose direction the sky is a haze running the streets emptied I fell no one saw me I walk. Anywhere. In tears the air stagnant continues to sting I am crying the sky remnant the gas smoke absorbed the sky I am crying. The streets covered with chipped bricks and debris. Because. I see the frequent pairs of shoes thrown sometimes a single pair among the rocks they had carried. Because. I cry wail torn shirt lying I step among them. No trace of them. *Except for the blood. Because. Step among them the blood that will not erase with the rain on the pavement that was walked upon like the stones where they fell had fallen. Because. Remain dark the stain not wash away. Because. I follow the crying crowd their voices among them their singing their voices unceasing the empty street.*[21]

This passage dramatically disrupts not only syntax but also the grammars of predication and causality fundamental to the novel and history: both presuppose closure (telos) and character (subject of development). Just as the passage portrays bodies that are wounded and separated, so too is syntax interrupted and truncated. There is a conspicuous absence of purposive narrative context, and no explanation for either the disrupted syntax or the fragmented bodies; there is only blood, as if blood that issues from both the breaking of syntax and limbs is the only language that emerges out of the violence of grammar. Blood is not merely the representation of violence but the trace whose stain, whose flow, and whose indelibility is the measure of what cannot be represented, is the index of the violence of historical representation itself. A subversion of predication occurs in the repeated separations of subjects from modifiers and the repeated dislocations of subject and predicate, as in "the stinging, it slices the air it enters," in which it is an unnamed firing which is the subject of "slices" and "enters" and which presumably results in "the stinging." Predication and causality are disrupted as well by the temporal inversion through which the stinging precedes the slicing and entering.

"Because," the conjunction conventionally used to express cause or reason, has a peculiar status in this passage. "Because" usually precedes a logical sequence or inference, indicating an unequivocal causal relationship, but here, the four repetitions of the conjunction defy this grammar and are followed by blood staining the pavement. In this sense, the inverted grammar (splitting—"because"—blood) registers the failure of temporal narrative, and the repetitions of "because" followed by blood ("that will not erase with the rain") assault causality as a trope of official history. They interrogate predication as one among several discursive orthodoxies for producing historical truth and ultimately target the violent regimes of official representation and narrative themselves: both the U.S. narrative of Korean emancipation from Japanese colonialism by U.S. intervention, on the one hand, and an official South Korean narrative about the rise of Korean nationalism and its role in the modernization of society and the capitalist economy, on the other.[22]

We have in this passage from *Dictée* a conception of history that treats the "historical" not as a continuous narrative of progress, maturity, and increasing rationality, not as a story of great moments and individuals, but as a surplus of materiality that exceeds textualization, that renders inoperable the vocabularies and grammars of nineteenth-century, post-Enlightenment narrative with its beliefs in the individual, reason, and the linear evolution of civilization. The materiality of history is, in this passage, what will not be ordered, what does not coagulate and cohere. This materiality does not become accessible with a mere change of perspective or even a shift to another narrative; it is not exclusively a question of creating more "accurate" narratives. Rather, "history" becomes "visible" not in its narrative representation but in its defiance of the dominant regimes of representability. Like the blood, which is itself not a "fixed" material but materiality's belated sign, it spreads, skews, seeps, and will not cohere into the developmental progress that narrative history and the novel demand.

Dictée's treatment of the relationship of a mobile, nonunivocal narrating subject to official events suggests that narrative accounts that give priority to elite groups against a backdrop of the institutions of government, political assembly, and the military are partial and obfuscating. It dramatizes the fact that the investigation of nonelite, popular activity requires not only a deviation from the well-documented, official account but also a transformation of historical understanding and a revaluation of what is considered to be significant. Such an investigation demands that we become literate in what may appear, through the lens of traditional representation, to be only confused, random, or violent incidents. Rather than provoking cynicism about the possibility of writing history, the challenge to representation signals the need for alternative projects of many kinds and suggests that the writing of *different* histories—of nonelites, of insurgencies, of women, from the "bottom up"—inevitably runs up against representation and linear narrative as problematic categories. Furthermore, in episodes that remember Korea retrospectively from the standpoint of the Korean immigrant to the United States and in others that recount the immigrant's return visit to a postwar, military-ruled South Korea, *Dictée* also refigures the national boundaries and cultural institutions that form "Asian Americans." The subject of *Dictée* cannot be narrated as a national subject within a single literary or historical tradition. Rather, in her text Cha fragments and recomposes the French, American, Japanese, and Korean cultural discourses that constitute both the material limits and the possibilities of her Asian American formation. In that recomposition, a double critique emerges: fragmented "flashes" of memory at once refuse the uniformity of the South Korean national project by invoking the heterogeneity of Korean people's histories, and they critique U.S. history's erasure of Korean people in national accounts. In the recomposition and redeployment of "history" as material memory, a new Asian American subject emerges.

■

> The tradition of the oppressed teaches us that the "state of emergency" in which we live is not the exception but the rule. — Benjamin, "Theses"

Jessica Hagedorn's 1990 *Dogeaters* is a Filipina American text that also radically alters the form and function of the novel and of historical narrative through explorations of alternative means for representing the history of "the popular." Like *Dictée*, it poses institutions of "official" historical representation against a notion of history as fragments and against the telling of history as a process of partial, imperfect recollection. *Dogeaters* thematizes the displacement of an Asian immigrant/Asian American narrator who "remembers" the Marcos era. It foregrounds the connections and discontinuities between her diasporic location and the Filipino nationalism that emerges as a consequence of and a challenge to Spanish colonialism (sixteenth century–1896), U.S. colonialism (1902–World War II), and neocolonial martial law (1954–1972). The Filipina American character Rio's national identifications with the United States and with the Philippines are each thematized, and yet disrupted, by the temporal and geographical dislocation of the narrator.[23] Rio's "recollections," from her standpoint as an immigrant to the United States, both mediate and defamiliarize the "homeland"; at the same time, the "Asian American" writing of a culturally heterogeneous and class-stratified Manila as her past grounds Rio in a multivalent collective memory that diverges repeatedly from the voice of the subject interpellated within a single national discourse. The collage structure of the text also interrupts the development of a national subject: *Dogeaters* places together discontinuous, simultaneous first- and third-person narratives about characters as different as a general, a senator's daughter, movie actors, a mixed-race "callboy," *bakla* (transvestite) hairdressers, and a department store salesgirl. An episodic multiperspectivism replaces character development; melodrama and pastiche parody realism. The integrity of "official" historical representations—such as an 1898 address by President William McKinley to justify his decision to invade the Philippines, news articles from the Associated Press, or an 1846 history of the Philippines by Jean Mallat—is subverted by the fragmented citation of these documents and by the juxtaposition and embedding of these fragments with other "popular" genres and in more "common" registers: transcripts from a radio melodrama *Love Letters*, scenes from Douglas Sirk's *All That Heaven Allows* and other Hollywood films, quotations from advertising, or bits of talk show or tabloid gossip.

In discussing *Dogeaters,* I focus on the role of gossip as a popular discourse that interrupts and displaces official representational regimes. Extravagant and unregulated, gossip functions as an "unofficial" discursive structure—or perhaps we might better characterize it as an antistructure or a destructuring discourse—running distinctly counter to the logic of verisimilitude and the organized subordination of written narrative. Though gossip is unofficial, I do not mean to imply that it occupies a terrain that is separate or discrete from official narratives; rather, gossip is peculiarly parasitic, pillaging from the official, imitating without discrimination, exaggerating, relaying. In this sense, gossip requires that we abandon binary notions of legitimate and illegitimate, discourse and counterdiscourse, or "public" and "private," for it traverses these classifications so as to render such divisions untenable. Rather than mere "postmodern" experimentation, *Dogeaters* disorganizes official history through its multiple performances of gossip, moving from particular citations and instantiations of gossip—*tsismis* (Tagalog for "gossip"), hearsay, anecdote, slander—to gossip's informal sites and institutions—the beauty parlor, the television talk show, the tabloid *Celebrity Pinoy*—to staging gossip as a trope of popular insurgency itself. By "gossip," I do not mean to refer to gossip practices that function as commentaries on, and primarily "domestic" excursions from, bourgeois propriety, of the sort we find in Austen's *Emma* or George Eliot's *Middlemarch*. Rather I wish to associate "gossip" in *Dogeaters* with the concept of "rumor," as elaborated by subaltern studies historians and others, to locate it as a public form of popular discourse in colonized societies in which relations of rule force popular modes of social organization (from subcultures to acts of insurgency) into unsanctioned sites and discourses. Historian Vicente Rafael, for example, has elaborated the importance of rumor in the Japanese-occupied Philippines as a strategy of the colonized nonelite classes for "fashioning alternative bases for recounting, and accounting for, their sense of deprivation." Rafael argues that unlike practices that seek to stabilize social institutions, rumor does not result in "the conservation of the social formation" but rather produces "evanescent communities."[24]

   In this regard, we might fruitfully extend Rafael's notion of rumor through the terms offered by historian Reynaldo Ileto in his "Outlines of a Nonlinear Emplotment of Philippine History." Ileto discusses the relationship between elite linear, developmental history and the popular knowledges, practices, and sites that are subjugated by this official account. He argues that "in examining historiography, criminality, epidemics, and popular movements, one has only begun to reflect upon those crucial moments when the state, or the historian, or whoever occupies the site of the dominant centres, performs a cutting operation: remembering/furthering that which it deems meaningful for its concept of development, and forgetting/suppressing the dissonant, disorderly, irrational, archaic, and subversive.[25] One focus of Ileto's critique is the internalization of European colonialist ideology evidenced in the developmental histories produced by the nineteenth-century Philippine nationalist elites who led the challenge to Spanish rule. He characterizes Teodoro Agoncillo's history of the Philippines as paradigmatic of this nationalist tradition, showing how it relies on the following categories in sequence: a golden age (pre-Hispanic society), the fall (conquest by Spain in the sixteenth century), the dark age (seventeenth and eighteenth centuries), economic and social development (nineteenth century), the rise of nationalist consciousness (post-1872 Katipunan revolt), the birth of the nation (1898), and either suppressed nationalism or democratic tutelage (post-1901, U.S. colonialism). After arguing that nineteenth-century discourses of modernization privileged a small elite and subjugated the knowledges of "others," a second focus of Ileto's work is the assembling of a "counterhistory" of the Philippines that gives priority to "irrational," disorderly, "popular" phenomena. A "history" that attends to the popular and regional activities of bandits provides an account of mobile, dispersed insurgency and of the official modes of regulation erected to police and suppress those insurgencies.

"Gossip" in Hagedorn's text responds to Ileto's call for more articulations of a "nonlinear emplotment of Philippine history." By featuring gossip as an element of and an organizing principle for social relations, *Dogeaters* offers scenes, dialogues, and episodes that are not regulated by plot, character, progress, or resolution. Both the gossip it features and the format of the novel itself move in a horizontal, or metonymic, contagion rather than through the vertical, or metaphorical, processes of referentiality and signification. Spontaneous, decentered, and multivocal, gossip is antithetical to developmental narrative. It seizes details and hyperbolizes their importance; it defies the notion of information as property. Gossip exemplifies both antinarrative and antirepresentational strategies that dehierarchize linear historical accounts, both orientalist and nationalist, with a popular, multiple record of very different kinds of activities and modes of social organization.

Gossip in *Dogeaters* is recognized as having superior authority and giving greater pleasure than other discourses: "Pucha signals me with her eyebrows, then whispers she'll call me first thing in the morning. We'll go over the night's *tsismis*, the juicy gossip that is the center of our lives. If the laundress Catalina is really the General's mother, then who is Apolinaria Cuevas? Who is the red-haired foreigner's wife *Tito* Severo is fucking?"[26]

Yet precisely owing to its popular status, members of the ruling oligarchy are also keenly aware of gossip and rely on it for the information on which they will base their economic and military decisions: "*Tsismis* ebbs and flows. According to a bemused Severo Alacran, richest of all the richest men and therefore privy to most of the General's secrets, the best *tsismis* is always inspired by some fundamental truth" (101). For those pragmatically in need of instruments with which to stay in power, gossip is acknowledged to be a more valuable discourse than a discourse of "truth." Yet defying possession by a single owner and moving easily across the class boundaries that express the concept of property, gossip is always in circulation, without assignable source and without trajectory or closure. Mobile and promiscuous, it collects significance as it travels from site to site; orality and speed make it "common" and yet difficult to detect or trace.

Gossip often plagiarizes, and in doing so satirizes, official civil institutions: government, marriage, family, the law. Adultery, bastardy, homosexuality, criminality, intoxication, profanity—each corresponds to the tropological structure of gossip, which cites the official and yet is in excess of it; these affinities underline the location of gossip as the terrain of these activities. As it is parasitic on the details of "private" life, it derides the separation of "public" and "private" spheres, transgressing these separations symbolic of bourgeois order. Since gossip is unwritten, it does not respond to demands for linguistic purity; it deviates from the laws of national languages, as well as from the linguistic separations of proper "high" language and "low" colloquialisms. In *Dogeaters,* gossip combines colloquial English with Tagalog and Spanish slang.[27] This hybrid text circulates in and around Manila, a city that is itself the expression of a Philippines colonized and occupied at different times by Spanish, Japanese, and U.S. powers.

> After dinner we drag ourselves to the adjoining living room for coffee, cigars, and Spanish brandy. "We're out of French cognac, I'm afraid," my mother apologizes. "Excellent, excellent. The French are overrated! Spanish brandy is actually the best in the world," Uncle Augustin says. . . . "Johnny Walker Black, on the rocks for me," my cousin Mikey says. . . .
> "That Johnny Walker is *sprikitik,* boss!" Mikey cracks up. . . .
> My mother turns to my father. "I don't get it, Freddie. What's the

difference between *putok* and *sprikitik?* Don't they both mean fake?"

My father thinks for a moment. "You might say Congressman Abad *sprikitiks* when he plays golf, but General Ledesma rewards his army with cases of *putok* liquor."

Tita Florence fans herself with a woven *pye-pye*. "*Dios mio,* Freddie. What are you making *bola-bola* about?" . . .

"The General is from a good family," *Tito* Augustin says to my mother. "Do you remember the Ledesmas from Tarlac?" My mother shakes her head. *Tita* Florence puts down her fan to correct her husband. "Wrong, Augustin, as usual. Nicasio is the outside son of Don Amado Avila and the laundress Catalina. I know because my mother is from the same town as the Avilas—"

My mother's eyes widen. "You mean he's actually Senator Avila's half-brother?"

"And the president's former chauffeur," *Tita* Florence nods triumphantly. (63–64)

The Saturday night talk of the Gonzaga clan exemplifies the many dimensions of gossip. This evening, the talk turns around the distinction between authenticity and inauthenticity—of ancestry, of nationality, of liquor, of sexual fidelity, of the military government—the liminal space that is indeed the "proper" site of gossip. Yet as Rio's father Freddie differentiates between the uses of the informal Tagalog terms "sprikitik" and "putok," the distinction between different orders of inauthenticity becomes crucial: on the one hand, acceptable acts of apparition or seeming and, on the other, the unacceptable counterfeit or the "bogus." Whereas sprikitik is associated with magic or spiritualism, putok connotes illegitimacy and scandal; Freddie's comparison ("Congressman Abad *sprikitiks* when he plays golf, but General Ledesma rewards his army with cases of *putok* liquor") establishes putok as a lower order of deception than the "abracadabra" magic of sprikitik. Thus, the gossip moves from one connotation of putok to the next: not only does General Ledesma give *putok* liquor labeled "Dewar's Scotch" or "Johnny Walker" to his soldiers (which "is so terrible, their guts rot and burn"), but the Gonzagas speak of the general as if he himself is a putok, an "outside son," a "former chauffeur" not part of the network of ruling families. Initially, the meditation on two orders of inauthenticity opens up an implicit subtext of the conversation—government power and rule; when the ruling military dictatorship is backed by the U.S. government, who sprikitiks and who is the putok? Who has the semblance of the usurper and who the semblance of the usurped? Gossip, as the instrument of the people, becomes the terrain for the critique of degrees of deception and for the organization of actions against the apparatuses of rule.

In another turn, the discussion of inauthenticity in relation to birth moves from the particularity of the general's illegitimate birth to the allegorical level of the heterogeneous cultures, languages, and races *in excess of* the legitimate nation provided for by the "birth" of the Philippines in 1898. In a country with seventy-one hundred known islands and eighty dialects and languages spoken, as well as a cultural and racial hybridity that has mixed Spanish, Malayan, Chinese, Arab, Hindu, North American, and others with "native" groups over the course of four centuries, the distinction between the "authentic" and the "inauthentic" may be less salient than the turn around different kinds of "seeming," the cultural, racial, and linguistic admixtures that are the contemporary expression of a history of colonial and commercial encounter in the Philippines. Like the composite, multileveled languages of the conversation, the drink itself is marked by the history of hybridizing colonial encounters.[28] The reverence for Spanish brandy, the taste for imported Johnny Walker Black, as well as the Tru-Cola and coffee they are drinking—each are what Nerissa Balce-Cortes has termed "metonyms of neocolonialism."[29] These metonyms condense and allude to different parts of the history of the Philippines: three centuries of Spanish rule, U.S. colonialism and the subsequent penetration of the Philippines by U.S. commodity capitalism, and the emergence of Philippine industries emulating U.S. products.

Daisy Avila, the "demure and solitary" daughter of the high-profile oppositional leader Senator Avila, begins as a dutiful daughter sequestered in the "private" family home and emerges into the alternative "public" sphere as a leader of armed insurgent guerrillas. Her first step toward this transformation takes place just before her twentieth birthday when she is crowned beauty queen of the Philippines. When Daisy denounces the beauty pageant as a farce on Cora Comacho's talk show *Girl Talk,* she "becomes a sensation, almost as popular as her father. The rock band Juan Tamad records a song dedicated to her, 'Femme Fatale.' Banned on the radio, the song surfaces on a bootleg label, Generik. It is an instant underground hit. Condemned as NPA [New People's Army] sympathizers, band members are rounded up by plainclothesmen from the President's Special Squadron Urban Warfare Unit" (109). Gossip produces figures around which other social discourses are organized. Daisy is just such a figure, and in this instance, the scandal of Daisy becomes a hub around which discourses of gender and sexuality, as well as discourses of counterinsurgency, revolve.

The representation of Daisy occurs always through forms of gossip—the tabloids report her marriage and divorce to Malcolm Webb, tsismis circulates about her pregnancy: "Daisy Avila is pregnant with Tito Alvarez' baby, Daisy Avila is secretly married to the President's only son, Daisy Avila is a junkie" (107). Headlines scream "Fickle Daisy in Hiding!" (111). This construction of "Daisy" reveals the decisively reactionary dimension of gossip, historically a key purveyor of the control and regulation of women's bodies, sexualities, and agency. As *woman*, Daisy is figured as carrier of community, and the gossip about her is concerned with the containment of her sexuality and with her transgressive movement across "private" and "public" domains as she changes from pious daughter to revolutionary. In this sense, while I focus on gossip in *Dogeaters* as an antirepresentational and antinarrative form, I would not suggest that it is anything like a counterethical system; we cannot understand gossip as intrinsically progressive or subversive. Nonetheless, Daisy's transgression of gendered roles and spheres is instantly linked with acts of political insurrection as well: indeed we might understand the eventual armed insurrection in which she participates as a mobilization which is not a univocal, linear development of politicization but which takes place according to gossip's model of spontaneous displacement and contagion. Revolutionary activity in *Dogeaters* is not teleologically narrated; it does not privilege heroes, martyrs, or the development of the revolutionary subject. The association in *Dogeaters* of insurrection with gossip may refer implicitly to a history of guerrilla strategies that were not centrally organized and to different modes of political practice that have been obscured by the stage of oppositional party nationalisms.[30]

Through its exploration of "gossip" as an antinarrative and antidevelopmental form, *Dogeaters* is a text that transforms the function of the novel and of historical narrative through explorations of alternative means of evoking a history of "the popular." Like *Dictée*, it suggests that the "subjugated knowledges" of the popular are not available in official narrative history; indeed, *Dogeaters* dramatizes the recollection of history as spasmodic hearsay and as an ongoing process of partial, imperfect recollection. In the displacement of the authority of official historical representation, *Dogeaters* rehistoricizes differently the material conditions of colonialism, neocolonialism, and continuing civil war. The antirepresentational strategies in Hagedorn's text propose an alternative aesthetic to the realist mode, and in that alternative, the text opens space for a different historical subject engaged with that aesthetic.

■

> History is the subject of a structure whose site is not homogeneous, empty time, but time filled by the presence of the now. — Benjamin, "Theses"

After meditating on "blood" and "gossip" as disruptions of official regimes of representation and narrative, I turn to Fae Myenne Ng's *Bone* (1993) to explore another mode through which Asian American writing addresses the problem of history. *Bone* confronts the narratives that have so often suppressed those events and peoples who do not conform to the logic of development and the equally vexing problem of how alternative records might adequately attend to those suppressed materials. Just as Ileto proposes a "nonlinear emplotment of history" that *maps*, rather than narrates, spaces of insurrection and suppression, I consider Ng's *Bone* as a novel that explores *space* as a category in which to read about the emergence of and the obstacles to Asian American social life over the past century. Meditations on the produced locality of community, records of the affective dimensions of the "everyday," excavations that trace the regulation and transformation of the physical and psychological spaces of otherness: all give priority to *space* over the temporality that is stressed by the traditional novel and official history. History in *Bone* is the history of place, an archaeology of the richly sedimented, dialectical space of urban Chinatown community. The buildings and streets, the relations between spaces, and the relations between human individuals and work, to leisure, to life and death are all material testimonies to the means through which U.S. society has organized Chinatown space to enhance production and to reproduce the necessary relations of production. But they testify equally to the means through which Chinatown society has reconfigured spatial discipline and has rearticulated the ethnic ghetto as a resistant, recalcitrant "historical" space. *Bone* exemplifies what Edward Soja has termed a "critical human geography," which excavates the uneven geography of locality within the pressures of universal temporalized history.[31]

San Francisco Chinatown, the site explored in *Bone*, emerged in the late nineteenth century in response to intense periods of anti-Chinese violence between 1870 and 1890 and the government's authorization of residential segregation in 1878. The old core area is the most densely populated: stores, restaurants, and family association houses that apparently have withstood the penetration of urban, industrial culture from the outside are concentrated on Grant Avenue and off Portsmouth Square. Since 1947 and the lifting of the restrictive covenant, Chinatown has grown beyond its old borders and through the valley that lies between Nob and Russian Hills west to Van Ness Street and eastward to the financial district; outlying satellites of Chinatown dot San Francisco and can be identified by the presence of Chinese businesses and grocery stores. Chinatown is a "social space" that is produced and reproduced over time in connection with the forces of production. Yet a social space cannot be adequately accounted for by simply describing its objects or its chronological history. As Henri Lefebvre reminds us, the mediations of groups, factors within knowledge, ideology, or the domain of representations must all be taken into consideration. Social space contains a great diversity of objects, and these objects are not merely things but also relations. Labor transforms these objects and their spatial relations; indeed, social space infiltrates, even collides with, the concept of production, becoming a central dimension of its content. Lefebvre writes, "No space disappears in the course of growth and development; the *worldwide does not abolish the local.*"[32] In other words, "Chinatown" is produced by the interrelation of spaces—from worldwide networks of markets of capital, labor, and commodities to national, regional, and local markets. Its space emerges as an expression of this heterogeneity and dialectic, with all its objects eloquently testifying to that spatial interrelation and ultimately calling into question the hierarchy of these networks of interrelated markets.

In the posthumously published essay "Of Other Spaces," Foucault discusses "heterotopias," those spaces of alterity that call into question the hierarchical organization of all other social space.[33] Foucault defines heterotopias as sites of crisis and deviation (prisons, sanitariums, or cemeteries) or sites that juxtapose several incompatible spaces or temporalities (the festival, museum, or colony). Heterotopias function in a critical relation to the binarized space that remains: they expose the untenability of the hierarchized divisions of space into domains of public and private, leisure and work, or legitimacy and illegitimacy. Chinatown can be considered such a space: a sedimented community space that condenses at once barbershop, boarding houses, and gambling halls (traces of late-nineteenth-century bachelor societies) with schools, churches, or family service businesses (signs of the transition to family society and the influx of women after World War II) and with the restaurants, stores, and factories in which newer Chinese immigrants work. Chinatowns are at once the deviant space ghettoized by the dominant configurations of social space and the resistant locality that signifies the internalization of "others" within the national space. The heterotopia of Chinatown challenges what Akhil Gupta and James Fergusen have called "the isomorphism" of space/place/culture/nation.[34] It marks the disunity and discontinuity of the racialized urban space with the national space. It is a space not spoken by or in the language of the nation.

The elaboration of space in *Bone* is permitted by the reverse chronology of the narrative. The novel focuses on the Leong family—the estranged and battling immigrant parents Mah and Leon and their three daughters, Leila, Ona, and Nina—as they come to terms with the suicide of the middle sister, Ona. If the overemphasis on temporality actively submerges and peripheralizes the "geographical" as a category of social life, then *Bone's* narrative reversal works to criticize the overdevelopment of temporal contextualization as a source of meaning. The narrative moves backward in time, in reverse approach to Ona's suicide. One effect of the reverse narration is that *causality* as a means of investigation is disorganized. Although Ona's death appears initially as the originating loss that would seem either to motivate the reverse chronology or to resolve a progressive one, when the event of the suicide is at last reached, it dissolves, apprehensible not as an origin but as a symptom of the Leong family's collective condition. The opening chapter represents the ongoing schism between Leon and Mah as if it were the effect of Ona's death, but as the chapters move backward, we learn that the painful divide between the parents precedes the death and is the result of the steady rhythm of loss that has been the mainstay of their lives: Mah's loss of her first husband, Lyman Fu; Leon's absences when he worked as a seaman; Leon's loss of his "original" history and antecedents upon immigration; his successive loss of jobs; his loss of Mah to her affair with Tommie Hom; and, finally, the loss of paternal authority that obliges his daughters to chaperone and care for him.

The novel investigates Chinatown space as a repository of layers of historical time, layers of functions, purposes, and spheres of activity. The Hoy Sun Ning Yung Benevolent Association, for example, is housed in a building that condenses many different activities into a space that is undifferentiated, in which leisure and work, family and business, coexist. If the rationality of production seeks to organize space as a sequence of actions that accomplish a certain "objective"—the production of an object, in this case, a garment—then the spatial contiguity of the building skews this rationality. Leila narrates her visit to the association:

> Friday after school, I walked down to the five-story building at 41 Waverly Place. The narrow staircase squeaked. I stepped aside on the first landing to let some Italian guys carrying white carnation wreaths pass. On the second floor, the rumble of machines and the odor of hot steamed linen made my nostrils feel prickly; these sensations brought back memories of working in Tommie Hom's sweatshop, helping Mah turn linen pockets. Ironing the interfacing for the culottes. The time I sewed my finger. The awful exactness of the puncture point where the needle broke nail and skin. An exacting pain.
>
> A racket of mah-jongg sounds, plastic tiles slapping and trilling laughter of winners filled the third floor. The fourth smelled of sweat. Sharp intakes of breath, sudden slaps, guys grunting. Master Choy, White Crane Gung-Fu Club.
>
> The office of the Hoy Sun Ning Yung Benevolent Association was like many other Chinatown family-association offices: family and business mixed up. To the right, a long counter; to the left, the reception area, made up of two hand-me-down sofas, old arm touching old arm. (75)

Though the prioritizing of the relations of production organizes the "private" space of the Leong home as a work space, the collective space of the Benevolent Association is not organized toward production as its sole end; work is not the privileged referent of its production of space. The Benevolent Association is a space of multiple functions, in which activities are simultaneous, not hierarchized or temporalized. Its condensed simultaneity of spaces ultimately comments on that organization of other social spaces that relegates Chinatown to the periphery serving the dominant center. Where the Benevolent Association overlaps one floor of activity on top of another, other buildings alternate and double activities into one space. Leila learns that the funeral house where Grandpa Leong was prepared was also a makeshift storefront with "nailed-together benches" and "stacks of boxes"; the funeral parlor doubled as Shing Kee's Grocery warehouse. Then the space went on to house other things: "Everybody's Bookstore, Master Kung's Northern-style Martial Arts Club, and the Chinese Educational Services" (83).

Doubling as family association and business, exercise space and work space, and space of life and of death, the hybrid space finds an analogue in the suitcase of papers that Leila's stepfather Leon keeps. In the informal "archive" of Leon's papers, we are offered an ethnological, bibliographical, and demographic space, a record of the everyday life within which Leon has lived, worked, dreamed, and remembered.

> I lifted the suitcase up on to the kitchen table and opened it. The past came up: a moldy, water-damaged paper smell and a parchment texture. . . .
>
> . . . This paper son saved every single scrap of paper. I remember his telling me about a tradition of honoring paper, how the oldtimers believed all writing was sacred. . . .
>
> I made paper files, trying to organize the mess. Leon the family man. Airmail letters from China, aerograms from Mah to Leon at different ports, a newsprint picture of Ona graduating from the Chinese Center's nursery school, of Nina in her "boy" haircut and an awful one of me and Mason.
>
> Leon the working man: in front of the laundry presser, the extractor; sharpening knives in the kitchen; making beds in the captain's

room. Leon with the chief steward. Leon with girls in front of foreign monuments.

A scarf with a colored map of Italy. Spanish pesetas in an envelope. Old Chinese money. Dinner menus from the American President Lines. The Far East itinerary for Matson Lines. A well-used bilingual cookbook. . . . Had Leon been a houseboy?

Selections from newspapers. From *The Chinese Times:* a picture of Confucius, a Japanese soldier with his bayonet aimed at a Chinese woman, ration lines in Canton, gold lines in Shanghai. From *Life* magazine: Hitler, Charlie Chaplin, the atom bomb. (57–59)

The suitcase of papers is a material archaeology of Leon's life, just as China-town is a sedimented site of collective memory for the Chinese in America. Sedimented space is an emblem for history as excavation rather than pro-jection, simultaneity rather than sequential time, and collective geography rather than individual biography. The suitcase of papers is also the record of the conversion of "blood" to "paper" that is required when Leon renounces his Chinese past to assume the legal identity of citizen. Leon Leong is a "paper son" who, like thousands of other Chinese, claimed a paper iden-tity in order to pass through the Angel Island immigrant detention cen-ter. According to U.S. law, the children of Americans were automatically citizens, even if they were born in a foreign country. After the 1906 San Francisco earthquake and fires destroyed municipal records, many young men purchased the birth certificates of American citizens of Chinese an-cestry born in China and then claimed they were citizens so as to enter the United States.[35] Leon had exchanged five thousand dollars and the promise to send Grandpa Leong's bones back to China for a "paper son" identity. After Grandpa Leong dies and his bones remain in the United States, Leon attributes the misfortune of Ona's death and all the losses to this debt. Contemplating the contents of the suitcase—Leon's affidavit of citizen-ship, remnants of travel and migration (maps, currency, cookbooks) and of work lives (pay stubs, diaries), along with receipts, photographs, letters, and newspaper clippings—Leila remarks: "I thought, Leon was right to save everything. For a paper son, paper is blood" (61). The paper in the suitcase is the residue, the trace of the "conversion" of Chinese into "Americans." The conversion can never be completed, and like the "blood" in *Dictée*, it retains "the physical substance of blood as measure, that rests as record, as document," becoming an integral part of the contemporary present. The paper archive, like Grandpa Leong's bones, is figured as the material trace of early Chinese immigrant life: a trace that paradoxically testifies to a loss of history, yet simultaneously marks the production of "community" that commences with the investment, through memory and narrative, in that loss.[37]

The Chinatown represented in *Bone* is a recalcitrant space that cannot be wholly or univocally translated. Its heterogeneity is not assimilable to the capitalist logic that would organize the ethnic ghetto for production; its contemporaneity does not yield to the gaze that seeks to exoticize it as antiquated artifact. The tourist, the voyeur, the immigration service may enter, but they are all deceived.

> From the low seats of the Camaro, I looked out. . . .
>
> . . . I thought, So this is what Chinatown looks like from inside those dark Greyhound buses; this slow view, these strange color combinations, these narrow streets, this is what tourists come to see. I felt a small lightening up inside, because I knew, no matter what people saw, no matter how close they looked, our inside story is something entirely different.[38]

In discussing blood as ground and figure of representation in *Dictée*, gossip as an antifiguration of narrative in *Dogeaters*, and Chinatown urban space as a disruption of overdeveloped temporalization in *Bone*, I have suggested that these Asian American novels displace the orthodoxies of both historical and novelistic representation and excavate the material histories that have been subjugated or erased by these aesthetics.[39] Engagement with the "past"—as catastrophe, as memory, as space—forms the core of all three projects. The three novelists do not seek through these engagements to find and represent an essential authenticity, to articulate the past "the way it really was." Rather, like Benjamin's historical materialist, they "seek to brush history against the grain." If historical narrative is, as Benjamin suggests, a narrative that has "empathy with the victor," the material memory of the unvictorious is not simply repressed by that narrative; it dialectically returns, to pressure and restructure precisely the regimes of uniformity that seek to contain it as representation.[40] In this sense, *Dictée, Dogeaters,* and *Bone* each suggest that the project of writing as a subject who remembers is not exclusively a matter of finding better modes of representing or renarrating those "histories" of colonialism, modernization, underdevelopment, and immigrant displacement from a posterior point. It is also to retrieve in places other than official history a repertoire of forms of memory, time, or counterhistory—these forms themselves an expression of the long encounter of situated forms of sociality with capitalist modernity— and to rearticulate them in culture in ways that permit the practices of subject and community not strictly governed by official modes. The next two chapters explore ways in which cultural forms, as the repository of countermemory and counterhistory, allow for the critical refiguration of conjunctions of domination. These critical refigurations both enable the formation of new subjects outside official dictations and dominations and make possible horizontal affiliations between such subjects.

Unfaithful to the Original:

The Subject of *Dictée*

If translation is to incorporate into the language and the spirit of a nation what it does not possess, or what it possesses in a different way, the first requirement is simple fidelity. This fidelity must be aimed at the real nature of the original . . . just as every good translation originates in simple and unpretentious love for the original.
    —Wilhelm von Humboldt, "A Theory of Translation" (1816)

To speak means to be in a position to use a certain syntax, to grasp the morphology of this or that language, but it means above all to assume a culture, to support the weight of a civilization. . . . Every colonized people— in other words, every people in whose soul an inferiority complex has been created by the death and burial of its local cultural originality—finds itself face to face with the language of the civilizing nation.
    —Frantz Fanon, *Black Skin, White Masks* (1957)

My experience as a writer coming from a culture of colonialism . . . my struggle to get wholeness from fragmentation while working within fragmentation, producing work which may find its strength in its depiction of fragmentation, through form as well as content, is similar to the experience of other writers whose origins are in countries defined by colonialism.
    —Michelle Cliff, *The Land of Look Behind* (1985)

Theresa Hak Kyung Cha's *Dictée* proposes questions that engage and disturb desires—critical desire, disciplinary desire, incorporative desire. An

128

Asian American text, a postcolonial text, and a woman's text, it evokes
alternately a girlhood education in French Catholicism, a brief history of
Korean nationalism during the Japanese colonial occupation, as well as
episodes from the narrator's displaced adulthood as a Korean American
immigrant and her return to a military-ruled South Korea. Inquiring into
the links between language and subjectivity, colonialism and nationalism,
and minority discourse and the transformation of hegemony, it interro-
gates these connections in terms of a terrain on which each connection
makes sense only within the context of its constitutive intersection with
other traversing relations. In this sense, it is impossible to reduce *Dictée* to
a single classification or preoccupation, for it resists such determination.
Indeed, the text repeatedly calls attention to the varied locations of its writing, at the boundaries of different cultures and geographies, across distinct
historical epochs; it enunciates the confluences and disjunctions, stresses
the myriad moments of conflict and interdependency. For this reason, *Dictée* deviates—in genre, themes, and style—from other narrative portraits of
postcolonials or of immigrants and women in the United States, present-
ing obstacles as well as opportunities for contemporary readers.

   Dictée is not a developmental narrative. Without a recognizable linearity
that depicts a unified subject's progress from youth to maturity, the text is
often broken, at times painfully disrupted. It prismatically fragments the
process of coming into speech—faltering hesitation is interspersed with
moments of fluency, followed again by intervals of stammering or interruption. The writing subject is elaborated as hybrid and multilingual, articulated in antagonism to the uneven determinations of the French, Japanese, and English languages and the colonial and imperial states of which
they are ideological apparatuses. Neither developmental nor univocal, the
subject of *Dictée* continually thwarts the reader's desire to abstract a notion
of ethnic or national identity—originating either from the dominant culture's interrogation of its margins or in emergent minority efforts to establish unitary ethnic or cultural nationalist examples. At the same time, because *Dictée* combines autobiographical and biographical fragments, photographs, historical narrative, calligraphy, and lyric and prose poems in a
complex, discontinuous weave, it blurs conventions of genre, further troubling the categories on which both dominant and ethnic literary canoniza-
tions depend.[1]

In particular, *Dictée* resists the core values of aesthetic realism—correspondence, mimesis, and equivalence—and approaches these notions as contradictions. Rather than constructing a narrative of unities and symmetries, with consistencies of character, sequence, and plot, it emphasizes instead an aesthetic of fragmented recitation and episodic nonidentity—dramatizes, in effect, an aesthetic of infidelity. Repetition itself is taken to its parodic extreme and disengaged as the privileged mode of imitation and realism. In *Dictée*, repetition more often marks the incommensurability of forms to their referents: improper recitations of the Catholic catechism or the marriage vow, interruptions of Japanese honorifics, and mispronunciations of the naturalization oaths of American citizenship all perform this function. To the extent that *Dictée* deviates generically from the realist novel of formation or education, it also thematizes the contradiction of an identity logic that privileges a developmental narrative as the mode of the subject's individual formation. In this sense, *Dictée*'s unfaithful relationship to realist aesthetic values also resonates with critiques of notions of individual and social equivalence: the student's pedagogical disobedience, the colonized subject's antagonism to the empire, the religious subject's incommensurability to God, and the citizen's discontinuity with the state—each provides a critique of identical equivalence as both a logic of domination and a legacy to be interrogated within the practices of resistance to domination. In addition, the formal fragmentation that underlies *Dictée*'s aesthetic also renders the text a complex object with regard to critical theories. While its critiques of identity engage with feminist, psychoanalytic, and Marxist discussions of subjectivity and ideology, in the overlapping layers of cultural and linguistic frames and the refusal of inference, deduction, and causality, *Dictée* unsettles the authority of any single theory to totalize or subsume it as its object.

Thus, in reading *Dictée*, we cannot escape the irony that the very ways in which the text presents a critical problem for the emergent fields of Asian American Studies, Third World Studies, or Women's Studies—particularly in how it problematizes the uniformity of ethnic, gendered, or nationalist identity and genre—constitute precisely the most powerfully suggestive critiques of dominant colonial and imperial interpellations. Its critique of identity invigorates an investigation of the degree to which a concept of unified nationalist membership may risk reproducing, in its very opposition to colonial and imperial rule, the notion of continuity between individual subject and the nation inherited from the ruling states themselves. At a historical moment when imperialist expansion continues to operate through a logic of identity that seeks to integrate to itself the heterogeneous and nonidentical "fragments" of third world peoples, an ongoing critique of such logic would appear to be a most urgent necessity. As a text that links Korean immigration to the United States with the record of Japanese colonialism and the American role in the Korean War and partition of Korea, *Dictée* contributes to this critique by making crucial connections between anti-immigrant sentiment in the United States and imperialist expansion in the third world. While rendering unavoidably explicit the traces of colonial and imperial damage and dislocation on the subject, it articulates a voice, in opposition to those dominations, that persistently refuses the assimilation of that subject to fictions of identity and development, writing this "subject" as a possible site for active cultural and ideological struggle.

Dictée, as its title suggests, proposes "dictation" as its emblematic topos. According to the rules of the dictation exercise, the student learns the vocabulary, idioms, and rules of grammar and syntax of the "foreign" language through rendering an oral example into a written equivalent. In the same process, the student internalizes the pedagogical mandate, in which learning consists in reproducing, and thereby conforming to, the morphology of the example, a process by which all students are iterated and abstracted as uniform, generically equivalent sites of those reproductions.[2] Dictation is at once a sign for the authority of language in the formation of the student; a model for the conversion of the individual into a subject of discourse through the repetition of form, genre, and example; and a metaphor for the many regulating reproductions to which the narrator is subject in spheres other than the educational. Ultimately, dictation provides the model by which the writing variously thematizes and negates the imperative to repeat. For not only does the logic of dictation itself provide a critique of the model of identical equivalence—in that the founding premise of dictation recognizes an initial incommensurability between the oral and the written, revealing the purported aim of that identical reproduction to be internally contradictory—but *Dictée* further exploits this contradiction through manifold deviations from the model. The subject of *Dictée* recites poorly, stutters, stops, and leaves verbs unconjugated. She fails to imitate the example and is unfaithful to the original.

The text begins with a dictation assignment in French, represented as if it were the first of many exercises performed during the narrator's childhood. The French grammar lesson dramatizes not only the indoctrination of the Korean narrator within a "foreign" Western language, but the "dictée"—as a paradigmatic instance of French educational influence on the Korean subject—also alludes to the long history of French Catholic missionary activity in Korea that dates from the early nineteenth century.[3]

> Aller à la ligne   C'était le premier jour   point   Elle venait de loin point   ce soir au dîner   virgule   les familles demanderaient   virgule   ouvre les guillemets   Ça c'est bien passé le premier jour   point d'interrogation   ferme les guillemets   au moins   virgule   dire le moins possible   virgule   la réponse serait   virgule   ouvre les guillemets   Il n'y a q'une chose   point   ferme les guillemets   ouvre les guillemets   Il y a quelqu'une   point   loin   point   ferme les guillemets

> Open paragraph   It was the first day   period   She had come from a far   period   tonight at dinner   comma   the families would ask comma   open quotation marks   How was the first day   interrogation mark   close quotation marks   at least to say the least of it possible comma   the answer would be   open quotation marks   there is but one thing   period   There is someone   period   From a far   period close quotation marks[4]

This initial representation of the dictation exercise deviates significantly from the model that demands faithful reproduction of the example. That is, even though the rules of dictation require that the "foreign" passage be reproduced verbatim, without recourse to the student's more familiar "native" language, the written equivalent of the oral French example is translated into another language, rather than into French. The translation of the French example into English breaks with the formal rules of dictation, and as English is itself an adopted "foreign" language for the Korean subject, the representation of the dictation is from the outset already a fictionalized amalgam that allegorizes the historical influences of both American imperialism and an earlier French missionary colonialism. The rendering of the dictation as a heterogeneous amalgam marks the subject of *Dictée* as a more complex site, a layered and shifting configuration, unevenly "dictated" by several Western colonial languages, French, as well as English.

In addition, the written passage reproduces not only the dictated text but also translates literally the teacher's punctuation instructions and grammar commands as part of the text itself. In fulfilling the task of dictation, the student is asked equally to submit to prohibitions against what cannot be said and to consent to closures which eliminate the unsayable and which refuse the indeterminate and inadmissible. That uniformity of genre depends on regulated omissions is emphasized in a description of the subject of punctuation: "*She would take on their punctuation. She waits to service this. Theirs. Punctuation. She would become, herself, demarcations. Absorb it. Spill it. Seize upon the punctuation. Last air. Give her. Her. The relay. Voice. Assign. Hand it. Deliver it. Deliver*" (4). In adhering to punctuation, the student agrees to the dictated rhythm of intervals, to enforced divisions and hierarchies. At the same time, to the extent that punctuation provides gaps, it also perforates the identical wholeness of the example and offers opportunities through which the student may alter or disrupt the lesson. Through these breaks and openings, the student intervenes in the model that requires both imitation and uniformity. Thus in the opening dictation the inclusion of the punctuation instructions within the English rendering of the text—"period," "comma," "interrogation mark" "close quotation marks"— submits, on the one hand, to the imperative of identical reproduction and yet, on the other, in the very literal inclusion of the punctuation instructions themselves, it "seizes upon the punctuation" to render explicit the disciplinary artifice of the dictation, exploiting the contingent spaces in the dictation in order to voice a "failed" subjection, affirming a departure from the pedagogical model of formation.

The English version of the text calls attention to itself as an inexact approximation of the French in other ways as well: certain commands are omitted from the last three lines of the translated section, and the translation of "au moins dire le moins possible" as "at least to say the least of it possible" reads as a stilted word-for-word translation that might have been rendered more freely or colloquially. Ironically, "faithful" verbatim translation does not "say it as simply as possible" and is often the least exact in transmitting the contextualized meaning of a phrase. Thus, the nonequivalence of the French and English text, here and foregrounded more dramatically still in other parts of *Dictée* (see, for example, "Urania/Astronomy"), thematizes the failure of translation as a topos of faithful reproduction. The discontinuity of the two examples evinces a disjunction in the process of translation, but the choice of English as the translating language further registers the increased suppression of the Korean language with the imposition of each Western colonial language. Indeed, following the frontispiece featuring Korean children's writing, romanized or ideogrammatic Korean appears rarely in *Dictée* in comparison with the greater portions in French and English.

Theories of translation, from discussions of biblical translation to those of comparative literature, include an ongoing polemic between those who assert that the translated text must be faithful "in letter" to the original and those who defend the translator's rights to creative artifice in the task of rendering the "spirit" of the original. At the root of most translation polemic is the ideal of equivalence, whether literal, spiritual, or cultural, which serves to hold up translation as an emblem for the *ethos* of fidelity.[5] Not only does this ethos level and minimize linguistic differences, but its presumption of equivalence masks the hierarchy of cultures operating in any differentiated linguistic relationship; the power of one nation-state to determine not merely the language but the material conditions of another people is rendered largely invisible.[6] In contrast, *Dictée* problematizes the premise of translation as fidelity, underscoring instead the ambivalence, or double valence, of the translation enterprise. In *Dictée*, translation is both an apparatus of cultural domination—the names of Korean subjects are forcibly translated into Japanese under Japanese colonialism, the narrator is "translated" as a namesake of Saint Thérèse—as well as the means by which the dictation is adulterated and resisted.[7] In the opening exercise, it is the female student who makes use of the artifice of translation to parody the French original, and the neutered translation of the female "quelqu'une" as "someone" precisely underscores female gender as the particularity that proves untranslatable. In the dictation, femininity constitutes the deviant detail that makes visible the normalization of masculinity in the English language, and female difference to the genre surfaces as the mark of an incommensurability that reveals the contradiction inherent in a logic of identical equivalence, subsuming not only the student to the example—the "native" Korean to the colonial languages—but also femininity to masculinity.[8]

Not only does the opening metaphor of dictation focus our attention on education as one site of subject formation, but the subsequent sections of the text elaborate dictation as a model for other processes through which cultural and ideological systems transform individuals into subjects, reminding us to read *Dictée* in terms of the differentiated layers of colonial and imperial languages within and against which it is written. *Dictée* portrays refusals of the demand for uniform subjectivity dictated by several languages, including the language of French Catholic missionary colonialism, the language imposed during the Japanese occupation of Korea from 1910 to 1945, as well as the English language of the United States, which becomes the narrator's eventual home and the imperial power responsible for the division of Korea in 1948. The text juxtaposes a series of sections that alternately depict subjects episodically and incompletely formed within linguistically and historically differentiated circumstances: for example, the first section thematizes the use of dictation and recitation in the conversion of the Korean student into a faithful French Catholic subject; the section "Clio/History" alludes to the civilizing of the "native" as colonial subject during the period of Japanese occupation; in "Melpomene/Tragedy," the narrator describes the incorporation of the individual into the Korean nationalist body during the Korean War; and in "Calliope/Epic Poetry," written from her standpoint as a Korean American returning to South Korea, the narrator recalls her naturalization as an immigrant into American citizenship. In the sense that each instance of subject formation is treated as uneven and unfinished, *Dictée* suggests that each of these "languages" determines the female/colonized/postcolonial/ethnic "subject" irregularly, leaving a variety of residues that remain uncontained by and antagonistic to the state apparatuses of domination and assimilation of which the French,

Japanese, and English languages are heterogeneous expressions. Further-more, as the earlier example of dictation illustrates, English language is paradoxically used to disrupt the French dictation. In this sense, antago-nisms to a particular demand for identical formation may be pronounced through recourse to another "language"—in this case, even a language of domination, English—or in the voicing of valences that are heterogeneous to that mode of formation, such as the untranslatable particularity of female gender.

The recent history of Korea is a uniquely complex record which suggests that the social space of modern Korea itself has been formed, unevenly and episodically, by its encounters with a variety of outside intrusions. At the turn of the century, the country first served as the battleground for wars fought by other powers, wars that in some cases had little or nothing to do with Korea—the Sino-Japanese War of 1894–1895, and then a decade later, the Russo-Japanese War of 1904–1905—and was subjected to non-Western colonial occupation and later to Western imperialism. When the Japanese occupied Korea in 1910, however, it was not without the brutal suppression of revolts and armed uprisings of a burgeoning, resistant Korean national-ist movement. The roots of this nationalism lay in the Tonghak Rebellion of 1884–1895, a mass movement born of discontent with the rigidly strati-fied society that had been in place since the Yi dynasty period, but the formation of modern Korean nationalism occurred only after the Japanese annexation and, more specifically, after the March First Movement of 1919. Many historians have argued that it was the negative force of Japanese rule that provided the context in which Korean nationalist consciousness arose in its modern form.[9] Throughout the period of Japanese colonialism, Korean nationalism was plagued by factions and divisions, however, and in the 1940s, moderate nationalists consolidated their power in the South. In the North, there emerged a much younger radical and Marxist leadership.[10] When Soviet and American troops entered Korea in 1945 for the purpose of dismantling Japanese power, they made use of and exacerbated these divi-sions among Korean nationalists. War between North and South broke out in 1950, with the South supported by American ground troops; soon after, the North received support from Communist China. For Korea, this war brought death, suffering, and devastation to the already divided nation. Unremitting hostility still divides the peninsula, and both sides remain heavily armed, despite the cease-fire and armistice of 1953, with Communist North Korea, increasingly isolated, rapidly becoming the more vulnerable of the two.[11] In the sense that Korean people have endured different and, in certain cases, conflicting state powers, modern Korea is itself inscribed by the history of multiply layered colonial determinations that *Dictée* elucidates in terms of the subject.

The Japanese government ruled Korea by means of a military dictatorship, through land administration that made a majority of the farming population heavily taxed tenant farmers; by censorship of newspapers and other publications; and, most significantly, through a carefully administrated educational system whose "objective was to educate loyal subjects for the Japanese emperor."[12] Schooling is an integral part of the state apparatus, and in the case of Japanese rule in Korea it functioned as a primary locus for socializing, and "dictating," subjects in the colonial language, culture, and hierarchy. E. Patricia Tsurumi suggests that education was at the center of the project of "Japanization" of Korea: "Koreans were to be transformed gradually into loyal Japanese subjects equipped for modern but humble life and work."[13] The education of Koreans in official Japanese culture equally depended on the erasure of native Korean cultural practices, acknowledged by the Japanese government to be of central importance to a viable Korean nationalism. Terauchi Masatake, the first governor-general, revealed this understanding in his 1910 statement: "Among the private schools, there are schools that teach songs and use other materials which encourage independence and incite rebellion against the Japanese empire. This is forbidden, and utmost care must be exercised to ensure that the prohibition of these activities is enforced."[14] We have seen in the discussion of the French dictation that the educational formation of the subject depends as much on the student's adoption of the example as it does on compliance with censoring prohibitions. Similarly, Japanese colonialist education required a forced fluency in Japanese, which silenced native Korean language and popular traditions, but the terms of the Korean subject's acculturation involved an internalization of the hierarchized subordination of Korean to Japanese colonialist culture.

In *Dictée*, the narrator emphasizes the role of education in the transformation of Koreans into loyal Japanese subjects in the description of her mother's experiences as a teacher during the occupation.

You are the first woman teacher to come to this village in six years. A male teacher greets you, he addresses you in Japanese. Japan had already occupied Korea and is attempting the occupation of China. Even in the small village the signs of their presence is felt by the Japanese language that is being spoken. The Japanese flag is hanging at the entry of the office. And below it, the educational message of the Meiji emperor framed in purple cloth. . . .

The teachers speak in Japanese to each other. You are Korean. All the teachers are Korean. . . . Fifty children to your class. They must speak their name in Korean as well as how they should be called in Japanese. . . . They force their speech upon you and direct your speech only to them. (48–50)

The signs of Japanese hegemony are ubiquitous in this description—the Japanese flag, the emperor's decree—and Japanese is not only the language regulating relations in the classroom but also the language in which Koreans must speak to one another outside that official classroom space. Not only is the mother herself "dictated" as a Japanese subject, but in her assigned role as teacher, she is also asked to require dictation, to pass on a legacy of submission to Japanese language and culture and to "reproduce" that compliance in her Korean students.[15] The forced translation of Korean names into Japanese is perhaps the most vivid emblem of colonial domination, marking as it does, at the level of the subject, the delegitimizing of Korean history, language, and experience that is performed through the colonial regulation of a variety of spheres—political, cultural, economic, and educational. The translation of the Korean name not only instantiates Japanese hegemony in the classroom but implicates as well the Korean subject in laws of hierarchy that organize the larger society in descending orders of privilege: not strictly the hierarchy of Japanese over Koreans but a hierarchy that places the emperor over officials, teachers, and students, on the one hand, and men over women and children, on the other. Elsewhere, the narrator comments that the pervasiveness of Japanese cultural education resulted in very material consequences that were, in turn, "textualized" through the bodies of Koreans: "Japan has become the sign. The alphabet. The vocabulary. . . . The meaning is the instrument, memory that pricks the skin, stabs the flesh, the volume of blood, the physical substance blood as measure, that rests as record, as document" (32). Throughout *Dictée*, it is often the physical body that bears the traces of colonial disfiguring and mutilation and is the literal and figural site from which different and often fragmented speech is uttered in resistance to the imposed competency in the colonizer's language. One recurring image of corporeal division is the violation of the physical organ of the tongue, as in the lines "Bite the tongue. Between the teeth. Swallow" (71) or "Cracked tongue" (75) or "Broken tongue/Pidgeon tongue" (158)—each crystallizing, in the ambiguous meaning of "tongue" as both organ and language, the relationship between linguistic colonialism and the material violences of which language can be only a painfully descriptive index.

This image of the broken, cracked, or divided tongue also foregrounds the central ambivalence of the colonized subject in relation to colonial languages. That is, throughout *Dictée*, the processes of coming to speech in the imposed languages of French, Japanese, or English are thematized as simultaneously a "forced fluency" that obliterates and silences differences and the instrumental means of voicing an oppositional utterance: moving through those forced fluencies—naming them through parody, disrupting signification, and composing coherence through fragmentation—Cha articulates a hybrid, nuanced, "unfaithful" voice.[16] The two valences of speaking (like the two valences of translation)—as forced fluency and as unfaithful voice—are dramatized in the relationship between the "unspeeched" mother and the writing subject. As if to intervene in the Japanese colonialist "dictation" of the mother-subject ("They force their speech upon you and direct your speech only to them"), the daughter addresses the writing of her text to her mother ("I write. I write you. Daily. From here. If I am not writing, I am thinking about writing. I am composing," 56). By renarrating *to the mother* her mother's silence during the colonial period, the daughter names and historicizes the loss of Korean language to her mother and to herself, constituting a retrospective mode of address—between postcolonial and colonial subject, between daughter and mother—which interrupts the unilateral dictation of the subject by the colonial state: "Mother, you are a child still. At eighteen. More of a child since you are always ill. They have sheltered you from life. Still, you speak the tongue the mandatory tongue like the others. It is not your own. Even if it is not you know you must. You are Bi-lingual. You are Tri-lingual. The tongue that is forbidden is your own mother tongue. You speak in the dark. In the secret. The one that is yours. Your own. . . . Mother tongue is your refuge" (45). The daughter addresses her mother as if the writing itself could reverse the roles of mother and child, as if she might, in turn, attend to her silenced mother by writing for her. However, the relationship between the narrating subject and the mother is always marked as disjoined rather than as identical or analogous, their positions separated by the distances of geography, different languages, and years. In recounting her mother's censoring by the colonial language, the narrator makes use of her own partial fluencies in English and French to revoice that censoring and to forge a new composite voice, a discontinuous voice. Through this voice, the narrating subject registers that she cannot perform a simple, untroubled recovery of the "mother tongue" either for herself or for her mother—any more than there exists, for Koreans or Korean Americans, an unproblematic return to a precolonial and unpartitioned Korean "homeland." Instead, the episodic renarrations of the division of her mother from that "mother tongue" construct an alternative, though fragmented and indirect, relationship of the subject to that "first language." The reformulated relationship of the postcolonial subject to the lost language and culture is the product of a double movement—mediated both through the "foreign" imposed tongues and through the figure of her mother who is at once divided origin and displaced destination of the writing ("To surpass overtake the hidden even beyond destination. Destination," 56). Rather than conforming to a nationalist narrative requiring an identification of the subject with the "original" nation, the subject addresses the mother through a paradox that at once both thematizes this identification by posing the mother as a figure for the homeland and yet figures the mother as a metonym rather than a metaphor, "re-membering" her as partial, disembodied, and missing ("The memory is the entire. The longing in the fact of the lost. Maintains the missing," 38). Furthermore, the "feminized" renarration of the subject-homeland relationship as a relationship between daughter and mother, as opposed to between son and father, also intervenes in the nationalist narrative that subordinates the feminine figuration of the motherland to the developmental progress of a masculine, nationalist state formation. This intervention echoes the "Clio" section, in which the account of the life of female nationalist leader Yu Guan Soon also "feminizes" and fragments the masculine narrative of Korean nationalism ("Guan Soon forms a resistant group with fellow students and actively begins her revolutionary work. There is already a nationally organized movement, who do not accept her seriousness, her place as a young woman, and they attempt to dissuade her," 30).[17] Indeed, we might understand the daughter's contradictory address to the mother as a deliberate, ironic "fetishism," refashioned without disavowal, simultaneously imagining the mother as both incomplete and completed, both partial and whole, in critical opposition to the "oedipalizing" dictation of the subject in the narratives not only of colonialism but of nationalism as well.[18]

To the degree that colonialism robs a colonized people of what Frantz Fanon calls "local cultural originality," it has often been the project of nationalism to restore these "origins" to the colonized, to claim the desired national status in terms of a precolonial integrity disrupted by the colonizer. However, even in its oppositionality as an organizing discourse enabling a subordinated people to rise up against domination, the nationalist narrative of "origins" has run the risk of reproducing the very logics of that colonialism against which it is articulated. Nationalism may be continuous with colonialism to the extent that it either constructs an analogy between the individual subject and the "original" body or adopts a narrative of progress that develops the emergent people into a "nation," for both formulations demand that difference and particularity be assimilated to an abstract and identical universality, a colonialist logic that founds the very basis of its effective hegemony.[19] In 1919, during the period of Japanese colonialism in Korea, such an identification between the subject and the nation was thematized in Korean nationalist leader Philip Jaisohn's declaration to the First Korean Congress that "the new provisional government of Korea is a personification of the will of the people of Korea."[20] In the section "Melpomene," the narrator emphasizes the degree to which South Korean nationalist narratives of identity tended to be continuous with Japanese colonialism by figuring the subject's subordination to the identity of the nation in the image of the soldier's military uniform: "You [the soldiers] are your post you are your vow in nomine patris you work your post you are your nation defending your country from subversive infiltration from your own countrymen. Your skin scorched as dark as your uniform as you stand you don't hear" (86). The first sentence, undivided by punctuation, suggests an almost algebraic series of equivalences. A logic of identity equates the single subject ("you") with the plural subject ("soldiers"), an equation which is confirmed by the operation of social service ("your post") and the recitation of fidelity ("your vow") and which ultimately produces the formal sum of the equation: the "nation." The soldier is called to serve by the South Korean fatherland ("in nomine patris"), and the identification between the subject and the nation is symbolized by the adoption of the uniform, the index of this operational equivalence. By wearing the uniform, each soldier is "spoken" as a formally equivalent site of loyal service to the national body of which he is a representative. The algebra of equivalence is actually an algebra of transformation, which divides all unlike variables into the "one," leaving behind heterogenous "remainders" of nonequivalence. It requires that the soldier/national subject suppress and subordinate differences both within his/her individual body as well as in the national body ("subversive infiltration from your own countrymen")—whether differences of gender, locality, religion, caste, or class—to the "uniform" (the "one form") of the national "personification." The insistence on national homogeneity would seem to be founded precisely on the recognition of social differences and internal divisions within the population the nation seeks to unify. That is, modern Korean nationalism began as a mass movement that for the first time involved people of all social classes, including younger generations and women. In addition, there were political differences among the nationalist leaders and controversies over differing strategy and policy regarding the establishment of a provisional government to coordinate the various Korean nationalist groups and to prepare for Korea's attainment of independence. These divisions were pronounced in the split between North and South, eventually the Korean War, and the continuing division of Korea.[21] Moreover, the metaphor of the military uniform to signify loyal relationship to the nation also calls explicit attention to the relationship between militarism and the construction of South Korean nationalism, suggesting

that both the logic of equivalence and the military means of its enforce-
ment are the legacies of Japanese and U.S. intervention: "You soldiers appear in green. Always the green uniforms the patches of camouflage. Trees
camouflage your green trucks you blend with nature the trees hide you you
cannot be seen behind the guns" (85). In the previous section, "Calliope,"
the narrator describes being interrogated as she passes through customs
on a return visit to the Republic of Korea after the war. Here again, the
image of the "uniform" underscores the links between nationalist and imperialist demands for identity: "They, the anonymous variety of uniforms,
each division, strata, classification, any set of miscellaneous properly uni
formed. . . . Their authority sewn into the stitches of their costume" (57).
Furthermore, the description of South Korean customs follows a paragraph
that evokes the rites of American citizenship, as if the two formations share
compatible logics to the degree that each requires a subordination of the
heterogeneous to the one.

The final incorporation of the nonidentical individual into uniform subjectivity, both thematized and contested by *Dictée*, is the transformation of
the Korean immigrant into an American citizen. In the "naturalization" of
the Korean immigrant as equal citizen, the subject is asked to internalize
an isomorphic analogy in which the relationship of identification between
the Korean immigrant and her Korean family is displaced first by an abstract identification between citizen-subject and the American state. This
internalization is instantiated through the oaths and rituals of naturalization and in the conferring of passports, documents, identification papers,
and photographs. Yet despite the ideological persuasiveness of such analo-
gized identifications, the discrepancy between the subject and the state is
exceedingly visible in this case of the female Korean immigrant, whose
language, history, national origin, race, and gender are at odds with the
formation offered by the promise of citizenship: "One day you raise the
right hand and you are American. They give you an American Pass port.
The United States of America. Somewhere someone has taken my identity
and replaced it with their photograph. The other one. Their signature their
seals. Their own image" (56). Rather than accepting the incorporation of
the citizen into the state, the narrator figures her transformation as a sub-
stitution in which "my identity" is taken away and superseded by "their

signature their seals. Their own image," in yet another subordination of the differentiated to the uniform. For the contract of citizenship is ultimately as contradictory as the other models we have discussed. If the notion of citizenship proposes the state as the unified body in which all subjects are granted membership, it simultaneously asks that individual differences (of race, ethnicity, class, gender, and locality) be subordinated to the general will of the collective polity. Indeed, the requirement for uniformity is most explicable in the context of American democracy, for it is under its ideology of pluralism that the notion of "equal citizenship" and of the subordination of private interests to the will of the majority in exchange for political representation make the most sense. As the critical discussion of citizenship in Chapter 1 demonstrated, the notion of the formally equivalent citizen in representative democracy suggests that all individuals of different constituencies have equal access to and are represented within the political sphere, while simultaneously masking the degree to which strata and inequalities continue to exist, particularly and precisely for the racial and ethnic immigrant populations to whom that notion holds out the promise of membership.[22] Liberal democracy maintains two facades that appear to represent a consensus of many different interests, while simultaneously facilitating the capitalist system in which one dominant class group prospers. In the United States, pluralism admits the existence of differences, yet it requires conformity to a public culture that tends to subordinate alternative cultures —not only racial and ethnic cultures but gay and lesbian cultures as well as working-class culture. The state apparatuses—schooling, communications media, the legal system—that assimilate immigrant individuals into citizenship are integral to the constitution of a state in which their racial and ethnic differences are silenced; hence, the important antagonisms of racial and ethnic immigrant cultures to the state in counterhegemonic critiques that do not exclusively reproduce pluralist arguments of inclusion and rights. As in the initial model of dictation, the discourse of equal citizenship under democracy is also inherently contradictory, for it holds out the state as an inclusive unity but asks for the suppression of particular and local differences as a requirement for representation by that state.

The model of dictation as the transformation of the individual into a formal but contradictory subject has much in common with the concept of "interpellation," which was first sketched by Louis Althusser in "Ideology and Ideological State Apparatuses" (1969). But because of the material and historical location of its production, *Dictée* is suggestive in a different manner than Althusser's essay. As an Asian immigrant cultural text, many of *Dictée*'s formal features imply links and questions that are excluded and undeveloped in Althusser's strictly theoretical formulation of interpellation. That is, in the multivocal, partial, and episodic turns from one narrative site to another and from one mode of narration to another—for example, in the juxtaposition of fragments of the narrator's childhood French lessons against epistolary recollections of her mother's young adulthood during the Japanese occupation and, then further, against aphoristically described scenes from the narrator's return from the United States to Korea as an adult—*Dictée* can be not only much more specific about the multiplicity and adjacency of determining ideological valences in the formation of subjects but also more precise regarding the connections and conflicts between historically differentiated sites of written subjectivity. Inasmuch as the nonlinear and nondevelopmental narrative of *Dictée* refuses closure and totalization, Cha continually subverts the identity of subjectivity and narrative, and in these particular deviations, she provides a more complicated and critical understanding of the incommensurability that constitutes the grounds for antagonism between the subject and the apparatuses of interpellation. Finally, the historical particularity of *Dictée*—authored by a woman at the intersection of Japanese colonialism, Korean nationalism, American imperialism, and Korean immigration to the United States—registers the importance of racial, colonial, and gender determinations in ways that are inevitably informed differently from Althusser's original theory of interpellation.

Althusser discusses interpellation as the process through which subjects internalize ideologies that "recruit" them as speakers or authors (he gives the examples of the police hailing a suspect with, "Hey, you there!" or Christ's address to the individual, "It is for you that I have shed this drop of my blood!").[23] Interpellation suggests that ideologies function through the subject, though it is defined as not accounting for the totality of subjective practice—that is, interpellation contains something akin to the psychoanalytic notion of splitting, but where psychoanalysis figures this splitting metaphorically as the "castration" of the subject upon entering language and social relations, in interpellation, this division is figured otherwise as a tension between an ideological demand for identification and the contradictory material conditions within which that demand is made.[24] Like Cha's notion of dictation, interpellation is inherently contradictory; the function of interpellation—the sublation of differences in order to reproduce generic subjects as equivalent units of abstract labor—attests to a contradiction between an always recognized ground of differences and capitalism's demand for formally identical subjects. In this sense, the concept of interpellation provides for the possibility that the designation of the subject by a particular ideology is not univocal or total. That is, a subject may be multiply hailed by several ideologies whose conditions of production are heterogenous and incommensurable, or alternatively, and perhaps more importantly, a subject may be insufficiently captured by an ideological formation such that an antagonism arises against that formation from the material conditions in which that interpellation takes place. Indeed, it might be said that it is often the demand for formally identical subjectivity that inflects extraneous differences with negative, oppositional significance in relationship to the ideological apparatuses whose function it is to regulate that identity. There are, in other words, what Althusser calls "bad subjects," inadequately interpellated subjects, who resist domination by deviating from the normative and whose misbehaviors "on occasion provoke the intervention of one of the detachments of the (repressive) State apparatus."[25]

A closer investigation of the instances of subject formation discussed in *Dictée* reveals that Cha episodically focuses on sites of interpellation that are not only multiple but are also hybrid, unclosed, and uneven. This focus suggests that resistances to the hegemony reproduced by interpellating structures are not located simply or exclusively in the antagonisms produced by their demands for identity but that it may also be the nonidentity of the irregularly multiple sites to those demands for uniformity which founds the condition of both inadequate interpellation and the subject's resistance to totalization. First, *Dictée* is more specific about multiple hailings, particularly about the conflicts and noncorrespondences between hailing apparatuses. Although they may intersect and coexist or be linked through the use of similar modes and logics, these apparatuses are often at odds with one another: in 1945, for example, the Japanese colonialist occupation of Korea was contested by the U.S. imperial interests in the area; in the 1960s and 1970s, the Catholic Church offered support to Korean student and worker protests against the authoritarian regimes of the Republic of Korea.[26] Second, *Dictée* suggests that, within this multiplicity, one site of interpellation may provide the means or instruments with which to disrupt another apparatus, as in the student's use of English to supplant the rules of French dictation or in the Korean American female narrator's critical stance with regard to the militaristic uniformity of South Korean nationalism.

In this sense, *Dictée* makes explicit that every social formation includes a multiplicity of social contradictions—of race, national origin, ethnicity, gender, or class—arising from heterogeneous origins and conditions, with certain contradictions taking priority over others at particular historical moments. Put otherwise, while the contradiction of capitalism may be said to be that it produces the conditions of its undoing in the forms of class struggle, the contradiction of colonialism that it "develops" the national bourgeoisie that will eventually rise up against the colonial system, or the contradiction of patriarchy that the sites in which women are exploited (for example, marriage, home, workplace) may paradoxically provide means for women to articulate opposition to patriarchy, these contradictions are uneven and nonequivalent, with a particular contradiction surfacing in relation to other contradictions in response to the material conditions of a given historical moment. Addressing the example of racial contradictions in Britain during the 1970s and 1980s, Stuart Hall has discussed the dynamic by which "a structure in dominance" takes priority or is "overdetermined" by the material conditions that perform a "double articulation" of class and race. In Hall's instructive analysis, racial and ethnic categories were, during this period, the prevailing forms in which the structures of domination and exploitation were lived, and he suggests that these structures were therefore necessarily contested through and by means of racial and ethnic categories and representations. He states this succinctly: "'Black,' then, exists ideologically only in relation to the contestation around those chains of meaning, and the social forces involved in that contestation. . . . The effect of the struggle over 'black,' if it becomes strong enough, is that it stops the society reproducing itself functionally, in *that* old way. Social reproduction itself becomes a contested process."[27] But *Dictée* extends this

notion a bit further by suggesting that in addition to the strategic and necessary attacks on the prevailing form of domination in the terms of that
domination, it may also be interventions from standpoints of alterity to the
structure in dominance that enable the displacement of that dominance. It
is with regard to this specific emphasis on the mobilization of "other" sites
of contradiction and the reappropriation of "other" artifices in the struggle
against a particular hegemony—of feminine alterity to Catholic interpellation or the use of English in a critique of French or Japanese colonialism—
that *Dictée* is the most illuminating.[28]

French Catholicism, for example, which the text represents as having
been most influential in the narrator's childhood, is not exclusively and entirely a religious apparatus of subject formation. Rather, French Catholic
conversion also makes use of the pedagogical interpellation of the Korean
subject in French, while the force of Catholic rites on that subject equally
depends on the long historical presence of French missionary colonialism
in Korea. In this instance, religion is articulated at an intersection with
pedagogical and colonial determinations; each demands different repetitions of the subject, and each is inextricably implicated in the forms of
fidelity demanded by the others. Those nonidentities that cannot be reduced in a single dictated formation of the subject—the unfaithful, the
female, the colonial other, the racially and linguistically other—are re-
trieved and revoiced in Cha's text as antagonisms heterogeneous to the
religious apparatus in dominance.

In *Dictée*, the Catholic narrative tells the subject that God has made "him"
"in his own likeness." In the confession as in the catechism, the faithful
subject "speaks" this equivalence between "man" and "God." But whereas
Althusser refers to the Christian religion as a paradigmatic example of ideology—the individual is transformed into a faithful "subject" (small *s*) in
accepting the metaphor between himself and the absolute, unique example
of God, the "Subject" (capital *s*)—Cha makes evident that the religious formation may coexist with pedagogical and colonial dictations and make use
of the logics of equivalence also instantiated by those dictations.[29] The emulation of God in the recitation of the example is a ritual that aims to produce faithful subjects as formally equivalent sites of that emulation. Like
the pedagogical and colonial, however, the premise of religious equivalence

carries in it ideological contradiction, for even as it imagines the communion of man and God, as embodied in the Eucharist, it presupposes sin as the original and fundamental condition that differentiates the fallen man from God's Example. This contradiction is exacerbated with regard to the subject of *Dictée*, who is distinctly nonequivalent to the Example in a variety of ways. Her "sins"—of female otherness, racial and ethnic Korean alterity, colonial difference—are articulated in an eloquent adulteration of the catechism: "*Q: GOD WHO HAS MADE YOU IN HIS OWN LIKENESS. A: God who has made me in His own likeness. In His Own Image in His Own Resemblance, in His Own Copy, in His Own Counterfeit Presentment, in His Duplicate, in His Own Reproduction, in His Cast, in His Carbon, His Image and His Mirror. Pleasure in the image pleasure in the copy pleasure in the projection of likeness pleasure in the repetition. Acquiesce, to the correspondance. Acquiesce*" (17–18). In multiplying the concept of "likeness," she responds to the catechism by submitting to the interpellative demand that she "repeat" and attest to the property of "likeness." At the same time, in alluding to forms of repetition that diminish or falsify the "original"—duplication, counterfeiting, carbon copy, and mirroring—she parodically thematizes the process of Catholic interpellation as a subordination of the multiple to the identical, the heteromorphic to the One. Repetition, taken to its extreme, discredits repeatability as the "proof" of equivalence and correspondence. Shoshana Felman has argued that if irony replaces the pathos required by repetition, the result is parody, which "decomposes" realism and its presumptions of faithful mimetic representation.[30] When the hypnosis of religious repetition is defamiliarized, repetition is revealed as cliché. Cliché betrays the arbitrariness of the sign and unsettles the authoritative discourse of equivalence. The subject's parodic response to "God who has made you in His own likeness" actually conforms to the conceptual premise of "likeness" and repetition, yet in the multiplication of synonyms and variants, it voices the female ("His . . . Reproduction"), racial ("His Carbon"), and colonial ("His Cast[e]") differences from the Catholic demand for formally identical, faithful subjects.

Female difference is further emphasized as one of the explicit obstacles to faithful religious subjection. As the narrator describes taking the host from the priest, she is struck that the marginalized physical location of the women in the church ("the women kneeling on the left side. The right side . . . their elongated tongues. In waiting. To receive. Him," 13) resonates with female nonequivalence to the masculine equations instantiated by the Eucharist: the wafer and wine are the metaphorical equivalents of the body and blood of Christ, administered by the priest who is the moral representative of Christ and the intermediary between the mortal and the divine: "The Host Wafer (His Body. His Blood.) His . . . . One gesture. Solid. For Him. By then he is again at the other end. He the one who deciphers he the one who invokes in the Name. He the one who becomes He. Man-God" (13). The "most grievous sins" (14) of female difference, sexual difference, and bodily procreative difference place women as eccentric to the "Man-God" continuum. The thematizing of female eccentricity calls attention to the male gender of the apparently ungendered equivalent subject formation, constituting a powerful form of articulating nonidentity in antagonism to the demand for uniformity.

Finally, *Dictée* is more specific about Althusser's rather cryptic allusion to ideology as "the imaginary representation of individuals to their real conditions of existence."[31] Rather than upholding a dyadic opposition of "imaginary" fictions to "real" material conditions, in her model of dictation Cha provides a means to understand this formulation that is ultimately more dynamic and useful than this binary interpretation.[32] That is, dictation, elaborated as the operation through which the subject internalizes ideology, suggests that ideology is a material site of struggle, that it locates the subject in social relations, but that it "captures" the subject precisely by means of its appeal to constructed imaginary equivalences or identifications. In *Dictée*, this "capture" is by no means monolithic or fixed. Rather, what we call the "subject" takes place in those articulated spaces of continuing contradiction between the ideological imperative to imagine equivalence and the material disruption of that equivalence, always in the process of both speaking and speaking against ideologies of imagined identification. For example, we might say that as ideology, liberal pluralism posits a relationship of analogical identification between the individual and the democratic state. This posited relationship in which the subject is "represented" either in or by the state is "imaginary," whether one takes "imaginary" strictly to mean fictional or whether one associates the term with the psychoanalytic Imaginary, a hypothetical phase recapitulated from the standpoint of language and social relations in which the ego "identifies" (or misidentifies, in Lacan's *méconnaissance*) with its specular image or with the displaced counterparts of the ego ideal, ideal ego, and superego.[33] It is with this latter psychoanalytic view—that identification involves a continual, repressed recognition of differentiation—that we can understand ideology to be, as Fredric Jameson describes it, an "indispensable mapping fantasy or narrative by which the individual subject invents a 'lived' relationship with collective systems."[34] That is, though the interpellation of the subject takes place in social relations, the process through which the subject is "captured" may be said to rely on a "fantasy" whose pleasurable erotic force derives from a fiction of identification (whether of specular duplication, transference, or relation of ego to its counterparts). This fiction, which both reveals and sutures the gap in the lived misidentification of difference as the same, is responsible for the production of universalities, harmonies, and gratifications. Imaginary identifications furnish the effects of pleasure that may be exploited by a state apparatus to enlist subjects in its operations and to dissuade them from active political resistance and antagonism. Against the ideological subsumption of difference and particularity to imaginary equivalence, *Dictée* suggests that it is precisely at the junctures of proposed equivalence that ideology may be interrupted and challenged and that specularity, homology, and identification are each vulnerable from the standpoint of differentiated social and material relations.[35]

Hence, the vulnerability of imaginary equivalence is evinced throughout *Dictée*—beginning with the revelation of the contradiction of dictation and the disjunction between the "original" and the translation—as well as in the incommensurabilities of the religious subject to God, the colonial subject to empire, the soldier to the nation, and the immigrant citizen to democratic pluralism. But the process of imagined identical reproduction is perhaps most disrupted by the rewritten relationship of the subject to the mother, which unsettles, as discontinuous and mediated, the metaphorizing of the subject-nation analogy through the specular relationship that is normally the privileged topos of the "mirror stage": the reflective dyad of mother and child. In *Dictée*, the relationship of the subject to the figure of the mother is never naturalized as an unmediated identification ("It seemed to resemble but it wasn't," 128). Rather, the writing thematizes union, but through a re-formulated notion of re-union that is displaced by departure, distance, and return. When there are repetitions, these repetitions cite, juxtapose, and decontextualize. *Dictée* makes use of analogy but reconceives analogy as being possible between unlike languages, histories, and bodies: "Eighteen years pass. I am here for the first time in eighteen years, Mother. We left here in this memory still fresh, still new. I speak another tongue, a second tongue. This is how distant I am. From then. From that time" (85).

If one of the aims of literary representation, with its premise of mimetic correspondence between the name and the thing, is to provide a fiction of reconciliation that resolves the material contradictions of differentiation in and between spheres other than the literary, *Dictée* suggests that every representation claiming such correspondence must bear anxious traces of the fundamental conditions of unmimetic irresolution. In its discontinuity, fragmentation, and episodic unfluency, *Dictée* attests to such irresolution, and its aesthetic of infidelity not only prompts the revelation of differences beneath the claim to verisimilitude but also, in disturbing the function of representation as reconciliation, returns us, as readers, to the material contradictions of lived political life.

Since the 1970s, notions of identity have provided the important models of social and political unity necessary for coherent liberation struggles. In feminist struggles, as well as in separatist or nationalist struggles against racism and colonialism, resistances to domination have been organized through identification with a common "origin" or common position in rela-tion to domination. These resistances to domination based on identity have been essential, and it seems inconceivable that they will diminish while the material conditions that produce them—racism, colonialism, capitalism, and sexism—not only continue but also, in particular regions and spheres, seem to have been refortified. At the same time, the urgent concerns of a politics of difference, rather than identity, have begun to demand atten-tion and dialogue: among feminists, greater attention is being given to the concerns of women of color. Within movements organized around race or ethnicity, the acknowledgment of differences of gender, class, and sexu-ality has not weakened those movements but has opened up new lines of affiliation with other groups whose cohesions are founded in other subordinations. Among nationalist movements, feminists have argued for reproductive rights, called attention to the gendered division of labor, and criticized religious fundamentalism as oppressive to women.[36] While these interrogations of heterogeneity, intersection, and multiplicity do not, and should not, supplant the earlier mode of identity politics, as struggles continue and extend their modes, sites, and forms of contestation—just as racism, colonialism, and sexism diversify and take new forms—the two differing political modes must engage, conflict, and necessarily shift each other's strategies and priorities. *Dictée* is a cultural object that catalyzes such an engagement; its elaboration of the multiplicity of subject formations, each articulated at an intersection with others, troubles the notion of an essential Asian American, female, or postcolonial subject; it opens critical debate and initiates what Stuart Hall has called "a critical politics, a politics of criticism."[37] This dialectic between the politics of identity and the politics of difference is, I would argue, of utmost importance, for it opens a terrain on which to imagine the construction of another politics, one which engages with rather than suppresses heterogeneities of gender, class, sexuality, race, and nation, yet which is also able to maintain and extend the forms of unity that make common struggle possible—a politics whose vision is not the origin but the destination.

Work, Immigration, Gender:

Asian "American" Women

Hello, my name is Fu Lee. I am 41 years old, married, and I have a 9-year old daughter. I have been living in Oakland Chinatown since I left Hong Kong 12 years ago. . . .

My eyes hurt from straining under poor lighting; my throat hurt because of the chemical fumes from the fabric dye. Sometimes, I would wear surgical masks so I don't have to breathe in all the dust from the fabric. My back never stopped hurting from bending over the sewing machine all day. Our boss was like a dictator. He was always pushing us to work faster. There was a sign in the shop that said, "No loud talking. You cannot go to the bathroom." When we did talk loudly or laugh during work, he would throw empty boxes at us and tell us to go back to work. When there was a rush order, we had to eat lunch at our work station.

Last year, my employer closed his shop and left us holding bad paychecks. We found out that he had filed for bankruptcy and had no intention of paying us our meager wages. The twelve Chinese seamstresses including myself were so mad. After working so hard under such horrendous working conditions, we should at least get our pay.

With the help of Asian Immigrant Women Advocates, we began searching for ways to get our pay.[1]

Mrs. Fu Lee's testimony at a community hearing initiated by Asian Immigrant Women Advocates (AIWA) in Oakland, California, describes the conditions of many Asian immigrant women working within the San

Francisco Bay Area garment industry: low-wage or unpaid labor, forced increases in productivity through long workdays or speedups, repetitive manual labor, occupational hazards and environmental toxins, and no union or collective bargaining protections. Before the Lucky Sewing Co. closed shop and left the sewing women with bad paychecks, Mrs. Lee and the other seamstresses were to have been paid $5 a dress; the subcontractor was paid $10 a dress, yet each dress was sold by Jessica McClintock, Inc. for $175. In the San Francisco Bay Area garment industry, women sew clothing that their meager wages, when they receive them, will not permit them to buy as commodities. The women work under physical conditions that are unsafe, unhealthy, and fatiguing. Furthermore, the policy of paying the worker by piece exploits the immigrant women in ways that extend beyond the extraction of surplus value from hourly, low-wage factory labor. The incentive to complete as many pieces as possible makes certain that the sewing woman will work overtime without compensation and will intensify her productivity even if it results in exhaustion or personal injury. Because many are non-English or little-English-speaking women and consider their employment options limited, because eight out of ten Chinatown immigrant families with multiple wage earners say they would "barely get by" if there were but one breadwinner in the family, these women are forced to accept the payment conditions dictated by the employer.[2]

Mrs. Lee, in collaboration with AIWA and the other women workers, has produced an important testimony that at once connects her life as a Chinese immigrant woman with her struggle as a worker who desires economic justice. Struggles for empowerment are often exclusively understood within the frameworks of legal, political, and economic institutions; the subjectivity of Mrs. Lee can be comprehended in relation to systemic oppression and systemic change. Yet an important link in this relation is the production of individual and collective subjectivities through cultural forms. In this sense, Mrs. Lee's testimony is compelling not only for the facts it relates, but also for the way it poses relations between those facts. The narrative progression charts a movement from being an aggrieved seamstress to forging a collective campaign for back pay; it inspires identification that has helped to build community solidarity around the immigrant garment workers. In addition, Mrs. Lee's testimony conveys the manner in which the factory extracted surplus value not only through her "labor" as an abstract form, but from using and manipulating her body itself: from her eyes that strained under poor lighting, her throat that hurt because of the chemical fumes from the fabric dye, and her back that ached from being bent over the sewing machine all day. Where Mrs. Lee's narrative evokes her conscious, embodied relation to work, it also refuses the isolation of each part as a separate site to be instrumentally exploited; her narrative integrates the sites of bodily exploitation as constitutive parts of the value of her labor, as well as of the process in which she becomes a political subject. Furthermore, as the narrative moves from her description of embodied exploitation to the decision to take collective political action, it alludes to her experiences as a woman, as a mother, as a Chinese immigrant, and as a worker, also refusing the atomization of the conditions that issue from patriarchal subordination, racialized immigration, segregation, and labor exploitation. Mrs. Lee's narrative does not reduce her political identity or actions to one cause or origin; it instead brings together the dimensions of her material and political subjectivity, and, in that process, illuminates the intersecting axes of exploitation she inhabits and the differentiating operations of contemporary capital that exploits precisely through the selection and reproduction of racial, cultural, and gender-specific labor power.

Forms of individual and collective narratives are not merely representations disconnected from "real" political life; nor are these expressions "transparent" records of histories of struggle. Rather, these forms—life stories, oral histories, histories of community, literature—are crucial media that connect subjects to social relations. In this book, I have argued that the contradictions of the political and economic spheres are manifested in Asian American cultural production as a material site of struggle, and Asian American critique is the dialectical politicization of these contradictions. Asian American culture is the medium through which alternatives to liberal citizenship in the political sphere are narrated, where critical subjects and collectivities can be reproduced in new configurations, with new coherences. To consider testimony and testimonial as constituting a "genre" of cultural production is significant for Asian immigrant women, for it extends the scope of what constitutes legitimate knowledges to include other forms and practices that have been traditionally excluded from both empirical and aesthetic modes of evaluation. Yet as Chandra Talpade Mohanty has observed of third world women's narratives, they are in themselves "not evidence of decentering hegemonic histories and subjectivities. It is the way in which they are read, understood, and located institutionally which is of paramount importance. After all, the point is not just 'to record' one's history of struggle, or consciousness, but how they are recorded; the way we read, receive, and disseminate such imaginative records is immensely significant."[3] "The way we read, receive, and disseminate" Mrs. Lee's testimony may be, in one context, to cite it as evidence in a hearing to grieve the abuse of Asian immigrant garment industry workers; in this context, Mrs. Lee's testimony contributed to AIWA's campaign that succeeded in establishing Jessica McClintock, Inc.'s responsibility for the subcontractor. In another, and not mutually exclusive, context, the way we read Mrs. Lee's testimony may be to place it in relation to other cultural forms that make use of different techniques of narration, such as Monique Thuy-Dung Truong's "Kelly," Theresa Hak Kyung Cha's *Dictée,* or Fae Myenne Ng's *Bone.* Such a reading need not level the differences between evidential forms that gain meaning on the horizon of the "empirical" and literary or art forms that are more commonly interpreted on the horizon of the "aesthetic." The aim is not to "aestheticize" the testimonial text but rather to displace the categorizing drive of disciplinary formations that would delimit the transgressive force of articulations within regulative epistemological or evaluative boundaries. This mode of reading and reception seeks to situate different cultural forms in relation to shared social and historical processes and to make active the dialectic that necessarily exists between those forms because of their common imbrication in those processes. It seeks to understand Asian American cultural production critically and broadly and to interpret the interconnections between testimony, personal narrative, oral history, literature, film, visual arts, and other cultural forms as sites through which subject, community, and struggle are signified and mediated. While specifying the differences between forms, this understanding of cultural production troubles both the strictly empirical foundations of social science and the universalizing tendencies of aesthetic discourse. In this mode, we can read testimony as more than a neopositivist "truth," as a complex mediating genre that selects, conveys, and connects "facts" in particular ways without reducing social contradiction or compartmentalizing the individual as a site of resolution. Likewise, we can read literary texts like the novel not merely as the aesthetic framing of a "private" transcendance but as a form that may narrate the dissolution or impossibility of the "private" domain in the context of the material conditions of work, geography, gender, and race. In this sense, cultural forms of many kinds are important media in the formation of oppositional narratives and are crucial to the imagination and rearticulation of new forms of political subjectivity, collectivity, and practice.

This notion of cultural production as a site for the formation of new political subjects serves to focus the next section, in which I discuss the current construction of Asian immigrant women's work within the context of what we might term the "racialized feminization of labor" in the global restructuring of capitalism. The location of Asian immigrant women's work —at the intersection of processes of immigration, racialization, labor exploitation, and patriarchal gender relations—marks that work as irreducible to the concept of "abstract labor," and distinguishes the subjectivity it constitutes as unassimilable to an abstract political identity or to a singular narrative of emancipation implied by that identity. Hence, it is often in cultural forms and practices, broadly defined, that we find the most powerful articulation of this complex subjectivity and through those forms and practices that an alternative "politicization" of that subject is mediated. Furthermore, the focus on women's work within the global economy as a material site in which several axes of domination intersect provides the means for linking Asian immigrant and Asian American women with other immigrant and racialized women. Asian immigrant and Asian American women are not simply the most recent formation within the genealogy of Asian American racialization; they, along with women working in the "third world," are the "new" workforce within the global reorganization of capitalism. In this sense, the active affiliations of Asian immigrant and Asian American women are informed by, yet go beyond, Asian American cultural identity as it has emerged within the confines of the U.S. nation. They are linked to an emergent political formation, organizing across race, class, and national boundaries, that includes other racialized and immigrant groups as well as women working in, and immigrating from, the neocolonized world.

From roughly 1850 to World War II, Asian immigration was the site for the eruptions and resolutions of the contradictions between the national economy and the political state, and, from World War II onward, the locus of the contradictions between the nation-state and the global economy. Hence, Asian immigrant women's work must be understood within the history of U.S. immigration policies and the attempts to incorporate immigrants into the developing economy, on the one hand, and within the global expansion of U.S. capitalism through colonialism and global restructuring, on the other. I argued in Chapter 1 that, in the first period, the contradiction between the economic need for inexpensive, tractable labor and the political need to constitute a homogeneous nation was "resolved" through the series of legal exclusions, disenfranchisements, and restricted enfranchisements of Asian immigrants that simultaneously "racialized" these groups as "nonwhites" as it consolidated immigrants of diverse European descent as "white." Because of the history in which economic forces and exigencies have been mediated through the legal apparatus that racializes and genders immigrant subjects, Asian immigrant and Asian American class struggles have always intersected with and been articulated through race and gender determinations. In the later period, the capital imperative has come into greater contradiction with the political imperative of the U.S. nation-state, with capitalism requiring an economic internationalism in order to increase labor and capital, and the state needing to be politically coherent and hegemonic in world affairs in order to determine the conditions of that internationalism. The expansion that led to U.S. colonialism and war in the Philippines, Korea, and Vietnam violently displaced immigrants from those nations; the aftermath of the repressed history of U.S. imperialism in Asia now materializes in the "return" of Asian immigrants to the imperial center. Both the racialized gendered character of Asian immigrant labor within the emergence of U.S. capitalism and U.S. colonial modes of development and exploitation in Asia provide the basis for understanding that U.S. capital has historically accumulated and profited through the differentiation of labor rather than through its homogenization; in the global expansion of the capitalist mode, the racial and gendered character of labor has been further exaggerated, refined, and built into the regime itself.

Since the 1980s, the globalization of capitalism has shifted many manufacturing operations to Asia and Latin America and has reorganized a mode of production that at one time employed a predominantly male U.S. labor force, white and black, in industrial manufacturing and employed white working-class and racialized women in assembly, blue- and pink-collar, and service work. In the search for cheaper, more "flexible" labor, this reorganization now recruits new immigrants, especially Asian and Latina women, to fill the insecure assembly and service-sector jobs within the United States that have emerged largely as a result of restructuring and "re-engineering." Just as the displacement of U.S. workers and increased immigration to the United States are an index of restructuring, so, too, has restructuring exacerbated both anti-immigrant nativism and the state's "need" to legislate "aliens" who have entered since 1965. Thus, the proletarianization of Asian and Latina immigrant women is a current instance of the contradiction between the globalization of the economy and the political needs of the nation-state; it takes place in conjunction with a gendered international division of labor that makes use of third world and racialized immigrant women as a more "flexible," "casual," "docile" workforce. Transnational industry's use of Asian and Latina women's labor—in Asia, Latin America, and the U.S.—is the contemporary site where the contradictions of the national and the international converge in an overdetermination of neo-colonial capitalism, anti-immigrant racism, and patriarchal gender stratification.

In this sense, the global restructuring of the capitalist mode of production can be understood to constitute a new social formation, one whose domain has extended beyond the nation-state to global markets and international circuits of exchange. In *Reading Capital*, Louis Althusser and Etienne Balibar extend Marx's original formulation of the relationship between the "mode of production" and the "social formation" by defining a social formation as the complex structure in which more than one mode of production, or set of economic relations, may be combined.[4] Their elaboration suggests not only that the situations of uneven development, colonialist incorporation, or global restructuring and immigration are each characterized by the combination of several simultaneous modes of production but that each constitutes a specific, historically distinct social formation (that includes economic, political, and ideological levels of articulation). The need to understand the differentiated forms through which capital profits through mixing and combining different modes of production suggests, too, that the complex structures of a new social formation may indeed require interventions and modes of opposition specific to those structures. One of the distinct features of the global restructuring of capital is its ability to profit not through homogenization but through the differentiation of specific resources and markets that permit the exploitation of gendered and racialized labor within regional and national sites. Part of this differentiation involves transactions between "national" and "international" sites which formalize new capital accumulation and production techniques that specifically target female labor markets where women are disciplined by state-instituted traditional patriarchy, whether in Malaysia or Guatemala, or by racialized immigration laws that target female immigrants in particular, such as in California. The global racialized feminization of women's labor is a new social formation characterized by the exploitation of women both in export-oriented production zones in Asia and Latin America *and* near the center of the market in the Silicon Valley, California, electronics industry, in the Los Angeles manufacturing district, and in the San Francisco Bay Area garment industry.

While some analysts of transnationalism argue that global capitalism has reached a near-universal extension and has incorporated all sectors into its logic of commodification, the situations of Asian and Latina women workers suggest that transnational capitalism, like nation-state capitalism and colonial capitalism before it, continues to produce sites of contradiction, and the dynamics of its own negation and critique.[5] For in the complex encounters between transnational capital and women within patriarchal gender structures, the very processes that produce a racialized feminized proletariat both displace traditional and national patriarchies and their defining regulations of gender, space, and work and racialize the women in relation to other racialized groups. These displacements produce new possibilities precisely because they have led to a breakdown and a reformulation of the categories of nation, race, class, and gender and in doing so have prompted a reconceptualization of the oppositional narratives of nationalism, Marxism, and feminism. The shift toward the transnationalization of capital is not exclusively manifested in the "denationalization" of corporate power or the nation-state, but perhaps more importantly, it is expressed in the reorganization of oppositional interventions against capital that articulate themselves in terms and relations other than the singular "national," "class," or "female" subject. Asian, Asian immigrant, and Asian American women occupy some of the sites of contradiction in the current international division of labor, and their agencies are critical to U.S. women of color activism, cross-border labor organizing, and third world and immigrant women's struggles.

Although Asian immigrant women have been in the United States since the nineteenth century, the greater numbers of Asian women immigrated after the mid-twentieth century, and the specific recruitment of women as a labor force has intensified since the Immigration and Nationality Act of 1965.[6] Since that time, along with African American and Mexican American women, Asian immigrant women have constituted an important low-paid workforce within the United States, "occupationally ghettoized" in menial, domestic, and reproductive labor, textile and garment industries, hotel and restaurant work, and a current mix of mass production, subcontracting and family-type firms. Because of their material, gender, and racial differentiation from the abstract citizen proposed by the U.S. political sphere, they remain at a distance from its nationalist narratives. Immigration laws help to produce a racially segmented and gender stratified labor force for capital's needs, inasmuch as such laws seek to resolve such inequalities by deferring them in the promise of equality on the political terrain of representation. While the official narratives of immigrant inclusion propose to assimilate immigrants as citizens, the conditions of Asian immigrant women in the United States directly contradict these promises of incorporation, equal opportunity, and equal representation. Asian "American" women, even as citizens, continue to be located at the cultural, racial, and political boundaries of the nation. Indeed, I use quotation marks here in order to signal the ambivalent identification that both U.S.-born Asian and Asian immigrant women have to the nationalist construction "American." For Asian immigrant women, the American contract of citizenship is quite evidently contradictory; if it proposes the state as the unified body in which all equal subjects are granted membership, it simultaneously asks that differences—of race, class, gender, and locality—be subordinated in order to qualify for membership in that democratic body.

At the same time, as a group formed through the intersecting processes of racialization, class exploitation, and gender subordination, Asian immigrant women are also differentially situated in relation to the political narratives of social movements organized around single forms of domination: for example, the liberal feminist critique of patriarchy, the trade union analysis of capitalism from the standpoint of class exploitation, and the critique of racism and internal colonialism from the standpoint of racialized minority subjects. From the early post-World War II years through the 1960s, political economy in the United States was dominated by the notion of development, and in that period, opposition to exploitation was primarily articulated in terms of class issues.[7] The 1960s marked, however, the beginning of a period in which the articulation of opposition became increasingly mediated by analyses of other forms of domination, not only capitalism and imperialism, but also patriarchy and racism.[8] Emerging out of this earlier moment in the capitalist mode of production, U.S. oppositional social movements of the 1970s—feminist, labor, civil rights and ethno-nationalist—produced narratives of political development for the subjects resisting domination within this earlier mode. According to these narratives, the "woman," "worker," and "racial or ethnic minority" subjects were said to develop from a prehegemonic, preclass identified position to that of politicized participants who could "grasp" their exploitation in relation to their function within patriarchy, capitalism, and racism. Asian immigrant and Asian "American" women, like other racialized women, have a different political formation than that prescribed by *either* narratives of liberal capitalist development and citizenship or the narratives proposed by these oppositional movements of the 1970s. The isolation of one axis of power, such as the exploitation of labor under capitalism, masks the historical processes through which capitalism has emerged in conjunction with, and been made more efficient by, other systems of discrimination and subordination—patriarchy, racism, and colonialism.[9] The Asian "American" woman and the racialized woman are materially in excess of the subject "woman" posited by feminist discourse, or the "proletariat" described by Marxism, or the "racial or ethnic" subject projected by civil rights and ethno-nationalist movements. This excess and differential places Asian American and other racialized women in critical, and dialectical, relationships to the subjects of feminism, Marxism, and ethnic nationalisms.

In this sense, Asian immigrant and Asian American women may be said to constitute the dialectical sublation of these earlier models of political subjectivity.

The particular location of racialized working women at an intersection where the contradictions of racism, patriarchy, and capitalism converge produces a subject that cannot be determined along a single axis of power or by a single apparatus, on the one hand, or contained within a single narrative of oppositional political formation, on the other. If Marxism proposes that the classical contradiction exists between capital and labor—a contradiction that permits the accumulation of surplus value through the exploitation of labor at the same time that it produces the class struggles that mark the points of crisis and vulnerability within capitalism—then the situation of racialized working women makes it apparent that we must always speak of more than one contradiction. We may speak of a racial contradiction by which the state claims to be a democratic body in which all subjects are granted membership, while racial, ethnic, and immigrant subjects continue to be disenfranchised and excluded from political participation in that state. Or we may speak of two sites of gender contradiction: the first in which the concept of abstract labor in political economy (that work is equivalent to pay) conflicts with unwaged female domestic labor in the home and unequal pay for women in the workplace; the second, a contradiction between the discourse of formal legal equality and the conditions under which a woman's choice to conceive or bear a child is an action that may still be contested by husband, father, or state. Furthermore, within the trajectory of liberal feminism, relative gains of some women in corporate, political, or professional domains accentuate the contradictory persistence of barriers to—and what Glenn has called "occupational ghettoization" of—poor women of color. Throughout lived social relations, it is apparent that labor is gendered, sexuality is racialized, and race is class-associated. A multiplicity of social contradictions with different origins converge at different sites within any social formation—the family, education, religion, communications media, sites of capitalist production—and each is uneven and incommensurable, with certain contradictions taking priority over others in response to the material conditions of a given historical moment. Singular narratives of consciousness aim at developing a subject position from which totalization becomes possible, whereas the cultural productions of racialized women seek to articulate multiple, non-equivalent, but linked determinations without assuming their containment within the horizon of an absolute totality and its presumption of a singular subject. U.S. women of color have located themselves in relationship to intersecting dominations, and these locations have been translated into powerful critical positions. From the 1980s, work by Audre Lorde, Cherríe Moraga, and the collective Asian Women United of California, for example, exemplify "situated" non-totalizing perspectives on conjoined dominations, as well as the emergence of politicized critiques of those conjunctions.[10]

The necessary alliances between racialized and third world women within, outside, and across the border of the United States grow out of the contemporary conditions of global capitalism under which immigrant women working in the garment industries of Los Angeles are virtually part of the same labor force as those employed in Asia or Latin America. The sweatshops of the garment industry located in San Francisco and Los Angeles, for example, employ immigrant women from Mexico, El Salvador, Guatemala, Hong Kong, South Korea, Thailand, and the Philippines, while in these countries of origin, U.S. transnational corporations are also conducting garment assembly work.[11] Women migrate from countries of origin formerly colonized by the United States, or currently neocolonized by U.S. corporate capital, and come to labor here as racialized women of color. In this sense, despite the obstacles of national, cultural, and linguistic differences, there are material continuities between the conditions of Chicanas and Latinas working in the United States and the women working in maquiladoras and low-cost manufacturing zones in Latin America, on the one hand, and Asian women working both within the United States and in Asian zones of assembly and manufacturing, on the other.

Thus, recent immigrant communities constitute the most evident sites for racialized women in the United States to intersect with women in the neocolonized world whose experiences are doubly determined by exploitation which traverses national boundaries. The important ongoing work of organizations like AIWA (Asian Immigrant Women Advocates) in the San Francisco Bay Area, in which second- and third-generation Asian American women work for the empowerment of immigrant Asian women workers in the garment, hotel, and electronics industries, or the Garment Workers' Justice Center in Los Angeles and La Mujer Obrera in El Paso, suggests some ways of thinking about the mutual processes of politicization that occur between racialized immigrant women in the United States and women in the third world. Groups like the Asian Law Caucus and the Coalition for Immigrant and Refugee Rights and Services have ongoing projects advocating immigrants rights.[12] AIWA is an innovative example of cross-generational women of different national origins, classes, and language backgrounds organizing in ways that address the particular conditions of Asian immigrant women workers.[13] While AIWA organizes Asian immigrant women around the more traditional labor issue of workers' rights—as in the successful campaign to pressure garment manufacturer Jessica McClintock, Inc.—AIWA also focuses on bringing Asian American and Asian immigrant women together as members of Asian communities and addresses issues that are of concern "outside" of the workplace, such as childcare, healthcare, language, and literacy. In addition, it should be emphasized that AIWA does not organize itself in a traditional hierarchy that would place "organizers" above "workers" or Asian American women above immigrant women; the reciprocally transformative relationship between Asian American organizers and Asian immigrant working women is expressly encouraged by AIWA's structure.[14] Miriam Ching Louie writes: "The challenge to AIWA organizers is to use the classes (in English) so that workers can reflect on their own lives, determine what is fair, visualize alternatives to oppressive conditions, and practice demanding their rights. . . . Organizers must also transform themselves in the process."[15]

While AIWA works with Asian immigrant and Asian American women, other projects create and maintain solidarity across racial and ethnic groups and across national boundaries: groups like the Border Workers Regional Support Committee (CAFOR) and the Coalition for Justice in the Maquiladoras (CJM) have helped Mexican maquiladora workers organize against U.S.- and Japanese-owned parent companies. The Support Committee for the Maquiladora Workers in San Diego organizes activists, a number of whom are Asian immigrant women, to assist in documenting the exploitative, unsafe working conditions of the maquiladoras, and to provide various support services for the mostly female Mexican workers.[16] Recently, the Support Committee assisted in retrieving the back wages for workers formerly employed at Exportadora de Mano de Obra in Tijuana, Mexico, by bringing suit in U.S. courts against the parent company National O-Ring, a division of American United Global Corporation. One hundred and eighty workers had lost their wages when National O-Ring suddenly closed the Exportadora plant in Tijuana, an act precipitated by the women workers having brought charges of sexual harassment against the company president. "Solidarity among workers should cross the border as easily as companies move production," says Mary Tong, director of the Support Committee for Maquiladora Workers. Asian "American" projects are changing in response to the changes in immigration and immigrant communities over the last two decades, as well as shifting to take on the difficult work of forging understanding and political solidarity between Asian and non-Asian groups across racial and national boundaries.

The work of Asian "American," Asian immigrant, and other racialized women organizing across national boundaries, formations, and displacements entails processes of learning, translation, and transformations of perspective. Chandra Mohanty has written about the movements *between* cultures, languages, and complex configurations of meanings and power: "Experience must be historically interpreted and theorized if it is to become the basis of feminist solidarity and struggle, and it is at this moment that an understanding of the politics of location proves crucial."[17] Asian American cultural forms, containing a repertoire of counter-history, memory, and resources for different narratives of new subjects and practices, are a medium for this critical historical interpretation. Rather than dictating that subjects be constituted through identification with the liberal citizen-formation of American national culture, Asian American cultural forms offer the possibility of subjects and practices constituted through dialectics of difference and disidentification. Rather than vertical determination by the state, these forms are suggestive of horizontal relations between subjects across national boundaries. As subjects occupying the contradictions of "the national-within-the-international," the location of Asian immigrant women is nonetheless the U.S. nation-state. Therefore, Asian immigrant women must struggle to understand not only the process of racialization within the U.S. national frame but also the different processes of other immigrant women who may already be a proletarianized gendered labor force in their "home" countries but within specifically nationally stratified sets of social relations there: the agencies of women in sites as different as South Korea, Sri Lanka, or Egypt are determined by their specific national histories of colonialism, decolonization, nationalist struggles, post-independence capitalist development, and multinational incursions.[18] Asian immigrant and Asian "American" women, as always, must be vigilant with regard to the dangers of universalizing nationalist notions of "womanhood" or struggle. The attention to "difference" vividly evoked by Audre Lorde's 1979 speech "The Master's Tools"—"community must not mean a shedding of our differences . . . [but] learning how to take our differences and make them strengths"[19]—is still, and all the more, crucial for Asian immigrant and Asian "American" women in the global instance of our contemporary moment.

Fae Myenne Ng's novel *Bone* (1993), like Mrs. Lee's testimony with which we began, portrays Chinatown sewing women who provide labor for a transnational consumer market in which they scarcely participate and who bring home work and solicit the help of children and relatives, making the "private" domestic space of the immigrant home an additional site of labor.

> Mah was too busy even to look up when I offered her lunch. She said she didn't have an appetite, so I put the aluminum packet of food on the water pipe, where it'd stay warm, and her thermos on the already-filled communal eating table.
>
> She wanted to teach me to do zippers so I could sew another dozen for her at home. . . .
>
> Back home, I started with the darts. I sewed the facing to the interfacing, the front to the back; then I had trouble with the zipper. I wasn't used to the slick gabardine fabric; my seams didn't match up, and the needle kept sliding over to the metal teeth. I undid the seam and tried again. This time the needle hit the metal zipper tab and jammed. I gave up afraid I might break the needle. Mah broke a needle once and its tip flew up and lodged so close to her eye that Luday and Soon-ping had to walk her over to Chinese hospital.[20]

The lives of the Leong family in Ng's novel are legibly imprinted by conditions of Mah's work as a sewing woman: from the central motif of the sewing machine in all of their lives, to the vulnerability of the immigrant home to capitalist penetration, to the tense contrast between the father Leon's difficulty staying steadily employed and Mah's "over-employment." The marriage of Leon and Mah mediates the changes in Chinatown immigrant community, gender, and work, as sweatshops first made use of Chinese male labor during the garment industry's growth from the 1920s though the 1940s and then turned increasingly to female labor after the 1946 modification of the Magnuson Act permitted Chinese wives and children to enter as non-quota immigrants and the Immigration Act of 1965 abolished Asian national origin quotas.[21] Finally, the family relations in *Bone* allegorize the conditions of immigrant life within the contradictions of the liberal nation-state as capitalism extends globally: the immigrant's lack of the civil rights promised to citizens of the nation permits the "private" space of the immigrant home to become a workplace that prioritizes the relations of production over Chinese family relations. In contradistinction to the traditional novel whose progressive narrative reconciliation of the individual to the social order symbolically figures the "private" domain as the resolution of struggles and conflicts in the nation, *Bone* "digresses" backward in time, narrating instead the erosion of the "private" sphere under the material pressures of racialized and gendered relations of production in a transnationally divided social space. From the breakdowns in communication between the parents to the various "flights" of the three daughters (emotional, mortal, and physical)—the novel allegorizes how the affective, cultural ties in the Leong family bear the weight of immigration laws, geographical segregation, and global flows of exchange.

   In associating a literary text like *Bone* with Mrs. Lee's testimony, I emphasize that a relation exists between these "literary" and "evidential" forms of narrative owing to their dialectical relationship to common historical and social processes. Both forms emerge in relation to a shift in the mode of production that expands by means of a deepened racialization, gendering, and fracturing of the labor force. Both elaborate the contradictions of this shift—in which the global "pulls" that bring immigrant women to work near the market's center also increases the regulation and segregation of those women by national laws and capital—but neither form seeks to "resolve" those contradictions in the development of a singular identity. Indeed, both Lee's testimony and Ng's novel suggest that the exploitation of immigrant seamstresses depends exactly upon the cultural, racial, and gendered qualities of the workforce, rather than on the reduction of their work as interchangeable "abstract labor" without characteristics; furthermore, as immigrant women, it is precisely those characteristics that are the material trace of their historical disenfranchisement from the political realm and that differentiate the seamstresses from the concept of the "abstract citizen." Therefore, in both immigrant narratives, opposition to garment industry exploitation is redressed neither through notions of the national citizen nor through strict identification with the proletarian class subject of traditional trade-unions. In other words, both Lee's testimony and Ng's novel refuse the separation of the economic, the political, and the cultural spheres dictated by the modern state, and neither narrative resolves in the formations of abstract subjects predicated on the modern separation of spheres. Rather, immigrant opposition articulates itself in forms and practices that integrate, yet move beyond, the political formations dictated by the modern institutions separating the political and economic spheres; the immigrant testimony and novel are cultural forms through which new political subjects and practices are narrated and through which new political actions are mediated. In their common interruption of the modern separation of spheres and the political formations dictated by that separation, these cultural forms produce conceptions of collectivity that do not depend upon privileging a singular subject as the representative of the group, conceptions of collectivity that do not prescribe a singular narrative of emancipation. Engagement with these cultural forms is not regulated by notions of identity or by modes of identification; a dialectic that presupposes differentiation and that crosses differences is always present as part of the process of engagement.

This dialectic of difference marks these texts as belonging to a new mode of cultural practice that corresponds to the new social formation of globalized capitalism. As I argued in Chapter 1, the contradictions of Asian American formation emerged in relation to the modern nation-state's attempt to resolve the contradictions between its economic and political imperatives through laws that excluded Asian immigrant laborers as "nonwhite aliens ineligible to citizenship" from the nineteenth to the mid-twentieth century. In that period, Asians entered along the economic axis, while the state simultaneously excluded Asians along racial and citizenship lines and thus distanced Asian Americans, even as citizens, from membership in the national culture. While official American cultural narratives aimed at reconciling the citizen to the modern nation-state, the material differentiation of Asian immigrants through racialization provided the conditions for Asian American cultural nationalism to emerge in the 1970s in contradiction to that official culture; Asian American cultural nationalism, as I discussed it in Chapters 2 and 3, is contestatory in the field of culture to the degree that culture operates in and for the modern state. Insofar as this notion of culture as an institution of the modern state remains in force, even today in its complex imbrication with "postmodern" global extensions and distortions, Asian American cultural nationalism as an oppositional mode continues to have significance in relation to both residual and recast modes of the "modern." For transnational capital is "parasitic" upon institutions and social relations of the modern nation-state, deploying its repressive and ideological apparatuses, manipulating the narratives of the liberal citizen-subject, as well as rearticulating modern forms of gender, temporality, and spatialization. This is nowhere clearer than in the contradiction within which global expansion precipitates the proliferation of anti-immigrant legislation, combining refortified policing of borders with ideological appeals to the racial basis of citizenship. Hence, Asian American cultural nationalism that emerged in opposition to racial exclusion continues to address these modern institutions within transnational capitalism. Yet at the same time, the current global restructuring— that moves well beyond the nation-state and entails the differentiation of labor forces internationally—constitutes a shift in the mode of production that now necessitates alternative forms of cultural practice that integrate yet move beyond those of cultural nationalism.

In the previous discussions, I have discussed such alternative forms of cultural practice, ranging from Christine Choy, Dai Sil Kim-Gibson, and Elaine Kim's video documentary of Korean immigrant women after the 1992 Los Angeles crisis, to Monique Truy-Dung Truong's Vietnamese American epistolary short fiction "Kelly," to Mrs. Fu Lee's testimony against the garment industry's abuse of Chinese immigrant women. Each engages with the dominant forces and formations that determine racialized immigrant women—in the city, the classroom, and the workplace—and simultaneously alter, shift, and mark possible resistances to those forces by representing not only cultural difference, but the convergence of differences, thereby producing new spaces and alternative formations. Culture in and for the modern state is not in itself "political," but the contradictions through which immigration brings national institutions into crisis produces immigrant cultures as oppositional and contestatory, and these contradictions critically politicized in cultural forms and practices can be utilized in the formation of alternative social practices.

These alternative forms of cultural practices are the *loci* of the culturally, racially, and gender specific qualities of the "class" formations of transnational capitalism. Since transnational capitalism does not work through the homogenization of the mode of production but operates through and because of the differentiations of culturally, racially, and gender specific forms and operations of work, its "class subjects" are not homogeneous. As corporations attempt to remain competitive in the global arena, the new patterns of flexible accumulation and mixed production that have emerged preserve and reproduce these specific differentiated forms of work. Immigration has intensified according to these new patterns of accumulation and production, and is now more than ever the site of the contradictions between the national state and the global economy. Just as these new patterns allow capital to exploit discrete sectors of the labor force in distinct ways and according to different means, the "class subject" of transnationalism cannot be politically and ideologically unified in any simple way but may be "unified" according to a process based on strategic alliances between different sectors, not on their abstract identity.[22] This shift in the mode of production must also shift our understanding of the terrain of politics itself: away from an exclusive focus on the abstract unified subject's relationship to the state or to capital, and toward those institutions, spaces, borders, and processes that are the interstitial sites of the social formation in which the national intersects with the international. The law, workplaces, schooling, community organizations, family, sexual life, churches, and popular culture are some of the sites which govern not only this intersection and the reproduction of racialized and gendered social relations along that intersection but which mediate the interruption and reorganization of those social relations, as well. These are the regulating sites through which "immigrants" are "naturalized" into "citizens" or through which "immigrants" are disciplined as "aliens" and "foreigners," but these are also the sites profoundly transformed by immigration and altered by the immigrant cultures and practices that emerge in contradiction to these regulating sites. In these sites, "immigrant acts" perform the dialectical unification across difference and critically generate the new subjects of cultural politics.

Epilogue

The tradition of the oppressed teaches us that the "state of emergency" in which we live is not the exception but the rule. We must attain to a conception of history that is in keeping with this insight. Then we shall clearly realize that it is our task to bring about a real state of emergency, and this will improve our position in the struggle against Fascism.
— Walter Benjamin, "Theses on the Philosophy of History"

. . . the state of emergency is also always a state of *emergence*.
— Homi Bhabha, *The Location of Culture*

In this book, I have wished to situate racialized immigrant formation within the context of national state institutions and the international forces of global economy as one site of a contemporary "state of emergency." As we have seen, immigration has been historically a *locus* of racialization and a primary site for the policing of political, cultural, and economic membership in the U.S. nation-state. Yet in our current moment, in the wake of California's Proposition 187, the proposed federal Personal Responsibility Act, and the federal immigration reforms that seek to restrict the rights and benefits of legal resident immigrants, we are witnessing a "re-racialization" of immigrants that constitutes "the immigrant" as the most highly targeted object of a U.S. nationalist agenda. The efforts to deny undocumented immigrants medical care and schooling and to prohibit legal immigrants from participating in state and federal programs are the newest forms of

174

surveillance and harassment for immigrant communities, particularly immigrant women, while these measures secure the conditions to ghettoize, marginalize, and extract low-wage labor from those same communities. In discussing Asian immigrant formation and Asian American culture, I have hoped to draw attention to how these conditions have dialectically produced the emergence of specific oppositional racial and cultural groupings and, perhaps more important, to how they give rise to the emergence of new subjects whose horizons of definition open up different possibilities for political practice and coalition. This is not to exceptionalize the racialization of Asians within the United States, it is rather to place the specific history of Asian American racialization in relation to other forms of racialization, those of African Americans, Chicanos/Latinos, Native Americans, and "white" Americans, in order to open possibilities of cross-race and cross-national projects.

In these discussions, I have treated a variety of literary and cultural productions as crucial media for alternative cultures and subjects and have tried to make connections between these alternatives and practical activist struggles for social change. This has required an investigation of the ways in which the history of immigrant racialization has produced cultural difference and material heterogeneity, which are rearticulated as interventions into dominant forms, whether those forms are the institution of citizenship, the traditional novel, the national historical narrative, or the transnational assembly line. The history of Chinese immigrant laborers who labored in mining and railroad construction yet were barred from citizenship is incommensurate with the narrative that reconciles the citizen to the nation. The lives of Japanese Americans, nominally recognized as citizens yet dispossessed of freedoms and properties explicitly granted citizens, cannot be narrated by the novel of formation that reconciles the individual to the social order. The U.S. colonization of the Philippines disrupts the national historical narrative, and the immigration of Filipinos to the United States after colonization contradicts the liberal narrative of political emancipation and citizenship. The interstitial situation of Asian immigrant women workers from South Korea, South Vietnam, Thailand, and Cambodia is the current instance of immigrant incommensurability with dominant forms of national citizenship, not only requiring different narratives of subject, community, and nation but generating a different political formation as well. This new political formation necessitates new modes of organizing and struggling and, in so doing, extends our understanding of the terrain of the "political."

I have argued that since the mid–nineteenth century, Asians have been admitted into the U.S. nation in terms of national economic imperatives, while the state has estranged Asian immigrants through racialization and bars to citizenship, thus distancing Asian Americans, even as citizens, from the terrain of national culture. Because it is the purpose of American national culture to form subjects as citizens, this distance has created the conditions for the emergence of Asian American culture as an alternative cultural site, a site of cultural forms that propose, enact, and embody subjects and practices not contained by the narrative of American citizenship. While I have suggested that an "aesthetic" characterizes the works of racialized oppositional cultures such as Asian American culture—one that is different from American modernist and postmodernist aesthetics—I have insisted on *de-aestheticizing* dominant understandings of Asian Americans in order to present a model for interpreting literature and culture as social forces, as nodes in a network of other social practices and social relations. We have considered here the social spaces of the university, the community, and the workplace, as well as literary, artistic, and cultural representations as crucial sites for studying the shaping, contesting, and transformation of race, gender, and identity.

Historically, the U.S. state has constructed different national "emergencies" around "the immigrant," which have, over time, generated emergent political formations. Our critical task now is to make the present *emergency* an active state of *emergence* in ways that respond to the contemporary conditions of global restructuring—conditions that exploit Asian workers both in Asia *and* in the deindustrialized United States, that bring new waves of immigrants from Asia and Latin America where precisely the United States has been a colonial or neocolonial power, and that intensify exploitation and worklessness in the United States in ways that exacerbate interracial urban conflicts. Our work begins with an engagement with the past, out of which we imagine, create, and dare to secure a future.

Notes

1 Immigration, Citizenship, Racialization: Asian American Critique

1 On the significance of the Vietnam War in the collective American imagina-
tion, see Susan Jeffords, *The Remasculinization of America: Gender and the Viet-
nam War* (Bloomington: Indiana University Press, 1989); Peter Ehrenhaus and
Richard Morris, eds., *Cultural Legacies of Vietnam: Uses of the Past in the Present*
(Norwood, N.J.: Ablex, 1990); Rick Berg and John Carlos Rowe, *The Vietnam
War and American Culture* (New York: Columbia University Press, 1991); and
Marita Sturken, *Tangled Memories: The Vietnam War, the AIDS Epidemic, and
the Politics of Remembering* (Berkeley: University of California Press, 1997).

2 Jeannie Barroga, "Walls," in *Unbroken Thread: An Anthology of Plays by Asian
American Women*, ed. Roberta Uno (Amherst: University of Massachusetts
Press, 1993). Barroga's play premiered at the Asian American Theatre Com-
pany, San Francisco, April–June 1989.

3 In her study of the Vietnam War Memorial and the collective processes of
memory, Marita Sturken discusses the critics' commentary characterizing the
monument's design as a "black gash of shame and sorrow" that symbolized
the open, castrated wound of this country's venture into an unsuccessful war,
a war that "emasculated" the United States in its ability to engage in foreign
conflicts. See Sturken, *Tangled Memories*.

4 In triangulating the affinities and differences between these different locations, the play frames an "Asian American panethnic" location. On the history
of the group formation "Asian American," see Yen Le Espiritu, *Asian American
Panethnicity: Bridging Identities and Institutions* (Philadelphia: Temple University Press, 1992).

5 The source of the second epigraph is Walter Benjamin, "Theses on the Philosophy of History," in *Illuminations*, ed. Hannah Arendt, trans. Harry Zohn
(New York: Schocken, 1969), 254.

6 The concept of the "immigrant" in American sociology and public policy has
historically signified "European immigrants," seeking to universalize the temporality of assimilation attributed to Irish Americans and Italian Americans to
the ethnic minority groups from the "third world." See Robert Blauner, "Colonized and Immigrant Minorities," in *Racial Oppression in America* (New York:
Harper, 1972). This use erases the heterogeneities and hierarchies within the

"immigrant" category and obscures the processes of racialization that the immigration process instantiates. In reappropriating the category from that history of meaning, I hope to rearticulate "immigration" as a historically specific process in which economic, gendering, and racializing forces converge.

Though my discussion focuses specifically on Asian Americans, the topos of immigration is crucial for Chicano and Latino formation as well. See, for example, Carl Gutierrez-Jones, *Rethinking the Borderlands: Between Chicano Culture and Legal Discourse* (Berkeley: University of California Press, 1995); and David G. Gutiérrez, *Walls and Mirrors: Mexican Americans, Mexican Immigrants, and the Politics of Ethnicity* (Berkeley: University of California Press, 1995).

7   U.S. orientalism of the twentieth century—the institutional, scholarly, and ideological representations of "Asia" and of "Asians in the United States"— may be rhetorically continuous but is materially discontinuous with an earlier European orientalism, which relied on representations of non-Western otherness as barbaric and incomprehensible, as well as with narrative teleologies of universal development. On European orientalism, see Lisa Lowe, *Critical Terrains: French and British Orientalisms* (Ithaca: Cornell University Press, 1991). U.S. orientalism makes use of some of the representational and narrative regimes of an earlier orientalism that mediated European colonialism, but it has been transformed by a quite different state apparatus and a different global and national context of material conditions, purposes, and possibilities.

Several fine works have elaborated the representations of the "yellow peril" in film, theater, and television. See Gina Marchetti, *Romance and the "Yellow Peril": Race, Sex, and Discursive Strategies in Hollywood Fiction* (Berkeley: University of California Press, 1993); James Moy, *Marginal Sights: Staging the Chinese in America* (Iowa City: University of Iowa Press, 1993); and Darrell Y. Hamamoto, *Monitored Peril: Asian Americans and the Politics of TV Representation* (Minneapolis: University of Minnesota Press, 1994).

8   David Palumbo-Liu examines the scientific racial discourse about Asians in the 1920s and the 1930s that constructed Asians as efficient workers. Some of this research was presented in the paper "Wetbacks and Re-essentialized Confucians" (Annual Meeting of the Association for Asian American Studies, Oakland, Calif., June 1995), and forms part of his work in progress, "Narrating Asian America: Cultural Politics and Subjectivities." Gary Okihiro's work on the Asian body also excavates extremely important material on nineteenth- and early-twentieth-century racial and biological discourses about Asians; see

Okihiro, "Reading Asian Bodies, Reading Anxieties" (paper presented at the Department of Ethnic Studies, University of California, San Diego, November 1995).

9   See Fred W. Riggs, *Pressures on Congress: A Study of the Repeal of Chinese Exclusion* (New York: Columbia University Press, King's Crown Press, 1950); Shirley Hune, "Politics of Chinese Exclusion: Legislative-Executive Conflict, 1876–1882," *Amerasia Journal* 9, no. 1 (1982): 5–27. Anti-Japanese exclusionist V. S. McClatchy declared: "Of all the races ineligible to citizenship, the Japanese are the least assimilable and the most dangerous to this country. . . . With great pride of race, they have no idea of assimilating in the sense of amalgamation. They do not come to this country with any desire or intent to lose their racial or national identity. . . . They never cease to be Japanese." Quoted in Ronald Takaki, *Strangers from a Different Shore* (New York: William Morrow, 1989), 209.

10   See British historian Charles H. Pearson, *National Life and Character: A Forecast* (New York: Macmillan, 1893), in which he warned of the impending peril of peoples of color in the tropics, led by Asians, and their invasion of the European temperate zone; and American Brook Adams, *The Law of Civilization and Decay: An Essay on History* (New York: Macmillan, 1898). See also Gary Y. Okihiro, *Margins and Mainstreams: Asian in American History and Culture* (Seattle: University of Washington, 1994).

Asians have been alternately subject to two processes of racist/nationalist constructions, what Etienne Balibar distinguishes as "internal racism" that figures racialized groups within a nation-state and "external racism" that is concerned with the construction of groups outside of the nation-state. See Balibar and Immanual Wallerstein, *Race, Nation, Class: Ambiguous Identities* (London: Verso, 1991). Takashi Fujitani has argued, in a similar vein, that the construction of Japanese Americans as a "model minority" is commensurate with the postwar modernization discourse about Japan as the "model" of capitalist development in Asia. See Fujitani, "Nisei Soldiers as Citizens: Japanese Americans in U.S. National, Military, and Racial Discourses," paper presented at "The Politics of Remembering the Asia/Pacific War," University of Hawaii at Manoa, Honolulu, Hawaii, September 1995.

11   In light of the ideological construction of the military subject, the situation of U.S. soldiers of color recruited for the wars in Asia is a complicated and powerful site in which the contradictions between U.S. nationalism and racial formation emerge. Ramón Saldívar writes, for example, of the Chicano sol-

dier in the Korean War in Rolando Hinojosa's *The Korean Songs;* see Saldívar, *Chicano Narrative: The Dialectics of Difference* (Madison: University of Wisconsin Press, 1990). George Mariscal is collecting essays on Chicano veterans of the Vietnam War that address the contradictions of race, class, and nationalism. Different contradictions arose for Asian Americans who served in the U.S. military. The Japanese American soldiers in World War II are discussed in Masayo Duus, *Unlikely Liberators: The Men of the 100th and 442nd* (Honolulu: University of Hawaii Press, 1987) and Tamotsu Shibutani, *The Derelicts of Company K* (Berkeley: University of California Press, 1978). K. Scott Wong's book-in-progress *"Americans First": Chinese Americans and the Second World War* considers the impact of the war on Chinese American veterans.

12 Vicente L. Rafael's discussion of the "immigrant imaginary" is suggestive in this regard. Rafael, "Cultures of Area Studies in the United States" (paper presented at the "Internationalizing Cultural Studies" conference, University of Hawaii at Manoa, 1994). An earlier version of this paper was published in *Social Text* 41 (Winter 1994): 91–111.

13 See King-kok Cheung's important study *Articulate Silences: Hisaye Yamamoto, Maxine Hong Kingston, Joy Kogawa* (Ithaca: Cornell University Press, 1993).

14 Attempts to exclude Asians began in 1855 in California, when the state legislature levied a capitation tax of fifty dollars on "the immigration to this state of persons who cannot become citizens thereof." An act in 1858 explicitly named "persons of Chinese or Mongolian races." In 1862, another act taxed Chinese to "protect free white labor against competition with Chinese coolie labor." Two acts passed in 1870 were directed against the importation of "Mongolian, Chinese, and Japanese females for criminal or demoralizing purposes" and of "coolie slavery." None of these laws had legal impact, as all were declared unconstitutional when tested in the higher courts. See Sucheng Chan, *Asian Americans: An Interpretive History* (Boston: Twayne, 1991), 54.

In 1882, 1884, 1886, and 1888, Congress passed Chinese exclusion acts, suspending immigration of Chinese laborers and barring reentry of all Chinese laborers who departed and did not return before the passage of the act. See Charles Gordon, "The Racial Barrier to American Citizenship," *University of Pennsylvania Law Review* 93 (1944–45): 237–58; and Milton Konvitz, *The Alien and the Asiatic in American Law* (Ithaca: Cornell University Press, 1946).

Exclusion efforts were then directed at Indians and Japanese. A geographical criterion was used to exclude Asian Indians, because their racial or ethnic status was unclear; the 1917 immigration act denied entry to people from a "barred zone" that included South Asia through Southeast Asia and islands in the Indian and Pacific Oceans, but excluded American possessions of the Philippines and Guam. The Immigration Act of 1924 barred entry of "aliens ineligible to citizenship"; because Japanese and other Asians were barred by the 1790 naturalization law stipulating that "whites only" could be naturalized as citizens, the 1924 act totally excluded them from immigration. See Gary R. Hess, "The 'Hindu' in America: Immigration and Naturalization Policies and India, 1917–1946," *Pacific Historical Review* 38 (1969): 59–79, reprinted in *Asian Indians, Filipinos, Other Asian Communities, and the Law*, ed. Charles McClain (New York: Garland, 1994); and Earl H. Pritchard, "The Japanese Exclusion Bill of 1924," *Research Studies of the State College of Washington* 2 (1930): 65–77, reprinted in *Japanese Immigrants and American Law*, ed. Charles McClain (New York: Garland, 1994).

The government did not have to exclude Koreans officially, because emigration from Korea had already been curbed by the Japanese colonial administration. Owing to U.S. colonization of the Philippines, Filipinos were "wards" of the United States and were called "nationals"; they were neither aliens nor citizens, and to exclude them required a change in their status. The Tydings-McDuffie Act of 1934 cut Filipino immigration to a quota of fifty persons per year, and all Filipinos in the United States were reclassified as "aliens." See Lee Houchins and Chang-su Houchins, "The Korean Experience in America, 1903–24," *Pacific Historical Review* 43 (1974): 548–75; and H. Brett Melendy, "Filipinos in the United States," *Pacific Historical Review* 43 (1974): 99–117, reprinted in McClain, *Asian Indians, Filipinos, Other Asian Communities, and the Law*. The U.S. exclusion of Filipino immigration was continually connected with the issue of Philippine independence from U.S. colonization; see Bruno Lasker, *Filipino Immigration* (Chicago: University of Chicago Press, 1931).

15 Neil Gotanda has discussed the legal history of the period from 1943 to 1950, during which Chinese exclusion was repealed and Chinese were granted citizenship and naturalization; see Gotanda, "Towards Repeal of Asian Exclusion: The Magnuson Act of 1943, the Act of July 2, 1946, the Presidential Proclamation of July 4, 1946, the Act of August 9, 1949, and the Act of August 1, 1950," in *Asian Americans in Congress: A Documentary History*, ed. Hyung Chan Kim (Westport, Conn.: Greenwood, 1995).

16 The 1965 immigration act removed "national origins" as the basis of American immigration legislation and was framed as an amendment to the 1952 McCarran-Walter Act. The 1965 act abolished "national origin" quotas and

specified seven preferences for Eastern Hemisphere quota immigrants: (1) un-married adult sons and daughters of citizens; (2) spouses and unmarried sons and daughters of permanent residents; (3) professionals, scientists, and artists of "exceptional ability"; (4) married adult sons and daughters of U.S. citizens; (5) siblings of adult citizens; (6) workers, skilled and unskilled, in occupations for which labor was in short supply in the United States; and (7) refugees from Communist-dominated countries or those uprooted by natural catastrophe. See Bill Ong Hing, *Making and Remaking Asian America through Immigration Policy, 1850–1990* (Stanford: Stanford University Press, 1993), appendix B. Since 1965, two million Asian quota immigrants, two million nonquota immigrants, and one million refugees outside the seventh preference have arrived. The subsequent 1975 Indochina Migration and Refugee Assistance Act, the 1980 Refugee Act, and the 1987 Amerasian Homecoming Act have facilitated Vietnamese, Cambodian, Lao, and Thai immigration and resettlement. See Chan, *Asian Americans,* 146–47.

17 Gary Y. Okihiro, *Margins and Mainstreams: Asians in American History and Culture* (Seattle: University of Washington Press, 1994). Okihiro argues that in the struggles for inclusion and equality, Asian Americans have helped preserve and advance the ideals of democracy and have thereby made the United States a freer place for not only Asian Americans but others as well.

18 On the conflicts and contradictions of contemporary immigration policies, see Wayne Cornelius, Philip Martin, and James Hollifield, eds., *Controlling Immigration: A Global Perspective* (Stanford: Stanford University Press, 1994). On the history of U.S. immigration law, see Kitty Calavita, *U.S. Immigration Law and the Control of Labor, 1820–1924* (London: Harcourt Brace Jovanovich, 1984). The legal dimensions of Asian immigration to the United States are discussed in Hing, *Making and Remaking Asian America.* The political economy of Asian immigration is discussed in Lucie Cheng and Edna Bonacich, eds., *Labor Immigration under Capitalism: Asian Workers in the United States before World War II* (Berkeley: University of California Press, 1984).
    On the history of contractual and consensual citizenship in the United States and its roots in English notions of natural and perpetual allegiance, see James Kettner, *The Development of the Concept of American Citizenship, 1608–1870* (Chapel Hill: University of North Carolina Press, 1978). On equal citizenship under the Constitution, see Kenneth Karst, *Belonging to America: Equal Citizenship and the Constitution* (New Haven: Yale University Press, 1989).

19 In taking up the concept of *contradiction,* I mean to adopt the Marxist concept

that describes the dialectic within which domination creates its own dynamic negation. For Marx, capitalism generates its own contradictions, the primary one being between capital and labor that precipitates proletarian consciousness and the overthrow of the capitalist system.

It will be evident in these chapters, however, that I depart from the singular, deterministic teleology associated with the more orthodox use of contradiction, for it proves inadequate for understanding the many sites of contradiction within historically situated social formations. While Marx proposes that the classical contradiction exists between capital and labor—a contradiction that permits the accumulation of surplus value through the exploitation of labor while it also produces class struggles—both the early conditions of Asian immigration within the still developing U.S. economy and the contemporary circumstances of Asian Americans within "postmodern" capitalist global economy make apparent that we must always speak of more than one contradiction that works in and through its articulation with other contradictions. In this chapter, for example, I elaborate the ways in which what might be theorized as economic contradiction is within the specificity of U.S. history also always a racial and gendered contradiction: the state claims to be a democratic body in which all subjects are granted membership, while the racialized immigrant workers from whom capital profits are historically excluded from political participation in the state. At the same time, the genealogy of exclusions and enfranchisements "genders" immigrant subjects in relation to the types of labor needed by capital; in the contemporary California economy, the anti-immigrant Proposition 187 makes clear that "legal" immigrant labor is constructed as "male," whereas "illegal" immigrant labor is constructed as "female" (see note 54 below, this chapter). Contradictions may be "antagonistic" or "nonantagonistic" according to their state of "overdetermination" or the ways in which contradictions converge. Louis Althusser has argued that in periods of "stability" the contradictions of the social formation are neutralized by displacement, whereas in a revolutionary situation (such as the 1917 Bolshevik movement in Russia), these contradictions may fuse or condense into a "rupture." Stuart Hall proposes that the material conditions of a given historical moment will bring one contradiction to the surface out of the convergence of contradictions. See Althusser, "Contradiction and Overdetermination," in *For Marx*, trans. Ben Brewster (London: Verso, 1969); and Hall, "Signification, Representation, Ideology: Althusser and the Post-Structuralist Debates," *Critical Studies in Mass Communication* 2, no. 2 (June 1985): 91–114.

20   On nineteenth-century Chinese immigrant labor, see Sucheng Chan, *This Bittersweet Soil: The Chinese in California Agriculture, 1860–1910* (Berkeley: University of California Press, 1986). See also Sucheng Chan, ed., *Entry Denied: Exclusion and the Chinese Community in America, 1882–1943* (Philadelphia: Temple University Press, 1991); Tomás Almaguer, *Racial Faultlines: The Historical Origins of White Supremacy in California* (Berkeley: University of California Press, 1994).

21   General John DeWitt stated that the Japanese were "an enemy race" whose "racial affinities were not severed by migration" and whose "racial strains" remained "undiluted" among second and third generations; cited in Chan, *Asian Americans,* 125. On the history of the internment of 110,000 Japanese immigrants and Japanese Americans during World War II, see Roger Daniels, Sandra C. Taylor, and Harry H. L. Kitano, eds., *Japanese Americans: From Relocation to Redress* (Seattle: University of Washington, 1986); Roger Daniels, *Concentration Camps, U.S.A.: Japanese Americans and World War II* (New York: Holt, Rinehart, and Winston, 1972); and Peter Irons, *Justice Delayed: The Record of the Japanese American Internment Cases* (Middletown: Wesleyan University Press, 1989).

22   In the first section of his 1946 novel *America Is in the Heart,* Carlos Bulosan describes the poverty and limited opportunity of the rural Philippines colonized by the United States, effectively demonstrating the power of the myths of American education, individualism, and developmentalism in the figures of Abraham Lincoln, Richard Wright, and the librarian—even before the narrator immigrates to America. Bulosan, *America Is in the Heart* (Seattle: University of Washington Press, 1973).

23   This is borne out in the historical separation of Filipino American political formation from "Asian American" movements in the 1960s. See Espiritu, *Asian American Panethnicity,* 103–9. For a coherent distinguishing of Filipino Americans, or "U.S. Filipinos," owing to the history of colonization and immigration, see Oscar V. Campomanes, ed., "The New Empire's Forgetful and Forgotten Citizens: Unrepresentability and Unassimilability in Filipino-American Postcolonialities," *Critical Mass* 47, no. 3 (September 1995): 145–200; and Theo Gonzalves, "'We Hold a Neatly Folded Hope': Filipino Veterans of World War II on Citizenship and Political Obligation," *Amerasia Journal* 21:3 (Winter 1995/1996): 155–174.

24   Theodor W. Adorno, *Negative Dialectics* (New York: Continuum, 1973), writes: "Aware that the conceptual totality is mere appearance, I have no way but to

break immanently, in its own measure, through the appearance of total identity. Since that totality is structured to accord with logic, however, whose core
is the principle of the excluded middle, whatever will not fit this principle,
whatever differs in quality, comes to be designated as a contradiction. Contradiction is nonidentity under the aspect of identity; the dialectical primary
of the principle of contradiction makes the thought of unity the measure of
heterogeneity. As the heterogeneous collides with its limit it exceeds itself.
Dialectics is the consistent sense of nonidentity. It does not begin by taking a
standpoint" (5).

25   Adorno writes: "A true preponderance of the particular would not be attain-
able except by changing the universal. Installing it as purely and simply extant
is a complementary ideology. It hides how much of the particular has come
to be a function of the universal—something which in its logical form it has
always been." Adorno, "Dynamics of Universal and Particular," in ibid., 313–14.
David Palumbo-Liu has an excellent discussion of the problem of the universal and the particular in relation to Asian American culture in "Universalisms
and Minority Culture," differences, 7, no. 1 (1995): 188–208. See also: Naoki
Sakai, "Modernity and Its Critique: The Problem of Universalism and Particularism," South Atlantic Quarterly 87: 475–504.

26   See William Preston Jr., Aliens and Dissenters: Federal Suppression of Radicals
(Urbana: University of Illinois Press, 1963).

27   See note 16 above on the seven preferences of the 1965 act. Eithne Luibheid has argued that while the 1965 act may have "opened" the United States
to new immigrants, it also produced differentiated categories of "the immigrant" for surveillance and regulation; Luibheid, "The 1965 Immigration and
Nationality Act: An 'End' to Exclusion?" positions (forthcoming). Leti Volpp
has observed that "the notion of citizenship is being used to assert a particular privilege that more recently was asserted through whiteness"; see Volpp,
"Immigration, Gender, and Violence: The Rest against the West" (paper presented at the annual meeting of the Association for Asian American Studies,
Oakland, Calif., June 1995).

28   Michel Foucault analyzed the discursive production and management of objects of knowledge through texts, social practices, laws, and institutions and
was concerned with the productive function of discursive exclusions and inclusions; paradoxically, for Foucault, both prohibitive policing and individual
"freedoms" granted by the liberal state institutions are forms through which
subjects and communities are regulated. See Foucault, Discipline and Punish,

trans. Alan Sheridan (New York: Vintage, 1979). In the context of U.S. immigration law, we can consider both the disenfranchisement of Asians as aliens
and the enfranchisement of Asians as citizens as forms of surveillance and
regulation.

29 I use the term "genealogy" in reference to Foucault's work. To revise the historiographical tendency to project progressions and totalities, Foucault elaborates the concept of genealogy as a series of moments or conjunctions wherein
it may be possible to analyze the coherence, logic, and specific types of relations within each moment or shift, neither imposing necessary causalities,
homogeneities, or analogies nor assuming that the same form of historicity
operates on all spheres of human society. Such series may overlap and intersect. He writes of a "new history" that "speaks of series, divisions, limits,
differences of level, shifts, chronological specificities, particular forms of re-
handling, and possible types of relation. This is not because it is trying to
obtain a plurality of histories juxtaposed and independent of one another: that
of the economy beside that of institutions, and beside these two those of science, religion, or literature. . . . The problem that now presents itself . . . is
to determine what form of relation may be legitimately described between
these different series: what vertical system they are capable of forming: what
interplay of correlation and dominance exists between them; what may be the
effect of shifts, different temporalities, and various rehandlings; in what distinct totalities certain elements may figure simultaneously; in short, not only
what series, but also what 'series of series'—or, in other words, what 'tables'
it is possible to draw up." Foucault, *The Archaeology of Knowledge*, trans. A. M.
Sheridan Smith (New York: Harper, 1972), 10. See also Foucault, "Nietzsche,
Genealogy, History," in *Language, Counter-Memory, Practice*, Donald Bouchard,
ed. (Ithaca: Cornell University Press, 1977).

In a separate essay on "governmentality," Foucault outlines a particular
"series"—namely, "government, population, political economy"—to advance
the thesis that since the eighteenth century, through government and its apparatuses, disciplinary societies in the West have replaced the former societies
ruled by sovereigns. Government—and the "political space" within techniques
of government—emerges as the disciplinary mode designed to manage population and to administer property. "This state of government which bears
essentially on population and both refers itself to and makes use of the in-
strumentation of economic *savoir* could be seen as corresponding to a type of
society controlled by apparatuses of security." Because governmentality as a

mode of social discipline cannot be fundamentally altered by contestations on the political terrain of government, our struggles must take the form of practices that demand the transformation of the "political" and the governmentality it upholds. Foucault, "Governmentality" (1978), in *The Foucault Effect: Studies in Governmentality*, ed. Graham Burchell, Colin Gordon, and Peter Miller (Chicago: University of Chicago Press, 1991).

30   My argument is indebted to the theory of racial formation and the racial state elaborated by Michael Omi and Howard Winant, *Racial Formation in the United States: From the 1960s to the 1990s* (New York: Routledge, 1994).

31   See David Roediger on the social construction of whiteness as masculinity, the historical relationship between "whiteness" and working-class formation, and between "whiteness" and "white ethnic" groups. Roediger, *The Wages of Whiteness: Race and the Making of the American Working Class* (London: Verso, 1991). Roediger identifies the historical links between masculinity, citizenship, and whiteness. See also: Michael Rogin, "Blackface, White Noise: The Jewish Jazz Singer Finds His Voice," *Critical Inquiry* 18 (Spring 1992): 417–453.

32   Chandra Talpade Mohanty's discussion of the interrelation of patriarchy with the racialized capitalist state argues that the definition of citizenship is always a gendered and racial formation. See Mohanty, "Cartographies of Struggle," in *Third World Women and the Politics of Feminism*, ed. Chandra Talpade Mohanty, Ann Russo, and Lourdes Torres (Bloomington: Indiana University Press, 1991). Zillah Eisenstein, *The Color of Gender: Reimaging Democracy* (Berkeley: University of California Press, 1994), also discusses the distinct and yet intertwined processes of "racialized patriarchy" and capitalism. See also: Eileen Boris, "The Racialized Gendered State: Constructions of Citizenship in the United States," *Social Politics* (Summer 1995): 160–180.

33   Chan, *Asian Americans*, 105–7; Hing, *Making*, 21–26. Throughout the nineteenth century, the number of Chinese women in the United States did not exceed five thousand, or 7 percent of the total Chinese population; the very small number of Chinese women who had immigrated before these bans were doubly bound by patriarchal controls inside Chinatowns and anti-Chinese racism outside. See Judy Yung, *Unbound Feet: A Social History of Chinese Women in San Francisco* (Berkeley: University of California Press, 1995); Gary Y. Okihiro, *Margins and Mainstreams*, Chapter 3.

The 1922 Cable Act demonstrates that the designation of U.S.-born female citizens was also a racialized designation, for while the Cable Act contained provisions for U.S.-born women of European or African descent to reclaim their citizenship in the event of divorce from a noncitizen spouse, or after the death of a noncitizen spouse, there were no such provisions for U.S.-born Asian immigrant women. See Virginia Sapiro, "Women, Citizenship, Nationality," *Politics and Society* 13 (1984): 1–26; Chan, *Asian Americans*, 106; Yung, *Unbound*, 168.

34   Karl Marx, *Capital: A Critique of Political Economy*, vol. 1 (New York: International Publishers, 1967), 768–69.

35   See, for example, Richard White, *It's Your Misfortune and None of My Own* (Tulsa: University of Oklahoma Press, 1991). White observes that the rural Chinese who achieved financial success did so as merchants, large tenant farmers, and labor contractors; their successes depended on their ability to command large numbers of Chinese workers at low wages (284). White writes, "In time, manufacturers themselves turned against the Chinese as Chinese merchants attempted to open factories in competition with white-owned factories" (341).

Daniel Rosenberg, "The IWW and Organization of Asian Workers in Early Twentieth Century America," *Labor History* 36, no. 1 (Winter 1995): 77–87, locates the source of anti-Japanese hostility in American middle-class fears of future competition with immigrant businessmen. Rosenberg argues, however, that against such hostility, the "IWW (Industrial Workers of the World) consistently worked for cooperation of Asian and non-Asian workers and that Asian Americans supported multiracial unionism. Such was the case in California's fruit and vegetable industries, from which arose the anarchist-led Fresno Labor League in 1908, with ties to the IWW, which had four thousand Japanese grape pickers in its initial membership" (78).

36   Marx writes that "abstract labour" is "absolutely indifferent to its particular specificity." Capital, according to Marx, can recognize the specificity of work tasks but not the particularities of laborers. Karl Marx, "Chapter on Capital," in *Grundrisse*, trans. Martin Nicolaus (New York: Penguin, 1973), 296–97. In a sense, contrary to the classical Marxist understanding that capital seeks "abstract labor," the use of Chinese immigrant labor demonstrates that even in the nineteenth century, U.S. capital profited precisely from the "flexible" racializing of Asian labor. Marx's elaboration of the "abstract citizen" in relation to the political state in "On the Jewish Question" is discussed later in this chapter.

37   For white workers, the surplus of Chinese labor lowered their wages and led to overproduction and unemployment that was expressed in general strikes in 1869, 1877, and 1886 and the organization of radical workers' groups. The crisis of overproduction and class conflict is discussed by Thomas J. McCor-

mick, *The China Market: America's Quest for Informal Empire, 1893–1901* (Chicago: Quadrangle, 1967); and William Appleman Williams, *The Contours of American History* (Chicago: Quadrangle, 1966). On anti-Chinese sentiment among white workers, see Alexander Saxton, *The Indispensable Enemy: Labor and the Anti-Chinese Movement in California* (Berkeley: University of California Press, 1971); and David Roediger, *Towards the Abolition of Whiteness* (London: Verso, 1994). For an important discussion of nineteenth-century white elite pro-Chinese positions and the construction of the white working class as "racist," see Grace Kyungwon Hong, "The Not-Working Class and Chinese Immigrant Labor: Discursive and Specular Projects of Containment in Bret Harte's *Overland Monthly* and Arnold Geuthe's Photographs," unpublished manuscript, San Diego, California, 1995.

38   On the Alien Land Laws, see Konvitz, *Alien and the Asiatic in American Law*, 157–70; Chan, *Asian Americans*, 95–96; Hing, *Making*, 212; and Charles McClain, ed., *Japanese Immigrants and the American Law: The Alien Land Laws and Other Issues* (New York: Garland, 1994).

39   Excellent documentation of these Chinese challenges is collected in Charles McClain, *In Search of Equality: The Chinese Struggle against Discrimination in Nineteenth-Century America* (Berkeley: University of California Press, 1994).

40   On the interconnections of race, class, and gender in relation to Asian Americans, see Yen Le Espiritu, *Asian American Women and Men: Labor, Laws, and Love* (Thousand Oaks, Calif.: Sage Publications, 1996).

41   Masao Miyoshi examines this contradiction in "A Borderless World? From Colonialism to Transnationalism and the Decline of the Nation-State," *Critical Inquiry* 19 (Summer 1993): 726–51. See also Robert B. Reich, *The Work of Nations: Preparing Ourselves for Twenty-First-Century Capitalism* (New York: Knopf, 1991).

42   On Asian immigrant communities to the United States following 1965, see Paul Ong, Edna Bonacich, and Lucie Cheng, eds., *The New Asian Immigration in Los Angeles and Global Restructuring* (Philadelphia: Temple University Press, 1994). These essays examine the ways that the global restructuring of capitalism has affected post-1965 Asian immigrant communities, pinpointing the contradictions of capitalist restructuring that produces a heterogeneous Asian immigrant population made up of both low-wage, service-sector and manufacturing laborers and what they call "middle-class professionals." I would want to modify this analysis of the class bifurcation of post-1965 Asian immigration through reference to the concept of the "white-collar proletariat," which de-

scribes U.S. capital's demotion and manipulation of skilled labor in the period of transition from entrepreneurial to corporate capitalism after the 1960s. See Samuel Bowles and Herbert Gintis, *Schooling in Capitalist America* (New York: Harper, 1976). Because trained Asian immigrants, in particular, are subject to this demotion and manipulation, the "white-collar proletarianization" of Asian-educated immigrant engineers or nurses needs to be distinguished from situations of U.S.-educated, white middle-class "professionals." Richard Appelbaum recalls Marx's distinction between "constant capital" (investment in machinery and equipment) and "variable capital" (the costs of living labor) in order to point to current transnational capitalist strategies for maximizing profits through exploitative "flexible" reorganization and management of skilled and semi-skilled labor. Variable capital is a crucial concept for understanding the use of lower-cost Asian immigrant professionals as one form of capital investment for the maximizing of surplus value. See Appelbaum, "Multiculturalism and Flexibility: Some New Directions in Global Capitalism," *Mapping Multiculturalism*, Avery Gordon and Christopher Newfield, eds. (Minneapolis: University of Minnesota Press, 1996).

Yet two additional political dimensions of the post-1965 immigrant group deserve mention. First, nations sending immigrants to the United States may often send off skilled, potentially disaffected workers as a safety valve in times of economic austerity, for it results in remittances for the "home" country, one of the key elements in the balance of payments for countries like the Philippines. Second, the U.S. government and business community has formal and informal relationships with the newly industrializing countries (NICs) in Asia; in return for low-wage industrialization and sources of investment, the immigration of Asian elites from those countries may be encouraged and protected. For instance, the U.S. government has protected members of the Korean CIA who have immigrated in order to monitor the politics of Korean American community; see Elaine H. Kim and Eui-Young Yu, *East to America: Korean American Life Stories* (New York: New Press, 1996); Nancy Abelmann and John Lie, *Blue Dreams: Korean Americans and the Los Angeles Riot* (Cambridge: Harvard University Press, 1995). Immigrants with ties to the Taiwanese government have also had active involvements with the repression of dissident activity in Chinatowns in the United States; see L. Ling-chi Wang's analysis, "The Structure of Dual Domination: Toward a Paradigm for the Study of the Chinese Diaspora in the United States," in *Amerasia Journal* 21, nos. 1 and 2 (1995): 149–69. In this regard, we must view the post-1965 immigrant popular as complex in both its political and economic profile.

43   See Aihwa Ong, "The Gender and Labor Politics of Postmodernity," *Annual Review of Anthropology 1991.* 20:279–309; Swasti Mitter, *Common Fate, Common Bond: Women in the Global Economy* (London: Pluto, 1986); and Maria Mies, *Patriarchy and Accumulation on a World Scale: Women in the International Division of Labor* (London: Zed, 1986). Ong and Mitter point out that the important features of the current global restructuring are "mixed production" and "flexible accumulation" that allow transnational corporations to fragment and separate the operations of production: labor-intensive parts of production can be sent to Asia and Latin America, where there is an abundance of low-wage, "docile" labor; if more profitable, the same fragmentation allows manufacturers to shift work to small subcontractors at the center of the market in the "first world," for smaller units can avoid problems with organized union labor and employment regulations. Mies argues that through these strategies, capital rearticulates patriarchal gender ideologies that relegate women to reproduction and domestic labor, leading to what she calls the "housewifization" of work.

44   Louis Althusser elaborates "overdetermination" as the convergence of different, nonequivalent contradictions that constitute a social formation or a "structure in dominance." The overdetermination of a contradiction is its relationship to its conditions of existence (i.e., the other contradictions) within the complex whole. The accumulation and exacerbation of all the historical contradictions produces a "weak link" that marks the vulnerability of the system; Althusser refers to the "'tangle' of Russia's internal and external contradictions" that precipitated the Bolshevik movement as a historical example of the accumulation and exacerbation of the historical contradictions of residual forms of medieval feudal exploitation in the countryside, large-scale capitalist production in the major cities, imperialist exploitation, and class struggles within the Russian ruling classes themselves. See Louis Althusser, "Contradiction and Overdetermination," in *For Marx*, trans. Ben Brewster (London: Verso, 1969).

45   William Appleman Williams wrote: "One of the central themes of American historiography is that there is no American Empire. Most historians will admit, if pressed, that the United States once had an empire. They then promptly insist that it was given away. But they also speak persistently of America as a World Power." Williams, "The Frontier Thesis and American Foreign Policy," *Pacific Historical Review* 24 (November 1955): 379–95. See also Amy Kaplan, "Left Alone with America: The Absence of Empire in the Study of American Culture," *Cultures of United States Imperialism*, ed. Amy Kaplan and Donald E. Pease (Durham: Duke University Press, 1993).

46   On the U.S. colonization of the Philippines (1898–1946), see Renato Constan-
tino, *The History of the Philippines: From the Spanish Colonization to the Second
World War* (New York: Monthly Review Press, 1975); Peter Stanley, *A Nation
in the Making: The Philippines and the United States, 1899–1921* (Cambridge:
Harvard University Press, 1974); Daniel B. Schirmer and Stephen Rosskamm
Shalom, eds., *The Philippines Reader: A History of Colonialism, Neocolonialism,
Dictatorship, and Resistance* (Boston: South End, 1987); and Vincente L. Rafael,
ed., *Discrepant Histories: Translocal Essays on Filipino Cultures* (Philadelphia:
Temple University Press, 1995). For a discussion of Filipino popular narrative
and the multiple determinations of colonialism, neocolonialism, gender, and
religion in the contemporary Philippines, see Eleanor M. Jaluague, "Escaping
Fantasy: Reconstructing Popular Memory and Consciousness in Lualhati Bautista's '*Gapo*,'" unpublished manuscript, San Diego, California, 1994. On the
ramifications of U.S. colonialism for Filipino Americans, see Campomanes,
"The New Empire's Forgetful and Forgotten Citizens.

47   On the American relation to China and Japan, see George M. Beckmann, *The
Modernization of China and Japan* (New York: Harper, 1962); see also McCormick, *The China Market: America's Quest for Informal Empire.*

48   See William Appelman Williams, *The Tragedy of American Diplomacy* (Cleveland: World Publishing, 1959); and Thomas J. McCormick, *America's Half-
Century: United States Foreign Policy in the Cold War and After,* 2d ed. (Baltimore: Johns Hopkins University Press, 1995).

49   Bruce Cumings, *The Origins of the Korean War* (Princeton: Princeton University Press, 1985); Marilyn Young, *The Vietnam Wars: 1945–1990* (New York:
Harper, 1991).

50   See Homi K. Bhabha, "The Other Question: Stereotype, Discrimination, and
the Discourse of Colonialism," in *The Location of Culture* (London: Routledge,
1994). In his elaboration of the colonialist stereotype, Homi Bhabha has relied on the psychoanalytic sense of fetishism, which reactivates the anxiety of
castration and sexual difference, whereas the racist scene mobilizes anxiety
about racial difference and the absence of racial purity that is expressed in
the anxious repetitive fixing of racialized difference in the fetish object of the
stereotype. In a significant departure from Bhabha's argument, I would locate
a "contradictory space" that disrupts the racist construction not exclusively in
the domain of phantasmatic anxiety about race but in the material conditions
of wars against Japan, in Korea, and in Vietnam, and the racialized gendered
division of labor in the domestic United States.

51 Gotanda, "Towards Repeal of Asian Exclusion."

52 Konvitz, *Alien and the Asiatic in American Law*, 80–97; Hing, *Making*, 226–29. Fred Riggs discusses anti-Asian legislation as "racial exclusion in euphemistic terms, so that those 'ineligible to citizenship' or 'natives of' certain geographical areas of Asia were excluded from immigration, thus extending the policy to cover all non-'white' peoples of Asia." Fred Riggs, *Pressures on Congress: A Study of the Repeal of Chinese Exclusion* (New York: Columbia University Press, King's Crown Press, 1950), 12–17.

53 Quotas were not specified by national origin, but through racialized ethnic categories such as "Chinese." In other words, the McCarran-Walter Act provided that one hundred ethnic Chinese persons enter annually; these Chinese originated from diverse nations. Even laws that repealed exclusion acts continued to "racialize" Asians. Neil Gotanda, "Towards Repeal of Asian Exclusion." See also Gotanda, "Our Constitution Is Colorblind," *Stanford Law Review*, 44, no. 1 (November 1991): 1–68.

54 Though Proposition 187 has been blocked by court procedures that are still determining if it is unconstitutional, its passage in November 1994 produced immediate and widespread effects: the sanctioning of increasingly violent patrolling of the border of the United States and Mexico; legalization of the inspection of immigrant minority communities; intimidation of communities against seeking routine or emergency medical care; and the use of fear of deportation further to exploit immigrant workers in low-wage domestic service, unsafe agricultural work, and menial repetitive assembly work. That Governor Pete Wilson ordered, the morning after the election, prenatal care and immunizations to be terminated for "illegal aliens" marks the degree to which this proposition is directed at immigrant women; anti-immigrant discourse proliferates images of racialized reproduction and feminized or infantilized bodily need as part of its campaign. But these images both acknowledge and disavow: they acknowledge the economic condition in which the "autonomy" of the white, middle-class male subject is dependent on the racialized and gendered division of labor, and they disavow that dependency by displacing it into the representational domains of racialized and sexualized stereotype.

55 Kitty Calavita analyzes the contemporary contradiction between anti-immigrant reactions juxtaposed with economic need for immigrant labor and the conflict between restrictionism, on the one hand, and the economic forces that accelerate illegal immigration, on the other. See Calavita, "U.S. Immigration and Policy Responses: The Limits of Legislation," in *Controlling*

Immigration: A Global Perspective, ed. Wayne Cornelius et al. (Stanford: Stanford University Press, 1994).

56   Omi and Winant, *Racial Formation in the United States,* 53–55.

57   According to Omi and Winant: "Racial *projects* do the ideological 'work' of making these links. *A racial project is simultaneously an interpretation, representation, or explanation of racial dynamics, and an effort to reorganize and redistribute resources along particular racial lines.* Racial projects connect what race *means* in a particular discursive practice and the ways in which both social structures and everyday experiences are racially *organized,* based upon that meaning." See ibid., 56.

58   Ibid., 105. See also George Lipsitz, *A Life in the Struggle: Ivory Perry and the Culture of Opposition* (Philadelphia: Temple University Press, 1988).

59   See Robert Allen, *Black Awakening in Capitalist America: An Analytic History* (Trenton, N.J.: Africa World Press, 1990); Carlos Muñoz, *Youth, Identity, Power: The Chicano Movement* (New York: Verso, 1989); Glenn Omatsu, "The 'Four Prisons' and the Movements of Liberation: Asian American Activism from the 1960s to the 1990s," in *The State of Asian America: Activism and Resistance in the 1990s,* ed. Karin Aguilar-San Juan (Boston: South End, 1994); Russell Leong, "To Open the Future," *Moving the Image: Independent Asian Pacific American Media Arts,* ed. Leong (Los Angeles: UCLA Asian American Studies and Visual Communications, 1991); L. Ling-chi Wang, "The Politics of Ethnic Identity and Empowerment: The Asian American Community since the 1960s," *Asian American Policy Review* (Spring 1991): 43–56.

60   In emphasizing *race* as the locus of struggle, the simultaneous class and gender struggles were less adequately addressed by the cross-race movements of the 1960s and 1970s. The fracturing of these movements was as much the result of these internal contradictions of gender and class as they were produced by external assaults by the FBI, the police, and conservative organizations.

61   Karl Marx, "On the Jewish Question," in *Marx-Engels Reader,* ed. Robert Tucker (New York: Norton, 1972), 32.

62   For analyses of the current global restructuring of capitalism and its cultural-spatial logics, see David Harvey, *The Condition of Postmodernity* (Cambridge: Basil Blackwell, 1990); Fredric Jameson, *Postmodernism, or, The Cultural Logic of Late Capitalism* (Durham: Duke University Press, 1991); and Edward W. Soja, *Postmodern Geographies: The Reassertion of Space in Critical Social Theory* (London: Verso, 1989).

63   See, for example, Melvin L. Oliver and Thomas M. Shapiro, *Black Wealth, White Wealth: A New Perspective on Racial Inequality* (New York: Routledge, 1995); and George Lipsitz, "Civil Rights Rhetoric and White Identity Politics," in *Cultural Pluralism, Identity Politics, and the Law* (forthcoming).

64   Jean-Jacques Rousseau, *The Social Contract*, trans. Maurice Cranston (Harmondsworth: Penguin, 1968).

65   In *The Sexual Contract* (London: Polity, 1988), Carole Pateman persuasively argues that the founding of civil society and the state through the social contract establishes male patriarchal right over women: "Women are not party to the original contract through which men transform their natural freedom into the security of civil freedom. Women are the subject of the contract. The (sexual) contract is the vehicle through which men transform their natural right over women into the security of civil patriarchal right" (6).

66   Marx, *Grundrisse*, 296.

67   See Max Horkheimer and Theodor W. Adorno, *The Dialectic of Enlightenment*, trans. John Cumming (New York: Seabury, 1972), especially "The Culture Industry: Enlightenment as Mass Deception"; and Fredric Jameson, "Reification and Utopia in Mass Culture," *Social Text* 1, no. 1 (1979): 130–48.

68   For a discussion of modernist aestheticism and the different historicity of the avant-garde, see Peter Bürger, *Theory of the Avant-Garde* (Minneapolis: University of Minnesota Press, 1984). On the possibilities of political art detached from notions of originality or authenticity that emerge from hybrid, residual sites, see Walter Benjamin, "The Work of Art in the Age of Mechanical Reproduction," in *Illuminations*.

69   George Lipsitz has used the term "families of resemblance" to evoke the relations between the styles and practices taken up by different subcultures of racialized groups. Rosalinda Fregoso's work, for example, elaborates the Chicana/Chicano film aesthetic, emphasizing the breaks with dominant forms and cultural codes that rearticulate history and collective memory rather than aspiring toward a notion of autonomous art. Lipsitz, *Time Passages: Collective Memory and American Popular Culture* (Minneapolis: University of Minnesota Press, 1990); Fregoso, *The Bronze Screen: Chicana and Chicano Film Culture* (Minneapolis: University of Minnesota Press, 1993).

70   Sau-ling Cynthia Wong, *Reading Asian American Literature: From Necessity to Extravagance* (Princeton: Princeton University Press, 1993), 13.

71   On other racialized minority sites of contradiction, see, for example, José David Saldívar, *The Dialectics of Our America: Genealogy, Cultural Critique, and*

Literary History (Durham: Duke University Press, 1991); Alfred Arteaga, ed., *An Other Tongue: Nation and Ethnicity in the Linguistic Borderlands* (Durham: Duke University Press, 1994); and Paul Gilroy, *The Black Atlantic: Modernity and Double Consciousness* (Cambridge: Harvard University Press, 1993).

72   Benjamin, "Theses on the Philosophy of History," in *Illuminations*.

73   Bertolt Brecht's critique of Georg Lukács's claims about the political subject produced by the aesthetic mode of realism is relevant in this regard. If shifts in the mode of production necessitate a new subject, then new aesthetic modes are required to accommodate the complex convergences and differentiations in the social formation. See Theodor W. Adorno et al., *Aesthetics and Politics*, afterword by Fredric Jameson (London: Verso, 1980).

74   Theodor W. Adorno, "Cultural Criticism and Society," *Prisms* (Cambridge: MIT Press, 1981); Herbert Marcuse, "A Note on Dialectic," in *The Essential Frankfurt School Reader*, ed. Andrew Arato and Eike Gebhardt (New York: Continuum, 1988). Asian American literary criticism has a distinguished history of critique that proceeds by way of this dialectical method. See Elaine Kim, *Asian American Literature: An Introduction to the Writings in Their Social Context* (Philadelphia: Temple University Press, 1982); and Wong, *Reading Asian American Literature*.

75   Judith Butler's and Homi K. Bhabha's elaborations of "performativity"—as a critical disruption of symbolic categories—are suggestive and helpful. See Butler, *Gender Trouble: Feminism and the Subversion of Identity* (New York: Routledge, 1990); Butler, "Critically Queer," *Bodies That Matter: On the Discursive Limits of "Sex"* (New York: Routledge, 1993); and Bhabha, "Disseminations," *The Location of Culture* (Routledge, 1994). See also Karen Shimakawa's work discussing Asian American theater representation as a cultural practice of "critical mimesis" that both thematizes and displaces the situation of Asian Americans as "abject" to the U.S. nation-state and American culture: Shimakawa, " 'made, not born': National Abjection and the Asian American Body on Stage" (Ph.D. diss., University of Washington, 1994).

76   Recent works that place Asian Americans within the international frames of global capitalism or neocolonialism are suggestive in this regard. Book-length studies include: Okihiro, *Margins and Mainstreams;* Ong, Bonacich, and Cheng, eds., *The New Asian Immigration in Los Angeles and Global Restructuring.* See also Kandice Chuh, "Toward a More Perfect Union: Transnationalizing Asian American and Postcolonial Studies," Ph.d. diss., University of Washington, 1996; Yen Le Espiritu, "Colonial Oppression, Labour Importation, and

Group Formation: Filipinos in the United States," *Ethnic and Racial Studies* 19, no. 1 (January 1996): 29–48; Helen Heran Jun, "Contingent Nationalisms: Renegotiating Borders in Korean and Korean American Oppositional Struggles," *positions* (forthcoming); Laura Hyun Yi Kang, "Compositional Subjects: Enfiguring Asian/American Women," Ph.D. diss., University of California, Santa Cruz, 1995; Min-Jung Kim, "'Moment of Danger': Continuities and Discontinuities between Korean Nationalism and Korean American Nationalism," *positions* (forthcoming); Colleen Lye, "Towards an Asian (American) Cultural Studies: Postmodernism and the 'Peril of Yellow Capital and Labor,'" in *Privileging Positions: The Sites of Asian American Studies*, ed. Gary Y. Okihiro, et al. (Pullman: Washington State University Press, 1995); and Viet Thanh Nguyen, "Representing Reconciliation: Le Ly Hayslip between Viet Nam and the United States," *positions* (forthcoming).

77   Saldívar, *Dialectics of Our America.*

78   Gilroy, *Black Atlantic*, 4.

79   The distinction between symbol and allegory can be elaborated through Raymond Williams's discussion of "reflection" and "mediation" in *Marxism and Literature* (London: Oxford University Press, 1977), which Williams poses suggestively as a contrast between Georg Lukács and Walter Benjamin's theories of art. Williams associates the symbol as much with the "ideal type" of traditional heroic narratives, as with the tendency toward "typification" in Lukács's concept of the "world-historical individual," or socialist realism's selection of the representative example situated within the constitutive and constituting processes of social and historical reality. In such typifications, there is a presumption of a knowable historical totality in terms of which the typification will be recognized, and symbolic figuration typifies "the elements and tendencies of reality that recur *according to regular laws*, although changing with the changing circumstances." (Lukács, quoted in Williams, 102, my emphasis). For Benjamin, however, social and historical processes are always mediated through "correspondences," rather than "types" that reflect a given social reality. Benjamin's concept of correspondences does not imply an analogy or homology between the figure and the totality but rather proposes a dialectic of displaced connections, a dialectic that considers the relation of parts to fractured wholes and seeks to be "historical" amid the losses and contingencies of history. Indeed, Benjamin elaborated the aesthetic ramifications of the difference between symbol and allegory in *Origin of German Tragic Drama* (New Left Books, 1977) and actually discusses allegory as always revealing a "cross-

ing of the border of a different mode. . . . Its intrusion could therefore be described as a harsh disturbance of the peace and *a disruption of law and order in the arts."* (177, my emphasis).

80 Dipesh Chakrabarty, "Postcoloniality and the Artifice of History: Who Speaks for 'Indian' Pasts?" *Representations* 37 (Winter 1992): 1–26, 10.

2 Canon, Institutionalization, Identity: Asian American Studies

1 Mas'ud Zavarzadeh and Donald Morton, eds., "Theory, Pedagogy, Politics: The Crisis of 'The Subject' in the Humanities," in *Theory Pedagogy Politics: Texts for Change* (Urbana: University of Illinois Press, 1991), 1.

2 Henry A. Giroux and Peter McClaren, eds., *Critical Pedagogy, the State, and Cultural Struggle* (Albany: State University of New York Press, 1989), "Introduction."

3 Martin Carnoy, "Education, State, and Culture in American Society," in Giroux and McClaren, *Critical Pedagogy*, 6.

4 Chela Sandoval, "U.S. Third World Feminism: The Theory and Method of Oppositional Consciousness in the Postmodern World," *Genders*, no. 10 (Spring 1991): 1–24; Kimberlé Crenshaw, "Demarginalizing the Intersection of Race and Sex: A Black Feminist Critique of Antidiscrimination Doctrine, Feminist Theory, and Antiracist Politics," *University of Chicago Legal Forum* (1989): 139–67; Evelyn Nakano Glenn, "The Dialectics of Wage Work: Japanese-American Women and Domestic Service, 1905–1940," *Feminist Studies* 6, no. 3 (Fall 1980): 432–71, and Glenn, "Racial Ethnic Women's Labor: The Intersection of Race, Gender, and Class Oppression," *Review of Radical Political Economics* 17, no. 3 (1983): 86–108.

5 See, for example, George Lipsitz, *Time Passages: Collective Memory and American Popular Culture* (Minneapolis: University of Minnesota Press, 1990); Rosalinda Fregoso, *The Bronze Screen: Chicana and Chicano Film Culture* (Minneapolis: University of Minnesota Press, 1993); Robin D. G. Kelley, *Race Rebels: Culture, Politics, and the Black Working Class* (New York: Free Press, 1994); Michael Omi and Howard Winant, *Racial Formation in the United States: From the 1960s to the 1990s* (New York: Routledge, 1994); and José David Saldívar, *Border Matters: Remaking American Cultural Studies* (Berkeley: University of California Press, forthcoming).

6 The historical sites for these alliances have been the demands for departments of ethnic studies, third world studies, or women's studies; other recent sites include the fight to maintain the University of California as a public university

that serves the racially and economically diverse constituency of California in light of the 1994 regents' decision to abolish affirmative action.

7   David Lloyd, "Genet's Genealogy: European Minorities and the Ends of Canon," in *The Nature and Context of Minority Discourse*, ed. Abdul Jan-Mohamed and David Lloyd (New York: Oxford University Press, 1990).

8   On the political situation of Hawaii and Hawaiian writing, see Haunani-Kay Trask, "Politics in the Pacific Islands: Imperialism and Native Self-Determination," *Amerasia* 16, no. 1 (1990): 1–19; Geraldine E. Kosasa-Terry, "The Politics of 'Local' Identity in Hawai'i" (paper presented at the annual meeting of the Association for Asian American Studies, June 1992); Stephen H. Sumida, *And the View from the Shore: Literary Traditions of Hawai'i* (Seattle: University of Washington Press, 1991); and Candace Fujikane, "Between Nationalisms: Hawaii's Local Nation and Its Troubled Racial Paradise," *Critical Mass* 1, no. 2 (1994): 23–57.

9   Frank Chin, Jeffrey Paul Chan, Lawson Inada, and Shawn Wong, eds., *Aiiieeeee!: An Anthology of Asian-American Writers* (New York: Doubleday, 1975); Shirley Geok-lin Lim, Mayumi Tsutakawa, and Margarita Donnelly, eds., *Forbidden Stitch: An Asian American Women's Anthology* (Corvallis, Oreg.: Calyx, 1989); Roberta Uno, ed., *Unbroken Thread: An Anthology of Plays by Asian American Women* (Amherst: University of Massachusetts Press, 1993).

10   Elaine Kim, *Asian American Literature: An Introduction to the Writings and Their Social Context* (Philadelphia: Temple University Press, 1982), xv.

11   Carlos Bulosan, *America Is in the Heart* (1943; reprint, University of Washington Press, 1973), 147.

12   Monica Sone, *Nisei Daughter* (Seattle: University of Washington Press, 1953), 238.

13   John Okada, *No-No Boy* (Seattle: University of Washington Press, 1976); Joy Kogawa, *Obasan* (Boston: David Godine, 1981).

14   For a more extensive interrogation of the ideology of healing in Asian American literature, see Shelley S. Wong, "Notes from Damaged Life: Asian American Literature and the Discourse of Wholeness" (Ph.D. diss., Department of Ethnic Studies, University of California, Berkeley, 1993); David Palumbo-Liu, "Model Minority Discourse and the Ideology of Healing," in *Minority Discourse: Ideological Containment and Utopian/Heterotopian Potential*, ed. Abdul JanMohamed (forthcoming).

15   Immigrants from South Asia are not a "new" group, having come to the United States since the late nineteenth century. Like other Asian immigrant groups,

South Asians were subject to exclusion acts and bars from citizenship. Because of the "Asiatic barred zone" established in 1917, the larger part of South Asian immigration has taken place after the Immigration and Nationality Act of 1965; the categories for immigration specified by this Act have affected the contours of the South Asian constituency in the United States. These immigration patterns, as well as historical conditions that distinguish South Asians from many other Asian immigrants, specifically British colonialism, explain in part the need for a separate articulation "South Asian American." Yet the links between South Asian and Asian American are now emerging; the inclusion of South Asian and Southeast Asian women writers in the 1989 anthology *Forbidden Stitch* widened and shifted the definition of Asian American women's literature. *Our Feet Walk the Sky: Women of the South Asian Diaspora*, edited by the Women of the South Asian Descent Collective (San Francisco: Aunt Lute Foundation, 1993) is one of the first collections of South Asia immigrant women's writings; in it, some pieces explore the relation between South Asian diasporic formation and "Asian American" formation. For a nuanced theoretical discussion of the links and continuities between South Asian immigrants and other Asian Americans, as well as the politics of differentiation, see Inderpal Grewal, "The Postcolonial, Ethnic Studies, and the Diaspora," *Social Text* 94, no. 4 (1994): 45–74.

16   See essays in Elaine Kim and Norma Alarcón, eds., *Writing Self/Writing Nation: Selected Essays on Theresa Hak Kyung Cha's DICTEE* (Berkeley: Third Woman Press, 1993).

17   Grace Hong, James Lee, David Maruyama, Jim Soong, and Gary Yee, eds., *Burning Cane*, special issue, *Amerasia Journal* 17, no. 2 (1991).

18   Monique Thuy-Dung Truong, "Kelly," *Amerasia Journal* 17, no. 2 (1991): 42.

19   On interpellation, see Louis Althusser, "Ideology and Ideological State Apparatuses," in *Lenin and Philosophy*, trans. Ben Brewster (New York: Monthly Review Press, 1971).

20   See Louis Althusser, "Contradiction and Overdetermination," in *For Marx*, trans. Ben Brewster (London: Verso, 1990), 99. For an elaboration of the unevenness of multiple contradictions, see Stuart Hall, "Signification, Representation, Ideology: Althusser and the Post-Structuralist Debates," *Critical Studies in Mass Communication* 2, no. 2 (June 1985): 91–114.

21   Antonio Gramsci, "Notes on Italian History," in *Selections from the Prison Notebooks*, ed. and trans. Quinton Hoare and Geoffrey Nowell Smith (New York: International Publishers, 1971).

3   Heterogeneity, Hybridity, Multiplicity: Asian American Differences

1   *Issei, nisei,* and *sansei* are Japanese terms meaning first-generation, second-generation, and third-generation Japanese Americans.

2   Janice Mirikitani, "Breaking Tradition," *Ikon* 9, *Without Ceremony: A Special Issue by Asian Women United* (1988): 9.

3   Lydia Lowe, "Quitting Time," *Ikon* 9, *Without Ceremony: A Special Issue by Asian Women United* (1988): 29.

4   See Elaine Kim, *Asian American Literature: An Introduction to the Writings and Their Social Context* (Philadelphia: Temple University Press, 1982).

5   Diana Chang, "The Oriental Contingent," in *The Forbidden Stitch,* ed. Shirley Geok-lin Lim, Mayumi Tsutakawa, Margarita Donnelly (Corvallis, Oreg.: Calyx, 1989), 171–77.

6   Stuart Hall, "Cultural Identity and Diaspora," in *Identity: Community, Culture, Difference,* ed. Jonathan Rutherford (London: Lawrence and Wishart, 1990), 225.

7   See the discussion of Michael Omi and Howard Winant in Chapter 1 of this volume.

8   Recent anthropological discussions of cultures as syncretic systems echo some of these concerns of Asian American writers. See, for example, Michael M. J. Fischer, "Ethnicity and the Post-Modern Arts of Memory," in *Writing Culture,* ed. James Clifford and George Marcus (Berkeley: University of California Press, 1986); and James Clifford, *The Predicament of Culture: Twentieth-Century Ethnography, Literature, and Art* (Cambridge: Harvard University Press, 1988). For an anthropological study of Japanese American culture that troubles the paradigmatic construction of kinship and filial relations as the central figure in culture, see Sylvia Yanagisako's *Transforming the Past: Kinship and Tradition among Japanese Americans* (Stanford: Stanford University Press, 1985).

9   Maxine Hong Kingston, *The Woman Warrior* (New York: Random, 1975), 6.

10   Wayne Wang, *Dim Sum* (1984).

11   See Peter Kwong, *Chinatown, N.Y.: Labor and Politics, 1930–1950* (New York: Monthly Review Press, 1979); and Victor G. Nee and Brett de Bary Nee, *Longtime Californ': A Documentary Study of an American Chinatown* (New York: Pantheon, 1972). Since the 1970s, the former Los Angeles "Chinatown" has been superseded demographically and economically by Monterey Park, the home of many Chinese Americans, as well as newly arrived Chinese from Hong Kong and Taiwan. On the social and political consequences of these changing demographics, see Timothy Fong, *The First Suburban Chinatown: The Remaking of*

Monterey Park, CA (Philadelphia: Temple University Press, 1993); and Leland Saito, "Contrasting Patterns of Adaptation: Japanese Americans and Chinese Immigrants in Monterey Park," in *Bearing Dreams, Shaping Visions,* ed. Linda Revilla, Gail Nomura, Shawn Wong, and Shirley Hune (Pullman: Washington State University Press, 1993).

12   Sucheng Chan, *This Bittersweet Soil: The Chinese in California Agriculture, 1860–1910* (Berkeley: University of California Press, 1986); Paul Ong, Edna Bonacich, and Lucie Cheng, eds. *The New Asian Immigration in Los Angeles and Global Restructuring* (Philadelphia: Temple University Press, 1994).

13   See Stuart Hall, "Signification, Representation, Ideology: Althusser and the Post-Structuralist Debates," *Critical Studies in Mass Communication* 2, no. 2 (June 1985): 91–114.

14   While California's "multiculturalism" is often employed to further an ideological assertion of equal opportunity for California's different immigrant groups, I am here pursuing the ignored implications of this characterization: that is, despite the rhetoric about increasing numbers of racialized immigrants racing to enjoy California's opportunities, for racialized immigrants, there is not equality but uneven opportunity, regulation, and stratification.

15   See Antonio Gramsci, *Selections from the Prison Notebooks,* ed. and trans. Quinton Hoare and Geoffrey Nowell Smith (New York: International Publishers, 1971).

16   The notion of "the dominant"—defined by Raymond Williams in a chapter discussing the "dominant, residual, and emergent" as "a cultural process . . . seized as a cultural system, with determinate dominant features: feudal culture or bourgeois culture or a transition from one to the other"—is often conflated in recent cultural theory with Gramsci's concept of "hegemony." Indeed, Williams writes in *Marxism and Literature* (Oxford: Oxford University Press, 1977), "We have certainly still to speak of the 'dominant' and the 'effective,' and in these senses of the hegemonic" (121), as if the "dominant" and the "hegemonic" are synonymous.

It is important to note, however, that in Gramsci's thought, "hegemony" refers equally to a specific hegemony (for example, bourgeois class hegemony), as it does to the process through which "emergent" groups challenging that specific hegemony assemble and contest the specific ruling hegemony.

17   See Antonio Gramsci, "History of the Subaltern Classes: Methodological Criteria," in *Prison Notebooks,* pp. 52–60. Gramsci describes "subaltern" groups as by definition not unified, emergent, and always in relation to the domi-

nant groups: "The history of subaltern social groups is necessarily fragmented and episodic. There undoubtedly does exist a tendency to (at least provisional stages of) unification in the historical activity of these groups, but this tendency is continually interrupted by the activity of the ruling groups; it therefore can only be demonstrated when an historical cycle is completed and this cycle culminates in a success. Subaltern groups are always subject to the activity of ruling groups, even when they rebel and rise up: only 'permanent' victory breaks their subordination, and that not immediately" (54).

18 "Hegemony" still remains a suggestive construct in Gramsci, however, rather than an explicitly interpreted set of relations. Within the current globalized political economy, it is even more important to specify which particular forms of challenge to an existing hegemony are significantly transformative and which forms may be neutralized or appropriated by that hegemony. We must go beyond Gramsci's notion of hegemony to observe that, in the present conjunction in which "modern" state forms intersect with "postmodern" movements of capital and labor, the social field is not a totality consisting exclusively of the dominant and the counterdominant but rather "the social" is an open and uneven terrain of contesting antagonisms and signifying practices, some of which are neutralized, others of which can be linked together to build pressures against an existing hegemony. See chapter 1, note 19.

19 Walter Adamson, *Hegemony and Revolution: A Study of Antonio Gramsci's Political and Cultural Theory* (Berkeley: University of California Press, 1980). Anne Showstack Sassoon, "Hegemony, War of Position, and Political Intervention," in *Approaches to Gramsci*, ed. Anne Showstack Sassoon (London: Writers and Readers, 1982). See Stuart Hall's reading of Gramsci, "Gramsci's Relevance for the Study of Race and Ethnicity," *Journal of Communication Inquiry* 10 (Summer 1986).

20 Frantz Fanon, *The Wretched of the Earth*, trans. Constance Farrington (New York: Grove, 1968), 94.

21 The work of Evelyn Nakano Glenn is outstanding in this regard; see especially "Occupational Ghettoization: Japanese-American Women and Domestic Service, 1905–1970," *Ethnicity* 8, no. 4 (December 1981): 352–86, a study of the entrance into and continued specialization of Japanese American women in domestic service and the role of domestic service in the "processing" of immigrant women into the urban economy.

22 See Trinh T. Minh-ha, *Woman, Native, Other: Writing Postcoloniality and Feminism* (Bloomington: Indiana University Press, 1989), 105.

23 See Angela Davis, "Interview," in *Worlds Aligned: The Politics of Culture in the Shadow of Capital*, ed. David Lloyd and Lisa Lowe (forthcoming).

24 See Elaine Kim, "'Such Opposite Creatures': Men and Women in Asian American Literature," *Michigan Quarterly Review* (Winter 1990): 68–93, for a comprehensive analysis of this debate between nationalism and feminism in Asian American discourse.

25 For an analysis of generational conflict in Chu's novel, see Ted Gong, "Approaching Cultural Change through Literature: From Chinese to Chinese American," *Amerasia* 7, no. 1 (1980): 73–86. Gong asserts that "the father/son relationship represents the most critical juncture in the erosion of a traditional Chinese value system and the emergence of a Chinese American character. Change from Chinese to Chinese American begins here" (74–75).

26 Wayne Wang's film production of *The Joy Luck Club* has taken liberties with Tan's novel, the novel already being a text that is somewhat dehistoricized and fanciful. See, for example, Sau-ling Cynthia Wong, "Sugar Sisterhood: Situating the Amy Tan Phenomenon," in *The Ethnic Canon: Histories, Institutions, and Interventions*, ed. David Palumbo-Liu (Minneapolis: University of Minnesota Press, 1995). Unfortunately, Wang's film moves in this direction and tends to exemplify, rather than criticize, the privatization and aestheticizing of the Chinese mother-daughter relationship.

27 Amy Tan, *The Joy Luck Club* (New York: Putnam, 1989). The cover review cited is by Alice Walker.

28 Peter Wang, *A Great Wall*, 1985.

29 Sau-ling Cynthia Wong, *Reading Asian American Literature: From Necessity to Extravagance* (Princeton: Princeton University Press, 1993); see chapter 3, "The Politics of Mobility."

30 Gayatri Chakravorty Spivak, "Subaltern Studies: Deconstructing Historiography," in *In Other Worlds* (New York: Routledge, 1988), 205.

31 Hall, "Cultural Identity and Diaspora," 226.

4 Imagining Los Angeles in the Production of Multiculturalism

1 See Giuliana Bruno, "Ramble City: Postmodernism and *Blade Runner*," *October* 42 (Summer 1987): 61–74.

2 On the relationship between aesthetic culture and political economy, see David Lloyd, "Analogies of the Aesthetic: The Politics of Culture and the Limits of Materialist Aesthetics," *New Formations* 10 (Spring 1990): 109–26.

3 On the logic of pluralism in critical discourse, see Ellen Rooney, *Seductive*

Reasoning: Pluralism as the Problematic of Contemporary Literary Theory (Ithaca: Cornell University Press, 1989).

4   Gramsci distinguishes hegemony from the violent imposition of rule, elaborating it as the process through which a particular group gains consent to determine the political, cultural, and ideological character of a state; pluralism elicits the consent of racial and ethnic groups through the promise of equal participation and equal citizenship. See Antonio Gramsci, *Selections from the Prison Notebooks*, ed. and trans. Quintin Hoare and Geoffrey Nowell Smith (New York: International Publishers, 1971). For further discussion of how Gramsci's concept of hegemony also includes within it the possible challenges by emergent groups, see Stuart Hall, "Gramsci's Relevance for the Study of Race and Ethnicity," *Journal of Communication Inquiry* 10 (Summer 1986).

5   The description of the "forgetting" of differentiated spheres recalls Horkheimer and Adorno's analysis of the "culture industry": "the idea of 'fully exploiting' available technical resources and the facilities for aesthetic mass consumption is part of the economic system which refuses to exploit resources to abolish hunger." Max Horkheimer and Theodor W. Adorno, *The Dialectic of Enlightenment*, trans. John Cumming (New York: Seabury, 1972), 139. Benjamin comments also on the production of art as distraction: "Distraction as provided by art presents a covert control of the extent to which new tasks have become soluable by apperception. Since, moreover, individuals are tempted to avoid such tasks, art will tackle the most difficult and most important ones where it is able to mobilize the masses. . . . The public is an examiner, but an absent-minded one." Walter Benjamin, "The Work of Art in the Age of Mechanical Reproduction," in *Illuminations*, ed. Hannah Arendt, trans. Harry Zohn (New York: Schocken, 1969), 240–41. For Horkheimer and Adorno, however, the analysis of the "forgetting" of historical differentiation is part of a critique of mass culture as deception and its undermining of society's emancipatory potential, whereas for Benjamin, technology and mass culture do not in themselves lead to deception or appropriation but can also be means, as with Brecht, of initiating political action. (In this it might be said that Benjamin portends postmodernism's "antiaesthetic" celebration of mass culture, technology, and the crisis of representation, as means of calling attention to the end of the autonomous aesthetic object, a critique of official representations and narratives, and the possibility of destructuring the order of representation; on a "postmodernism of resistance," see Hal Foster, introduction to *The Anti-Aesthetic: Essays on Postmodern Culture* [Port Townsend,

Wash.: Bay Press, 1983].) For a very persuasive discussion of the ideological and utopian functions of mass culture, see Fredric Jameson, "Reification and Utopia in Mass Culture," *Social Text* 1, no. 1 (1979): 130–48.

6 On racialized spatial discipline in Los Angeles, see Edward W. Soja, *Postmodern Geographies: The Reassertion of Space in Critical Social Theory* (London: Verso, 1989); Mike Davis, *City of Quartz: Excavating the Future in Los Angeles* (London: Verso, 1990); and Michael S. Murashige, "Race, Resistance, and Contestations of Urban Space" (Ph.D. diss., Department of English, University of California, Los Angeles, 1995).

7 Hal Foster, "The Problem of Pluralism," *Art in America*, January 1982, 9–15.

8 *Sa-I-Gu*, prod. Christine Choy, Elaine Kim, and Dai Sil Kim-Gibson, Cross Current Media, 1993, video. Distributed by National Asian American Telecommunications Association, 346 Ninth Street, 2d Floor, San Francisco, Calif. 94103.

9 Althusser's notion of structure-in-dominance describes a social formation that expresses the convergence of multiple yet asymmetrical contradictions, one of which is dominant at a particular historical moment varying according to the overdetermination of the contradictions and their uneven development. See Louis Althusser, *For Marx*, trans. Ben Brewster (London: Verso, 1969), and Louis Althusser and Etienne Balibar, *Reading 'Capital'*, trans. Ben Brewster (London: Verso, 1979).

10 Elaine Kim, "Home Is Where the Han Is," in *Reading Rodney King, Reading Urban Uprisings*, ed. Robert Gooding-Williams (New York: Routledge, 1993), 216.

11 For studies that attach the different histories of racial and ethnic communities to neighborhoods, urban history, labor movements, community practices, and popular cultural forms such as rap, rock and roll, low-riding, or graffiti, see Davis, *City of Quartz;* George Lipsitz, *Time Passages: Collective Memory and American Popular Culture* (Minneapolis: University of Minnesota Press, 1990); and Murashige, "Race, Resistance, and Contestations of Urban Space."

12 Jeff Chang, "Race, Class, Conflict, and Empowerment: On Ice Cube's 'Black Korea,'" *Amerasia Journal* 19, no. 2 (1993): 87–107.

5 Decolonization, Displacement, Disidentification: Writing and the Question of History

1 Frantz Fanon, *Black Skin, White Masks*, trans. Charles Lam Markmann (London: Pluto, 1986), 17–18.

2   The following studies investigate the interpellating function of the novel in the formation of the individual, the family, the nation, and the empire: Franco Moretti, *The Way of the World: The Bildungsroman in European Culture* (London: Verso, 1987); Benedict Anderson, *Imagined Communities: Reflections on the Origin and Spread of Nationalism* (London: Verso, 1983); David Lloyd, *Nationalism and Minor Literature: James Clarence Mangan and the Emergence of Irish Cultural Nationalism* (Berkeley: University of California Press, 1987); Nancy Armstrong, *Desire and Domestic Fiction: A Political History of the Novel* (New York: Oxford University Press, 1987); Roddey Reid, *Families in Jeopardy: Regulating the Social Body in France, 1750–1910* (Stanford: Stanford University Press, 1993); Jenny Sharpe, *Allegories of Empire: The Figure of Woman in the Colonial Text* (Minneapolis: University of Minnesota, 1993); and Edward Said, *Culture and Imperialism* (New York: Knopf, 1993).

3   Buchi Emecheta, *The Joys of Motherhood* (London: Allison and Busby, 1979).

4   Michelle Cliff, *Abeng* (New York: Dutton, 1984). Colonial education in *Abeng* is discussed further in Tejaswini Niranjana, " 'History, Really Beginning': The Compulsions of Post-Colonial Pedagogy," in *The Lie of the Land: English Literary Studies in India*, ed. Rajeswari Sunder Rajan (Delhi: Oxford University Press, 1992).

5   E. P. Thompson, *The Making of the English Working Class* (Harmondsworth: Penguin, 1968). On the teaching of "English literature" as an apparatus of the British colonial project in India, see Gauri Viswanathan, *Masks of Conquest: Literary Study and British Rule in India* (New York: Columbia University Press, 1989); and Ania Loomba, "Criticism and Pedagogy in the Indian Classroom," in Rajan, *Lie of the Land.*

6   See John Dower, *War without Mercy: Race and Power in the Pacific War* (New York: Pantheon, 1989).

7   See Nick Browne, "Race: The Political Unconscious in American Film," *East-West Film Journal* 6, no. 1 (January 1992): 5–16; and Gina Marchetti, *Romance and the "Yellow Peril": Race, Sex, and Discursive Strategies in Hollywood Film* (Berkeley: University of California Press, 1993).

8   See Chandra Talpade Mohanty, "Cartographies of Struggle," in *Third World Women and the Politics of Feminism*, ed. Chandra Talpade Mohanty, Ann Russo, and Lourdes Torres (Bloomington: Indiana University Press, 1991); and Aihwa Ong, "The Gender and Labor Politics of Postmodernity," *Annual Review of Anthropology* 20 (1991): 279–309.

9   Hayden White, *Metahistory: The Historical Imagination in Nineteenth-Century*

Europe (Baltimore: Johns Hopkins University Press, 1973); Dominick LaCapra, *History and Criticism* (Ithaca: Cornell University Press, 1985); Jean-François Lyotard, *The Postmodern Condition: A Report on Knowledge* (Minneapolis: University of Minnesota Press, 1984).

10   Edward Said, *Orientalism* (New York: Random, 1979).

11   Dipesh Chakrabarty, "Postcoloniality and the Artifice of History: Who Speaks for 'Indian' Pasts?" *Representations* 37 (Winter 1992): 1–26; Gyan Prakash, "Writing Post-Orientalist Histories of the Third World," *Society for Comparative Study of Society and History* 32, no. 2 (1990): 383–408; Tejaswini Niranjana, *Siting Translation: History, Post-Structuralism, and the Colonial Context* (Berkeley: University of California Press, 1992); David Lloyd, *Anomolous States: Irish Writing in the Postcolonial Moment* (Durham: Duke University Press, 1993).

12   See Gyanendra Pandey, "Peasant Revolt and Indian Nationalism," in *Selected Subaltern Studies*, ed. Ranajit Guha and Gayatri Chakravorty Spivak (Oxford: Oxford University Press, 1988); Reynaldo Ileto, "Outlines of a Nonlinear Emplotment of Philippine History," in *Reflections on Development in Southeast Asia*, ed. Lim Teck Ghee (Singapore: ASEAN Economic Research Unit, Institute of Southeast Asian Studies, 1988).

13   Kumkum Sangari and Sudesh Vaid, *Recasting Women: Essays in Indian Colonial History* (New Brunswick: Rutgers University Press, 1990).

14   Eric Goldman, *The Crucial Decade—and After, 1945–1960* (New York: Vintage, 1960), 148, 152, 172, and 173.

15   James C. Thomson, Peter W. Stanley, and John Curtis Perry, *Sentimental Imperialists: The American Experience in East Asia* (New York: Harper, 1981), 236.

16   Frantz Fanon, *The Wretched of the Earth*, trans. Constance Farrington (New York: Grove, 1968).

17   I have learned from Winifred Woodhull's critique of French poststructuralism in terms of its reiteration within some Francophone postcolonial writing. See Woodhull, *Transfigurations of the Maghreb: Feminism, Decolonization, and Literature* (Minneapolis: University of Minnesota Press, 1993).

18   Bipan Chandra, "Colonialism, Stages of Colonialism, and the Colonial State," *Journal of Contemporary Asia* 10, no. 3 (1980): 272–85. For other discussions that have differentiated "postcolonial" or "third world" texts and contexts from "postmodernism," see Kumkum Sangari, "The Politics of the Possible," in *The Nature and Context of Minority Discourse*, ed. Abdul JanMohamed and David Lloyd (New York: Oxford University Press, 1990); E. San Juan Jr., "Mapping the Boundaries: The Filipino Writer in the USA," *Journal of Ethnic Studies*

19, no. 1 (Spring 1991): 117–31; Carolyn Hau, "*Dogeaters,* Postmodernism, and the 'Worlding' of the Philippines," in *Philippine Post-Colonial Studies: Essays on Language and Literature,* ed. Christina Pantoja Hidalgo and Priscelina Patajo-Legasto (Manila: University of the Philippines, 1993); and Rey Chow, "Postmodern Automatons," in *Feminists Theorize the Political,* ed. Judith Butler and Joan Scott (New York: Routledge, 1992).

19 Earlier Asian American novels also make this detour. As I argue in Chapter 3, even novels that can be said to conform more closely to the formal criteria of the bildungsroman, such as Carlos Bulosan's *America Is in the Heart* (1943), John Okada's *No-No Boy* (1957), or Louis Chu's *Eat a Bowl of Tea* (1961) express a remarkable contradiction between the demand for a univocal developmental narrative and the historical specificities of immigrant experiences.

20 For accounts of Japanese colonialism and Korean nationalist opposition, see, for example, Michael Robinson, "Ideological Schism in the Korean Nationalist Movement, 1920–1930: Cultural Nationalism and the Radical Critique," *Journal of Korean Studies* 4 (1982–83): 241–68; and Bruce Cumings, "The Legacy of Japanese Colonialism in Korea," in *The Japanese Colonial Empire, 1895–1945,* ed. Ramon H. Myers and Mark R. Peattie (Princeton: Princeton University Press, 1984).

21 Theresa Hak Kyung Cha, *Dictée* (New York: Tanam, 1982), 81–82. My emphasis.

22 See Chungmoo Choi, "The Discourse of Decolonization and Popular Memory: South Korea," *positions* 1, no. 1 (Spring 1993): 77–102.

23 On Filipino American identity, see Enrique Bonus, "Locating Filipino-American Identities: Ethnicity and the Politics of Space in Southern California" (Ph.D. diss., Department of Communications, University of California, San Diego, in progress. Bonus's work explores the important part played by Filipino immigrant nostalgia and longing for the "homeland" in the construction of ethnic and national group identity.

24 See Vicente L. Rafael, "Anticipating Nationhood: Collaboration and Rumor in the Japanese Occupation of Manila," *Diaspora* 1, no. 1 (Spring 1991): 67–82; and Gayatri C. Spivak, "Subaltern Studies: Deconstructing Historiography," in *In Other Worlds* (New York: Routledge, 1988).

25 Ileto, "Nonlinear Emplotment of Philippine History," 154.

26 Jessica Hagedorn, *Dogeaters* (New York: Penguin, 1990), 66.

27 See Vicente L. Rafael, "Taglish, or, the Phantom Power of the Lingua Franca," *Public Culture* 8, no. 1 (Fall 1995): 101–26.

28   By "hybridity," I do not mean simply cultural or linguistic mixing or "ambivalence" but rather a material form that expresses the sedimented traces of a
complex history of violence, invasion, exploitation, deracination, and imposed
rule by different colonial and neocolonial powers. On Philippine hybridity, see
Nick Joaquin, *Culture and History: Occasional Notes on the Process of Philippine
Becoming* (Manila: Solar Publishing, 1988).

29   In an excellent discussion of *Dogeaters* and Ninotchka Rosca's *State of War* as
texts that make use of "the postmodern idiom" in the project of forging "alternative historiographies," Nerissa Balce-Cortes argues that the metonyms of
neocolonialism that figure everywhere in *Dogeaters*—the mestizo "half-breed"
elite, the commodified subaltern bodies of Joey Sands and Boy-Boy—are
themselves residues that found an "alternative historiography." Balce-Cortes,
"Imagining the Neocolony," *Critical Mass: A Journal of Asian American Cultural
Criticism* 2, no. 2 (Spring 1995): 95–120.

30   On decentered insurgent movements in the Philippines, see Amado Guerrero, "Specific Characteristics of Our People's War," in *Philippine Society and
Revolution* (Manila: International Association of Filipino Patriots, 1979).

31   Edward W. Soja, *Postmodern Geographies: The Reassertion of Space in Critical
Social Theory* (London: Verso, 1989). See Fae Myenne Ng, *Bone* (New York:
Hyperion, 1993).

32   Henri Lefebvre, *The Production of Space*, trans. Donald Nicholson-Smith (Cambridge, Mass.: Basil Blackwell, 1991), 86.

33   Michel Foucault, "Of Other Spaces," trans. Jay Miskowiec, *Diacritics* 16, no. 1
(Spring 1986): 22–27.

34   Akhil Gupta and James Fergusen, "Beyond 'Culture': Space, Identity, and the
Politics of Difference," *Cultural Anthropology* 7, no. 1 (February 1992): 6–22.

35   Him Mark Lai, Genny Lim, and Judy Yung, eds., *Island Poetry and History
of Chinese Immigrants, 1910–1940* (San Francisco: Hoc Doi Chinese Cultural
Foundation, 1980).

36   Cha, *Dictée*, 32.

37   In relation to German history and the Holocaust, Eric Santner associates
mourning with the historical "task of integrating damage, loss, disorientation,
decenteredness into a transformed structure of identity, whether it be that of
an individual, a culture, or an individual as a member of a cultural group."
Santner, *Stranded Objects: Mourning, Memory, and Film in Postwar Germany*
(Ithaca: Cornell University Press, 1990), xiii. Though the ostensive narrative
drive of *Bone* appears to be the mourning of Ona, it seems important to recast

that representation of individual or familial mourning as an echo of the "community" mourning of the loss of Chinese American history, of which Grandpa Leong's bones are the emblem.

38   Ng, *Bone*, 145.

39   While I want to underscore the potential access to historical understanding that such texts as *Dictée*, *Dogeaters*, and *Bone* provide, I do not mean to privilege Asian American "literature" over Asian American "history." The discussion of historical narratives would need to take place elsewhere, but it might be said here that just as Asian American literature emerges out of the contradiction between, for example, racialization and U.S. narratives of citizenship, so too do Asian American histories. This contradiction expresses itself in the historiographical work by John Cheng, John Kuo Wei Tchen, Nayan Shah, or K. Scott Wong, for example, on Chinatowns, immigrant labor history, masculinity, and community life, which provide alternatives to univocal, totalizing historical modes. For a crucial discussion of Asian American historiography and the need to recenter new historical subjects and to place Asian Americans within a global historical landscape, see Gary Y. Okihiro, *Margins and Mainstreams: Asians in American History and Culture* (Seattle: University of Washington Press, 1994).

40   Walter Benjamin, "Theses on the Philosophy of History," in *Illuminations*, ed. Hannah Arendt, trans. Harry Zohn (New York: Schocken, 1969).

6   Unfaithful to the Original: The Subject of *Dictée*

1   *Dictée* stands in contrast to Asian American novels of formation such as Carlos Bulosan's *America Is in the Heart* (1943), Monica Sone's *Nisei Daughter* (1953), Louis Chu's *Eat a Bowl of Tea* (1961), or Maxine Hong Kingston's *The Woman Warrior* (1975). Its formal deviations from the genre allegorize the practical importance of recognizing heterogeneities of national origin, language, generation, gender, and class within the Asian American constituency.

2   For an analysis of the pedagogical assimilation of students into capitalism through the reproduction of generic citizen-individuals, see Martin Carnoy, "Education, State, and Culture in American Society," in *Critical Pedagogy, the State, and Cultural Struggle*, ed. Henry A. Giroux and Peter McLaren (Albany: State University of New York Press, 1989); and Herbert Gintis and Samuel Bowles, "Contradiction and Reproduction in Educational Theory," in *Education and the State: Schooling and the National Interest*, ed. Roger Dale et al. (Sussex: Falmer Press and the Open University, 1981).

3   On the history of French Catholic missionary colonialism in Korea, see Charles Dallet, *Histoire de l'église de Corée*, 2 vols. (Paris: Victor Palmé, 1874); John F. Cady, *The Roots of French Imperialism in Eastern Asia* (Ithaca: Cornell University Press, 1954); and Eric O. Hanson, *Catholic Politics in China and Korea* (Maryknoll, N.Y.: Orbis, 1980). Although Cha learned French after emigrating to the United States, the representation in *Dictée* of the narrator's French language instruction and Catholic training is not located or historicized in this way. Within the sequence of *Dictée*, the indoctrination in French Catholicism is represented as a part of the narrator's childhood education and precedes the sections on Japanese colonialism, Korean nationalism, and the depiction of the adult narrator's return to divided Korea after the Korean War. This sequence suggests that the initial section on French Catholic education alludes to French Catholic missionary colonialism in Korea.

4   Theresa Hak Kyung Cha, *Dictée* (New York: Tanam, 1982), 1.

5   For examples of the constitutive positions of this polemic, see Brower, ed., *On Translation* (New York: Oxford University Press, 1966); and André Lefevere, ed., *Translating Literature: The German Tradition* (Assen: Van Gorcum, 1977).

6   Some nineteenth-century theories do discuss translation as a means of cultural conquest in the building of national integrity; see Friedrich Nietzsche, and Karl Vossler, essays in Lefevere, *Translating Literature*.

7   Norma Alarcón has observed of the Mexican and Chicano traditions that the paradigm of translation is rendered as a female figure whose sexual and reproductive difference connotes this subversive ambivalence, expressed in the paradoxical formulation "traddutora, traditora" ("translatoress, traitoress"). See Alarcón, "Traddutora, Traditora: A Paradigmatic Figure of Chicana Feminism," *Cultural Critique* 13 (Fall 1989): 57–87. On the relationship of translation to colonialism, see Vicente L. Rafael, *Contracting Colonialism: Translation and Christian Conversion in Tagalog Society under Early Spanish Rule* (Ithaca: Cornell University Press, 1988); and Tejaswini Niranjana, *Siting Translation: History, Post-Structuralism, and the Colonial Context* (Berkeley: University of California Press, 1992).

8   In subsequent sections, *Dictée* further explores the valence of female "untranslatability" in numerous voicings of the antagonism of female particularity to the closure and telos of the masculine narrative form. In the section "Clio/History," the renarration of the life of female nationalist leader Yu Guan Soon, interspersed with excerpts from F. A. McKenzie's history *The Tragedy of Korea*, is "unfaithful" both to the formal unity of the official "paternal" Ameri-

can history, on the one hand, and, in feminizing the nationalist narrative, "unfaithful" and unsuitably companionable to the male body of Korean nationalism, on the other. The daughter's address to her mother as a metonym for the Korean "motherland," in "Calliope/Epic Poetry," intervenes in the oedipalizing demands of both colonialist and nationalist discourses; in "Erato/Love Poetry," the husband's patriarchal right to the wife's body in the marriage contract is questioned and displaced.

9   See Chong-Sik Lee's history of Korea under Japanese colonialism, *The Politics of Korean Nationalism* (Berkeley: University of California Press, 1963); E. Patricia Tsurumi, "Colonial Education in Korea and Japan," in *The Japanese Colonial Empire, 1895–1945*, ed. Ramon H. Myers and Mark R. Peattie (Princeton: Princeton University Press, 1984); and Bruce Cumings, "The Legacy of Japanese Colonialism in Korea," in Myers and Peattie, *Japanese Colonial Empire.*

10   See Michael Robinson, "Ideological Schism in the Korean Nationalist Movement, 1920–1930: Cultural Nationalism and the Radical Critique," *Journal of Korean Studies* 4 (1982–83): 241–68; and Cumings, "Legacy of Japanese Colonialism in Korea."

11   For an outstanding analysis of the legacy of colonialism in South Korea, see Chungmoo Choi, "The Discourse of Decolonization and Popular Memory: South Korea," *positions* 1, no. 1 (Spring 1993): 77–102.

12   Lee, *Politics of Korean Nationalism*, 97.

13   Tsurumi, "Colonial Education in Korea and Japan," 294.

14   From Ono, *Chosen kyoiku mondai kanken*, 31, quoted in ibid., 296.

15   In a poem by Michelle Cliff, female creole teachers in British schools in Jamaica are also described as being forced to occupy a similarly "reproductive" role: "They were passing on to those of us who were light-skinned the creole heritage of collaboration, assimilation, loyalty to our betters. We were expected to be willing subjects in this outpost of civilization." See Cliff, "If I Could Write This in Fire, I Would Write This in Fire," in *The Land of Look Behind* (Ithaca: Firebrand, 1985), 61.

16   Cliff alludes to a similar "history of forced fluency" in the British West Indies under which she "received the message of anglocentrism, of white supremacy, and . . . internalized it"; Cliff suggests that the "fury" against such forced fluency "breaks apart sharply into a staccato poetry—direct, short, brilliantly bitter—as if measured prose would disintegrate under her fury." See ibid., 12–15.

17   For greater discussion of the conjunction of Korean feminism and Korean anticolonialism during the nationalist period, see Elaine Kim, "Poised on the In-

Between: A Korean American's Reflections on *Dictée*," in *Writing Self/Writing Nation: Selected Essays on Theresa Hak Kyung Cha's DICTEE*, ed. Elaine Kim and Norma Alarcón (Berkeley: Third Woman Press, 1993); and Kumari Jayawardena, *Feminism and Nationalism in the Third World* (London: Zed, 1986), 213–25.

18 By fetishism, I am referring loosely to the psychoanalytic logic of a fixation that disavows "castration," or incomplete wholeness of the mother, by substituting another object in place of the "missing" part. See Sigmund Freud, *An Outline of Psycho-Analysis* (New York: Norton, 1949), 60; J. Laplanche and J.-B. Pontalis, "Splitting of the Ego," in *The Language of Psycho-Analysis* (London: Hogarth, 1973). Oedipalization, in turn, is that internalization of the law of castration that separates the child and mother and places the "son"/subject in subordinated relation to the "father"/state. Thus defined, oedipalization (and fetishism, to the extent that disavowal confirms the logic of castration) is integral to and determining of the formation of the masculine subject within both the colonial and nationalist narratives. We might say that colonialism incorporates the male subject into the colonial state according to a relationship that is not dissimilar to the family's oedipalization of the son. The subject becomes a citizen when he identifies with the paternal state and accepts the terms of this identification by subordinating his identification with the precolonial, "preoedipal" motherland. Nationalisms may inherit this oedipal narrative to the degree that they leave the social institutions of patriarchy uninterrogated. Such nationalisms demand that the nationalist citizen identify with the new state or "fatherland," while relegating the "woman" to the symbolic register of figuring the nation.

In contrast to the masculine subject's fetishism that confirms the logic of oedipalization, I suggest that in *Dictée* the daughter's renarration of the mother as homeland and origin—yet as homeland and origin to which the subject's relationship is always already disrupted, broken, and problematized—can be conceived as a rewriting of "fetishism" from a site of difference that displaces both colonialist and nationalist oedipal narratives. For a discussion of the possibility of "female fetishism" within the French literary tradition, see Emily Apter, *Feminizing the Fetish: Psychoanalysis and Narrative Obsession in Turn-of-the-Century France* (Ithaca: Cornell University Press, 1991).

19 Beginning with Frantz Fanon's critique of the relationship between bourgeois nationalism and colonialism in *The Wretched of the Earth*, trans. Constance Farrington (New York: Grove, 1968), subsequent discussions of nationalism have

explored the ways in which the national narrative may function doubly as a fiction of unity for both the colonial power and the emergent population. See Benedict Anderson, *Imagined Communities: Reflections on the Origin and Spread of Nationalism* (London: Verso, 1983); David Lloyd, *Nationalism and Minor Literature: James Clarence Mangan and the Emergence of Irish Cultural Nationalism* (Berkeley: University of California Press, 1987); Mary Layoun, "Fictional Formations and Deformations of National Culture," *South Atlantic Quarterly* 87, no. 1 (Winter 1988): 53–73; Homi K. Bhabha, ed. *Nation and Narration* (London: Routledge, 1990).

The case of Korean nationalisms is vastly more complicated than the nationalisms of former French and British colonies, because Korean nationalist influences were and are both Western and non-Western and because the division of Korea and the involvement of outside powers in the governing of both North Korea and South Korea have further exacerbated the factionalized nature of its nationalist practices. On this question, see Lewis H. Gann, "Western and Japanese Colonialism: Some Preliminary Comparisons," in Myers and Peattie, *Japanese Colonial Empire;* and Sonia Ryang, "Historian-Judges of Korean Nationalism," *Ethnic and Racial Studies* 13, no. 4 (October 1990): 503–26.

20   From *Proceedings of the First Korean Congress,* 1919, quoted in Lee, *Politics of Korean Nationalism,* 144.

21   See Lee, *Politics of Korean Nationalism.*

22   On the history of contractual and consensual American citizenship and its roots in English notions of natural and perpetual allegiance, see James Kettner, *The Development of the Concept of American Citizenship, 1608–1870* (Chapel Hill: University of North Carolina Press, 1978). On the notion of equal citizenship under the constitution, see Kenneth Karst, *Belonging to America: Equal Citizenship and the Constitution* (New Haven: Yale University Press, 1989).

23   See Louis Althusser, "Ideology and Ideological State Apparatuses," in *Lenin and Philosophy,* trans. Ben Brewster (New York: Monthly Review Press, 1971).

24   It seems more productive to consider *Dictée*'s portraits of the process by which individuals are transformed into formal but contradictory subjects in terms of Althusser's notion of "interpellation," rather than in the psychoanalytic language of subjectification, because where the former suggests a varied set of ideological apparatuses, the latter largely depends on the acceptance of a universalizing and ahistorical narrative of oedipalization. Lacanian notions of splitting, fetishism, or transference, on the one hand, or Luce Irigaray's notion

of the plural lips of the female body/text, on the other, both provide suggestive ways for reading *Dictée*—as a refusal of fluency to reiterate the splitting of
the subject upon the entry into language, the "re-membering" of the mother's
body in opposition to the narrative of oedipalization. But the psychoanalytic
explanations do not account for colonialism, racism, and assimilation in the
processes of subjectification. See, for example, Jacques Lacan, "The Agency of
the Letter in the Unconscious. . . ," in *Ecrits* (New York: Norton, 1977); and
Luce Irigaray, *This Sex Which Is Not One*, trans. Catherine Porter, with Carolyn
Burke (Ithaca: Cornell University Press, 1985).

Psychoanalysis may tell us that naming constitutes a splitting, that with the
entry into language the mother's voice acquires the status of an *objet petit a*
without which the subject can never be whole and for which it consequently
yearns. But it is insufficient for explaining the historical power of the Catholic
catechism in Asia or the power of the Japanese occupation to refuse Korean
subjects their Korean names. And it certainly falls short of giving us the means
to differentiate spheres and registers such that we might understand how the
U.S. government's division of Korea in 1948 both does and does not resonate
with the narrator's attempts to underscore and suture her subjective splits.

25 Althusser, "Ideology" in *Lenin and Philosophy*, 181.

26 See Eric O. Hanson, *Catholic Politics in China and Korea* (Maryknoll, N.Y.:
Orbis, 1980), chapter 8.

27 Stuart Hall, "Signification, Representation, Ideology: Althusser and the Post-
Structuralist Debates," *Critical Studies in Mass Communication* 2, no. 2 (June
1985): 113. For the general discussion of the uneven development of contradictions, see Louis Althusser, "Contradiction and Overdetermination," in *For
Marx*, trans. Ben Brewster (London: Verso, 1969).

28 With respect to this notion of "other spaces," I have found Foucault's notion
of "heterotopia" suggestive; see Michel Foucault, "Of Other Spaces," trans. Jay
Miskowiec, *Diacritics* 16, no. 1 (Spring 1986): 22–27. On the colonized popula-
tion's reappropriation of the *technai* of colonialism in efforts to decolonize, see
Frantz Fanon's discussion of the Algerian use of the radio during the French-
Algerian War, in *A Dying Colonialism*, trans. Haakon Chevalier (New York:
Grove, 1967).

29 Althusser states: "God thus defines himself as the Subject *par excellence*, he
who is through himself and for himself ('I am that I am'), and he who inter-
pellates his subject . . . the interpellated-called recognizes that he is a subject, a subject *of* God, *a subject through the Subject and subjected to the Subject*.

The proof: he obeys him." See Althusser, "Ideology," in *Leninism and Philosophy*, 179.

30 See Shoshana Felman, *La Folie et la chose littéraire* (Paris: Seuil, 1978), 166: "La répétition ironique déplace la répétition pathétique. Au lieu de «montrer» le réel dans un geste faussement innocent, le roman décompose celui-ci, décompose—du réel—précisément l'image «représentée», l'idéologie de la représentation mimétique!"

31 Althusser, "Ideology," in *Lenin and Philosophy*, 162.

32 Paul Smith, for example, interprets Althusser as proposing this dyadic opposition between "imaginary" and "real," in which the "real" is understood to be "historically real conditions" as opposed to something like "false consciousness." See Smith, *Discerning the Subject* (Minneapolis: University of Minnesota Press, 1988), 21. *Dictée* offers a way of interpreting Althusser's use of "imaginary" and "real" that is more dynamic and less dyadic, in which the imaginary is not merely false but makes use of the "real" and provides the modes through which the subject conceives of itself in the "real," and the "real" is not static but a historical complex of relations.

33 See Lacan, "The Mirror Stage as Formative Function. . . ," in *Ecrits*.

34 Fredric Jameson, "Imaginary and Symbolic in Lacan: Marxism, Psychoanalytic Criticism, and the Problem of the Subject," *Yale French Studies* 55/56 (1977): 394.

35 Elsewhere, Althusser also suggests not only that the ideological notion of equivalence is determined by an imaginary specularity that can be disrupted but that the relationship between social contradictions and the ideological representation of identity is vulnerable as well, precisely as an imaginary, or specular, relationship: "But what, concretely, is this uncriticized ideology if not simply the 'familiar,' 'well-known,' transparent myths in which a society or an age can recognize itself (but not know itself), the mirror it looks into for self-recognition, precisely the mirror it must break if it is to know itself? What is the ideology of a society or a period if it is not that society's or period's consciousness of itself, that is, an immediate material which spontaneously implies, looks for and naturally finds its forms in the image of a consciousness of self living the totality of its world in the transparency of its own myths?" See Althusser, "The 'Piccolo Teatro': Bertolazzi and Brecht," in *For Marx*, trans. Ben Brewster (London: Verso, 1969), 144. In other terms, Homi K. Bhabha has described the interruption of an imaginary specular identity as a difference between the aural and the visual or inscriptive—alluding, as it were, to a

difference between the aural-oral dimension of the Imaginary and the linguistic terms of the Symbolic. In Bhabha's conception, the determination of the "subject" as the specular duplicate of the authoritative "Subject" always contains such a gap or fissure: "Where the aural is contending with the visual or the inscriptive, the time of turning and the time of fixing, in all these things, it is impossible to derive the individualist subject." See Bhabha, "Location, Intervention, Incommensurability: A Conversation," *Emergences* 1 (1989): 87.

36   On the intersections of antiracist, feminist, labor, gay, and anticolonialist struggles and the relationship of these intersections to identity politics, see Gloria Anzaldúa, ed., *Making Face, Making Soul*/Haciendo Caras: *Creative and Critical Perspectives by Women of Color* (San Francisco: Aunt Lute, 1990); Gloria Hull, Patricia Bell Scott, and Barbara Smith, eds., *All the Women Are White, All the Blacks Are Men, but Some of Us Are Brave* (New York: Feminist Press, 1982); bell hooks, *Ain't I a Woman: Black Women and Feminism* (Boston: South End, 1981); Deborah K. King, "Multiple Jeopardy, Multiple Consciousness: The Context of a Black Feminist Ideology," *Signs* 14, no. 1 (1988): 42–72; Kimberlé Crenshaw, "Demarginalizing the Intersection of Race and Sex: A Black Feminist Critique of Antidiscrimination Doctrine, Feminist Theory, and Antiracist Politics," *University of Chicago Legal Forum* (1989): 139–67; Stuart Hall, "New Ethnicities," *ICA Documents* 7 (1988): 27–31; Sunil Gupta, "Black, Brown, and White," in *Coming on Strong: Gay Politics and Culture*, ed. Simon Shepherd and Mick Wallis (London: Unwin Hyman, 1989), 163–79; Elaine Kim, " 'Such Opposite Creatures': Men and Women in Asian American Literature," *Michigan Quarterly Review* (Winter 1990): 68–93; Evelyn Nakano Glenn, *Issei, Nisei, War Bride: Three Generations of Japanese American Women in Domestic Service* (Philadelphia: Temple University Press, 1986); Lata Mani, "Multiple Mediations: Feminist Scholarship in the Age of Multinational Reception," *Inscriptions* 5 (1989): 1–23; Chela Sandoval, "U.S. Third World Feminism: The Theory and Method of Oppositional Consciousness in the Postmodern World," *Genders*, no. 10 (Spring 1991): 1–24; Gemma Tang Nain, "Black Women, Sexism, and Racism: Black or Antiracist Feminism?" *Feminist Review*, no. 37 (Spring 1991): 1–22; Clara Connolly, "Washing Our Linen: One Year of Women against Fundamentalism," *Feminist Review*, no. 37 (Spring 1991): 68–77; Nanneke Redclift and M. Thea Sinclair, eds., *Working Women: International Perspectives on Labour and Gender Ideology* (London: Routledge, 1991).

37   See Hall, "New Ethnicities," 28.

7 Work, Immigration, Gender: Asian "American" Women

This chapter is dedicated to Lydia Lowe.

1 Testimony from Asian Immigrant Women's Advocates (AIWA), *Immigrant Women Speak Out on Garment Industry Abuse: A Community Hearing Initiated by Asian Immigrant Women Advocates, May 1, 1993, Oakland, California* (Oakland: AIWA, 1993). Mrs. Fu Lee is one of twelve women who were not paid by a sweatshop contracted by manufacturer Jessica McClintock, Inc. AIWA organized a long-term campaign that secured pay for these women and revealed garment industry abuse of immigrant women workers.

2 See Chalsa Loo, *Chinatown: Most Time, Hard Time* (New York: Praeger, 1991).

3 Chandra Talpade Mohanty, "Cartographies of Struggle: Third World Women and the Politics of Feminism," in *Third World Women and the Politics of Feminism* (Bloomington: Indiana University Press, 1991), 34.

4 Althusser and Balibar, "On the Basic Concepts of Historical Materialism," in *Reading Capital* (London: Verso, 1968).

5 On transnationalism and the capitalist mode of production, see, for example, David Harvey, *The Condition of Postmodernity* (Oxford: Basil Blackwell, 1990); Fredric Jameson, *The Geopolitical Aesthetic: Cinema and Space in the World System* (Bloomington: Indiana University Press, 1992). For analyses of third world and racialized women's work in the global economy, see Aihwa Ong, *Spirits of Resistance and Capitalist Discipline: Factory Women in Malaysia* (Albany: State University of New York Press, 1987) and "The Gender and Labor Politics of Postmodernity," *Annual Review of Anthropology* 20 (1991): 279–309; Swasti Mitter, *Common Fate, Common Bond: Women in the Global Economy* (London: Pluto, 1986); Maria Mies, *Patriarchy and Accumulation on a World Scale: Women in the International Division of Labor* (London: Zed Press, 1986).

6 Sucheta Mazumdar, "General Introduction: A Woman-Centered Perspective on Asian American History," in *Making Waves*, ed. Asian Women United of California (Boston: Beacon Press, 1989).

7 See Arturo Escobar's "Imagining a Post-Development Era? Critical Thought, Development and Social Movements," *Social Text* 31/32 (1992): 20–56.

8 See Nancy Hartsock, "The Feminist Standpoint: Toward a Specifically Feminist Historical Materialism," in *Money, Sex, and Power* (Boston: Northeastern University Press, 1985); Catharine Mackinnon, "Feminism, Marxism, Method, and the State: An Agenda for Theory," *Signs* 7 (1982): 515–544; Robert Blauner, *Racial Oppression in America* (New York: Harper, 1972); Mario Barrera, *Race and Class in the Southwest* (Notre Dame: University of Notre Dame Press,

1979); Rodolfo Acuna, *Occupied America: A History of Chicanos* (New York: Harper, 1981).

9   Theorists such as Chela Sandoval, Angela Davis, and Evelyn Nakano Glenn have articulated critiques of single-axis political organization by suggesting that an exclusive gender politics may obscure class hierarchy and racialization, while an exclusive class politics may ignore gender stratification, racialization, and homophobia. Chela Sandoval, "US Third World Women: The Theory and Method of Oppositional Consciousness in the Postmodern World," *Genders* 10 (Spring 1991): 1–24; Angela Davis, *Women, Race, and Class* (New York: Random House, 1981); Evelyn Nakano Glenn, "Racial Ethnic Women's Labor: The Intersection of Race, Gender, and Class Oppression," *Review of Radical Political Economics*, Vol. 17, no. 3 (1983): 86–109. Moreover, the critique established by many women of color has consistently argued against both the hierarchization of oppressions as well as the false unification of women of color as impediments to theorizing and organizing movements for social change.

10 See Audre Lorde, "The Master's Tools Will Never Dismantle the Master's House," Cherríe Moraga and Gloria Anzaldúa, eds. *This Bridge Called My Back: Writings by Radical Women of Color* (Watertown: Persephone Press, 1981); Asian Women United of California, *Making Waves: An Anthology of Writings by and about Asian American Women* (New York: Beacon, 1989). These women of color cultural texts propose new subjects and new political formations. Whereas the normative notion of the subject of liberal society assumes an individual "oedipalized" by family relations and the state, these texts suggest that racialized women are differently formed and articulated, defined by a "disidentification" with the national citizen-subject formation and constituted through lateral movements across distances and disjunctions. On the subject "women of color," see Norma Alarcón, "The Theoretical Subject(s) of 'This Bridge Called My Back' and Anglo-American Feminism," in Anzaldúa, *Making Face, Making Soul*/Haciendo Caras: *Creative and Critical Perspectives by Women of Color*, ed. Gloria Anzaldúa (San Francisco: Aunt Lute, 1990).

11 For discussions of the global garment and electronics industries and the use of women's labor for assembly, see Committee for Asian Women, *Many Paths, One Goal: Organizing Women Workers in Asia* (Hong Kong: CAW, 1991); June Nash and Maria Patricia Fernandez-Kelly, eds., *Women in the International Division of Labor* (Albany: State University of New York Press, 1983); Maria Patricia Fernandez-Kelly, *For We Are Sold, I and My People: Women and Industry on Mexico's Frontier* (Albany: State University of New York Press, 1983);

Edna Bonacich, "Asians in the Los Angeles Garment Industry," in *New Asian Immigration in Los Angeles and Global Restructuring* (Philadelphia: Temple University Press, 1994); Richard P. Appelbaum, "Multiculturalism and Flexibility: Some New Directions in Global Capitalism," in *Mapping Multiculturalism*, Avery Gordon and Christopher Newfield, eds. (Minneapolis: University of Minnesota, 1996); and Laura Ho, Catherine Powell, and Leti Volpp, "(Dis)Assembling Women Workers' Rights Along the Global Assemblyline: Human Rights and the Garment Industry," *Harvard Civil Rights-Civil Liberties Law Review* 31, no. 2 (forthcoming).

12   Asian Law Caucus, 468 Bush Street, 3rd floor, San Francisco CA 94108; Coalition for Immigrant and Refugee Rights and Services, 995 Market Street, 11th floor, San Francisco 94103.

13   Asian Immigrant Women's Advocates (AIWA), 310-8th Street, Suite 301, Oakland CA 94607.

14   See Lydia Lowe, "Paving the Way: Chinese Immigrant Workers and Community-based Labor Organizing in Boston," *Amerasia Journal*, Vol. 18, no. 1 (1992); Glenn Omatsu, "The 'Four Prisons' and the Movements of Liberation: Asian American Activism from the 1960s to the 1990s," in *State of Asian America: Activism and Resistance in the 1990s*, Karin Aguilar-San Juan, ed. (Boston: South End Press, 1994).

15   Miriam Ching Louie, "Immigrant Asian Women in Bay Area Garment Sweatshops: 'After Sewing, Laundry, Cleaning and Cooking, I Have No Breath to Sing,'" *Amerasia Journal* 18 (1992): 14. For other discussions of Asian women's labor in the garment industry, see Chalsa Loo and Paul Ong, "Slaying Demons with a Sewing Needle: Feminist Issues for Chinatown's Women" in Loo, *Chinatown: Most Time, Hard Time* (New York: Praeger, 1991); and Diane Yen-Mei Wong and Dennis Hayashi, "Behind Unmarked Doors: Developments in the Garment Industry," in *Making Waves*. See also *Through Strength and Struggle*, a video documentary that tells the story of Chinese immigrant women workers and the P & L and Beverly Rose Sportwear shutdowns; by Chinese Progressive Association Workers Center, 164 Lincoln Street, 2nd floor, Boston MA 02111.

16   Support Committee for Maquiladora Workers, 3909 Center Street, Suite 210, San Diego CA 92103; Mary Tong, Director.

17   Chandra Talpade Mohanty, "Feminist Encounters: Locating the Politics of Experience," in *Destabilizing Theory*, Michelle Barrett and Anne Phillips, eds. (Stanford: Stanford University Press, 1992).

18 See for example, Kumari Jayawardena's *Feminism and Nationalism in the Third World* (London: Zed, 1986), a social history of women's work and women's activities in feminist, nationalist, and labor movements in Turkey, Egypt, India, Sri Lanka, Indonesia, the Philippines, China, Korea, Vietnam, and Japan. For analyses of segmented labor and occupational segregation of women within different "third world" national locations, see *Working Women: International Perspectives on Labour and Gender Ideology*, Nanneke Redclift and M. Thea Sinclair, eds. (London: Routledge, 1991). *Third World Women and the Politics of Feminism*, Chandra Talpade Mohanty, Ann Russo, and Lordes Torres, eds. (Bloomington: Indiana University Press, 1991) contains important accounts of different "third world" feminisms in the context of the specific upheavals of decolonization, national liberation struggles, and transnational capitalism. On the cultural dimensions of women's positions within transnationalism, see Inderpal Grewal and Caren Kaplan, eds., *Scattered Hegemonies: Postmodernity and Transnational Feminist Practices* (Minneapolis: University of Minnesota, 1994).

19 Audre Lorde, "The Master's Tools," *op. cit.*

20 Fae Myenne Ng, *Bone* (New York: Hyperion, 1993), 178–79.

21 For an in-depth study of the transition from bachelor society to family society in San Francisco Chinatown, see Victor G. Nee and Brett de Bary Nee, *Longtime Californ': A Documentary Study of an American Chinatown* (New York: Pantheon, 1972).

22 On the possibilities of "cultural struggle" within the contradictions of the "postmodern" political economy, see Aihwa Ong, "The Gender and Labor Politics of Postmodernity," *Annual Review of Anthropology* 20 (1991): 279–309; Donna Haraway, "A Cyborg Manifesto," in *Simians, Cyborgs, and Women* (London: Routledge, 1989); George Lipsitz, *Dangerous Crossroads: Popular Music, Postmodernism and the Poetics of Place* (London: Verso, 1994); David Lloyd and Lisa Lowe, eds., *Worlds Aligned: The Politics of Culture in the Shadow of Capital* (forthcoming).

Bibliography

Abelmann, Nancy, and John Lie. *Blue Dreams: Korean Americans and the Los Angeles Riots.* Cambridge: Harvard University Press, 1995.

Acuna, Rodolfo. *Occupied America: A History of Chicanos.* New York: Harper, 1981.

Adams, Brook. *The Law of Civilization and Decay; an Essay on History.* New York: Macmillan, 1895.

Adamson, Walter. *Hegemony and Revolution: A Study of Antonio Gramsci's Political and Cultural Theory.* Berkeley: University of California Press, 1980.

Adorno, Theodor W. *Negative Dialectics.* New York: Continuum, 1973.

——. *Prisms.* Cambridge: MIT Press, 1981.

Adorno, Theodor W. et al. *Aesthetics and Politics.* Afterword by Fredric Jameson. London: Verso, 1980.

Alarcón, Norma. "Traddutora, Traditora: A Paradigmatic Figure of Chicana Feminism," *Cultural Critique* 13 (Fall 1989): 57–87.

——. "The Theoretical Subject(s) of 'This Bridge Called My Back' and Anglo-American Feminism." In *Making Face, Making Soul/Haciendo Caras: Creative and Critical Perspectives by Women of Color,* ed. Gloria Anzaldúa. San Francisco: Aunt Lute, 1990.

Allen, Robert. *Black Awakening in Capitalist America: An Analytic History.* Trenton, N.J.: Africa World Press, 1990.

Almaguer, Tomás. *Racial Faultlines: The Historical Origins of White Supremacy in California.* Berkeley: University of California Press, 1994.

Althusser, Louis. *For Marx.* Trans. Ben Brewster. London: Verso, 1969.

——. *Lenin and Philosophy.* Trans. Ben Brewster. New York: Monthly Review Press, 1971.

Althusser, Louis, and Etienne Balibar. *Reading 'Capital'.* Trans. Ben Brewster. London: Verso, 1979.

Anderson, Benedict. *Imagined Communities: Reflections on the Origin and Spread of Nationalism.* London: Verso, 1983.

Anzaldúa, Gloria, ed. *Making Face, Making Soul/Haciendo Caras: Creative and Critical Perspectives by Women of Color.* San Francisco: Aunt Lute, 1990.

Appelbaum, Richard P. "Multiculturalism and Flexibility: Some New Directions in Global Capitalism." *Mapping Multiculturalism.* Avery Gordon and Christopher Newfield, eds. Minneapolis: University of Minnesota Press, 1996.

Apter, Emily. *Feminizing the Fetish: Psychoanalysis and Narrative Obsession in Turn-of-the-Century France.* Ithaca: Cornell University Press, 1991.

Armstrong, Nancy. *Desire and Domestic Fiction: A Political History of the Novel.* New York: Oxford University Press, 1987.

Arteaga, Alfred, ed. *An Other Tongue: Nation and Ethnicity in the Linguistic Border-lands.* Durham: Duke University Press, 1994.

Asian Immigrant Women's Advocates (AIWA). *Immigrant Women Speak Out on Garment Industry Abuse. A Community Hearing Initiated by Asian Immigrant Women Advocates, May 1, 1993, Oakland, California.* Oakland: AIWA, 1993.

Asian Women United of California. *Making Waves: An Anthology of Writings by and about Asian American Women.* New York: Beacon, 1989.

Balce-Cortes, Nerissa. "Imagining the Neocolony," *Critical Mass: A Journal of Asian American Cultural Criticism* 2, no. 2 (Spring 1995): 95–120.

Balibar, Etienne, and Immanuel Wallerstein. *Race, Nation, Class: Ambiguous Identities.* London: Verso, 1991.

Barrera, Mario. *Race and Class in the Southwest.* Notre Dame: University of Notre Dame Press, 1979.

Barroga, Jeannie. "Walls." In *Unbroken Thread: An Anthology of Plays by Asian American Women,* ed. Roberta Uno. Amherst: University of Massachusetts Press, 1993.

Beckmann, George M. *The Modernization of China and Japan.* New York: Harper & Row, 1962.

Benjamin, Walter. *Illuminations.* Ed. Hannah Arendt, trans. Harry Zohn. New York: Schocken, 1969.

———. *Origin of German Tragic Drama.* Trans. John Osborne. London: New Left Books, 1977.

Berg, Rick, and John Carlos Rowe. *The Vietnam War and American Culture.* New York: Columbia University Press, 1991.

Bhabha, Homi K. "Location, Intervention, Incommensurability: A Conversation." *Emergences* 1 (1989): 63–88.

———. *The Location of Culture.* London: Routledge, 1994.

———, ed. *Nation and Narration.* London: Routledge, 1990.

Blauner, Robert. "Colonized and Immigrant Minorities." In *Racial Oppression in America.* New York: Harper, 1972.

Bonus, Enrique. "Locating Filipino-American Identities: Ethnicity and the Politics of Space in Southern California." Ph.D. diss., Department of Communications, University of California, San Diego, in progress.

Boris, Eileen. "The Racialized Gendered State: Constructions of Citizenship in the United States." *Social Politics* (Summer 1995): 160–80.

Bowles, Samuel, and Herbert Gintis. *Schooling in Capitalist America.* New York: Harper, 1976.

———. "Contradiction and Reproduction in Educational Theory." In *Education and the State: Schooling and the National Interest,* ed. Roger Dale et al. Sussex: Falmer Press and the Open University, 1981.

Brower, Reuben A., ed. *On Translation.* New York: Oxford University Press, 1966.

Browne, Nick. "Race: The Political Unconscious in American Film." *East-West Film Journal* 6, no. 1 (January 1992): 5–16.

Bruno, Giuliana. "Ramble City: Postmodernism and *Blade Runner*." *October* 42 (Summer 1987): 61–74.

Bulosan, Carlos. *America Is in the Heart*, 1946. Reprint, Seattle: University of Washington Press, 1973.

Bürger, Peter. *Theory of the Avant-Garde*. Minneapolis: University of Minnesota Press, 1984.

Butler, Judith. *Gender Trouble: Feminism and the Subversion of Identity*. New York: Routledge, 1990.

———. *Bodies That Matter: On the Discursive Limits of "Sex."* New York: Routledge, 1993.

Cady, John F. *The Roots of French Imperialism in Eastern Asia*. Ithaca: Cornell University Press, 1954.

Calavita, Kitty. *U.S. Immigration Law and the Control of Labor, 1820–1924*. London: Harcourt Brace Jovanovich, 1984.

———. "U.S. Immigration and Policy Responses: The Limits of Legislation." In *Controlling Immigration: A Global Perspective*, ed. Wayne Cornelius et al. Stanford: Stanford University Press, 1994.

Campomanes, Oscar V. "The New Empire's Forgetful and Forgotten Citizens: Unrepresentability and Unassimilability in Filipino-American Postcolonialities." *Critical Mass* 47, no. 3 (September 1995): 145–200.

Carnoy, Martin. "Education, State, and Culture in American Society." In *Critical Pedagogy, the State, and Cultural Struggle*, ed. Henry A. Giroux and Peter McClaren. Albany: State University of New York Press, 1989.

Cha, Theresa Hak Kyung. *Dictée*. New York: Tanam, 1982.

Chakrabarty, Dipesh. "Postcoloniality and the Artifice of History: Who Speaks for 'Indian' Pasts?" *Representations* 37 (Winter 1992): 1–26.

Chan, Sucheng. *This Bittersweet Soil: The Chinese in California Agriculture, 1860–1910*. Berkeley: University of California Press, 1986.

———. *Asian Americans: An Interpretive History*. Boston: Twayne, 1991.

———, ed. *Entry Denied: Exclusion and the Chinese Community in America, 1882–1943*. Philadelphia: Temple University Press, 1991.

Chandra, Bipan. "Colonialism, Stages of Colonialism, and the Colonial State." *Journal of Contemporary Asia* 10, no. 3 (1980): 272–85.

Chang, Diana. "The Oriental Contingent." In *The Forbidden Stitch*, ed. Shirley Geok-lin Lim, Mayumi Tsutakawa, and Margarita Donnelly. Corvallis, Oreg.: Calyx, 1989.

Chang, Jeff. "Race, Class, Conflict, and Empowerment: On Ice Cube's 'Black Korea.'" *Amerasia Journal* 19, no. 2 (1993): 87–107.

Cheng, Lucie, and Edna Bonacich, eds. *Labor Immigration under Capitalism: Asian*

Workers in the United States before World War II. Berkeley: University of California Press, 1984.

Cheung, King-kok. *Articulate Silences: Hisaye Yamamoto, Maxine Hong Kingston, Joy Kogawa.* Ithaca: Cornell University Press, 1993.

Chin, Frank, Jeffrey Paul Chan, Lawson Inada, and Shawn Wong, eds. *Aiiieeeee!: An Anthology of Asian-American Writers.* New York: Doubleday, 1975.

Choi, Chungmoo. "The Discourse of Decolonization and Popular Memory: South Korea." *positions* 1, no. 1 (Spring 1993): 77–102.

Chow, Rey. "Postmodern Automatons." In *Feminists Theorize the Political,* ed. Judith Butler and Joan Scott. New York: Routledge, 1992.

Choy, Christine, Elaine Kim, and Dai Sil Kim-Gibson, prods. *Sa-I-Gu.* Cross Current Media, 1993.

Chu, Louis. *Eat a Bowl of Tea.* Seattle: University of Washington Press, 1961.

Chuh, Kandice. "Toward a More Perfect Union: Transnationalizing Asian American and Postcolonial Studies." Ph.d. diss., University of Washington, 1996.

Cliff, Michelle. *Abeng.* New York: Dutton, 1984.

———. *The Land of Look Behind.* Ithaca: Firebrand, 1985.

Clifford, James. *The Predicament of Culture: Twentieth-Century Ethnography, Literature, and Art.* Cambridge: Harvard University Press, 1988.

Committee for Asian Women (CAW). *Many Paths, One Goal: Organizing Women Workers in Asia.* Hong Kong: CAW, 1991.

Connolly, Clara. "Washing Our Linen: One Year of Women against Fundamentalism." *Feminist Review,* no. 37 (Spring 1991): 68–77.

Constantino, Renato. *The History of the Philippines: From the Spanish Colonization to the Second World War.* New York: Monthly Review Press, 1975.

Cornelius, Wayne, Philip Martin, and James Hollifield, eds. *Controlling Immigration: A Global Perspective.* Stanford: Stanford University Press, 1994.

Crenshaw, Kimberlé. "Demarginalizing the Intersection of Race and Sex: A Black Feminist Critique of Antidiscrimination Doctrine, Feminist Theory, and Antiracist Politics." *University of Chicago Legal Forum* (1989): 139–67.

Cumings, Bruce. "The Legacy of Japanese Colonialism in Korea." In *The Japanese Colonial Empire, 1895–1945,* ed. Ramon H. Myers and Mark R. Peattie. Princeton: Princeton University Press, 1984.

———. *The Origins of the Korean War.* Princeton: Princeton University Press, 1985.

Dallet, Charles. *Histoire de l'église de Corée.* 2 vols. Paris: Victor Palmé, 1874.

Daniels, Roger. *Concentration Camps, U.S.A.: Japanese Americans and World War II.* New York: Holt, Rinehart, and Winston, 1972.

Daniels, Roger, Sandra C. Taylor, and Harry H. L. Kitano, eds. *Japanese Americans: From Relocation to Redress.* Seattle: University of Washington Press, 1986.

Davis, Angela. *Women, Race, and Class.* New York: Random House, 1981.

————. "Interview." In *Worlds Aligned: The Politics of Culture in the Shadow of Capital*, ed. David Lloyd and Lisa Lowe (forthcoming).

Davis, Mike. *City of Quartz: Excavating the Future in Los Angeles*. London: Verso, 1990.

Dower, John. *War without Mercy: Race and Power in the Pacific War*. New York: Pantheon, 1989.

Duus, Masayo. *Unlikely Liberators: The Men of the 100th and 442nd*. Honolulu: University of Hawaii Press, 1987.

Ehrenhaus, Peter, and Richard Morris, eds. *Cultural Legacies of Vietnam: Uses of the Past in the Present*. Norwood, N.J.: Ablex, 1990.

Eisenstein, Zillah. *The Color of Gender: Reimagining Democracy*. Berkeley: University of California Press, 1994.

Emecheta, Buchi. *The Joys of Motherhood*. London: Allison and Busby, 1979.

Escobar, Arturo. "Imagining a Post-Development Era? Critical Thought, Development, and Social Movements." *Social Text* 31/32 (1992): 20–56.

Espiritu, Yen Le. *Asian American Panethnicity: Bridging Identities and Institutions*. Philadelphia: Temple University Press, 1992.

————. "Colonial Oppression, Labour Importation, and Group Formation: Filipinos in the United States." *Ethnic and Racial Studies* 19 (January 1996): 28–48.

————. *Asian American Women and Men: Labor, Laws, and Love*. Thousand Oaks, Calif.: Sage, 1996.

Fanon, Frantz. *A Dying Colonialism*. Trans. Haakon Chevalier. New York: Grove, 1967.

————. *The Wretched of the Earth*. Trans. Constance Farrington. New York: Grove, 1968.

————. *Black Skin, White Masks*. Trans. Charles Lam Markmann. London: Pluto, 1986.

Felman, Shoshana. *La Folie et la chose littéraire*. Paris: Seuil, 1978.

Fernandez-Kelly, Maria Patricia. *For We Are Sold, I and My People: Women and Industry on Mexico's Frontier*. Albany: State University of New York Press, 1983.

Fischer, Michael M. J. "Ethnicity and the Post-Modern Arts of Memory." In *Writing Culture*, ed. James Clifford and George Marcus. Berkeley: University of California Press, 1986.

Fong, Timothy. *The First Suburban Chinatown: The Remaking of Monterey Park, CA*. Philadelphia: Temple University Press, 1993.

Foster, Hal. "The Problem of Pluralism." *Art in America*, January 1982, 9–15.

————, ed. *The Anti-Aesthetic: Essays on Postmodern Culture*. Port Townsend, Washington: Bay Press, 1983.

Foucault, Michel. *The Archaeology of Knowledge*. Trans. A. M. Sheridan Smith. New York: Harper, 1972.

————. "Nietzsche, Genealogy, History." In *Language, Counter-Memory, Practice*, ed. Donald Bouchard. Ithaca: Cornell University Press, 1977.

————. "Governmentality" (1978). In *The Foucault Effect: Studies in Governmentality*, ed. Graham Burchell, Colin Gordon, and Peter Miller. Chicago: University of Chicago Press, 1991.

————. *Discipline and Punish*. Trans. Alan Sheridan. New York: Vintage, 1979.

————. "Of Other Spaces." Trans. Jay Miskowiec. *Diacritics* 16, no. 1 (Spring 1986): 22–27.

Fregoso, Rosalinda. *The Bronze Screen: Chicana and Chicano Film Culture*. Minneapolis: University of Minnesota Press, 1993.

Freud, Sigmund. *An Outline of Psycho-Analysis*. New York: Norton, 1949.

Fujikane, Candace. "Between Nationalisms: Hawaii's Local Nation and Its Troubled Racial Paradise." *Critical Mass* 1, no. 2 (Spring/Summer 1994): 23–57.

Fujitani, Takashi. "Nisei Soldiers as Citizens: Japanese Americans in U.S. National, Military, and Racial Discourses." Paper presented at "The Politics of Remembering the Asia/Pacific War," University of Hawaii at Manoa, Honolulu, Hawaii, September 1995.

Gann, Lewis H. "Western and Japanese Colonialism: Some Preliminary Comparisons." In *The Japanese Colonial Empire, 1895–1945*, ed. Ramon H. Myers and Mark R. Peattie. Princeton: Princeton University Press, 1984.

Gilroy, Paul. *The Black Atlantic: Modernity and Double Consciousness*. Cambridge: Harvard University Press, 1993.

Giroux, Henry A., and Peter McClaren, eds. *Critical Pedagogy, the State, and Cultural Struggle*. Albany: State University of New York Press, 1989.

Glenn, Evelyn Nakano. "The Dialectics of Wage Work: Japanese-American Women and Domestic Service, 1905–1940." *Feminist Studies* 6, no. 3 (Fall 1980): 432–71.

————. "Occupational Ghettoization: Japanese-American Women and Domestic Service, 1905–1970." *Ethnicity* 8, no. 4 (December 1981): 352–86.

————. "Racial Ethnic Women's Labor: The Intersection of Race, Gender, and Class Oppression." *Review of Radical Political Economics* 17, no. 3 (1983): 86–108.

————. *Issei, Nisei, War Bride: Three Generations of Japanese American Women in Domestic Service*. Philadelphia: Temple University Press, 1986.

Goldman, Eric. *The Crucial Decade—and After, 1945–1960*. New York: Vintage, 1960.

Gong, Ted. "Approaching Cultural Change through Literature: From Chinese to Chinese American." *Amerasia* 7, no. 1 (1980): 73–86.

Gonzalves, Theo. "'We Hold a Neatly Folded Hope': Filipino Veterans of World War II on Citizenship and Political Obligation." *Amerasia Journal* 21, no. 3 (Winter 1995/1996): 155–174.

Gordon, Charles. "The Racial Barrier to American Citizenship." *University of Pennsylvania Law Review* 93 (1944–45): 237–58.

Gotanda, Neil. "A Critique of 'Our Constitution Is Colorblind.'" *Stanford Law Review* 44, no. 1 (November 1991): 1–68.

———. "Towards Repeal of Asian Exclusion: The Magnuson Act of 1943, the Act of July 2, 1949, the Presidential Proclamation of July 4, 1946, the Act of August 9, 1949, and the Act of August 1, 1950." In *Asian Americans in Congress: A Documentary History*, ed. Hyung Chan Kim. Westport, Conn.: Greenwood Press, 1995.

Gramsci, Antonio. *Selections from the Prison Notebooks.* Ed. and trans. Quinton Hoare and Geoffrey Nowell Smith. New York: International Publishers, 1971.

Grewal, Inderpal. "The Postcolonial, Ethnic Studies, and the Diaspora." *Social Text* 94, no. 4 (1994): 45–74.

Grewal, Inderpal, and Caren Kaplan, eds. *Scattered Hegemonies: Postmodernity and Transnational Feminist Practices.* Minneapolis: University of Minnesota Press, 1994.

Guerrero, Amado. "Specific Characteristics of Our People's War." In *Philippine Society and Revolution.* Manila: International Association of Filipino Patriots, 1979.

Gupta, Akhil, and James Fergusen. "Beyond 'Culture': Space, Identity, and the Politics of Difference." *Cultural Anthropology* 7, no. 1 (February 1992): 6–22.

Gupta, Sunil. "Black, *Brown*, and White." In *Coming on Strong: Gay Politics and Culture*, ed. Simon Shepherd and Mick Wallis. London: Unwin Hyman, 1989.

Gutiérrez, David G. *Walls and Mirrors: Mexican Americans, Mexican Immigrants, and the Politics of Ethnicity.* Berkeley: University of California Press, 1995.

Gutierrez-Jones, Carl. *Rethinking the Borderlands: Between Chicano Culture and Legal Discourse.* Berkeley: University of California Press, 1995.

Hagedorn, Jessica. *Dogeaters.* New York: Penguin, 1990.

Hall, Stuart. "Signification, Representation, Ideology: Althusser and the Post-Structuralist Debates." *Critical Studies in Mass Communication* 2, no. 2 (June 1985): 91–114.

———. "Gramsci's Relevance for the Study of Race and Ethnicity." *Journal of Communication Inquiry* 10 (Summer 1986).

———. "New Ethnicities." *ICA Documents* 7 (1988): 27–31.

———. "Cultural Identity and Diaspora." In *Identity: Community, Culture, Difference*, ed. Jonathan Rutherford. London: Lawrence and Wishart, 1990.

Hamamoto, Darrell Y. *Monitored Peril: Asian Americans and the Politics of TV Representation.* Minneapolis: University of Minnesota Press, 1994.

Hanson, Eric O. *Catholic Politics in China and Korea.* Maryknoll, N.Y.: Orbis, 1980.

Haraway, Donna. "A Cyborg Manifesto." In *Simians, Cyborgs, and Women.* London: Routledge, 1989.

Hartsock, Nancy. "The Feminist Standpoint: Toward a Specifically Feminist Historical Materialism." In *Money, Sex, and Power*. Boston: Northeastern University Press, 1985.

Harvey, David. *The Condition of Postmodernity*. Cambridge: Basil Blackwell, 1990.

Hau, Carolyn. "*Dogeaters*, Postmodernism, and the 'Worlding' of the Philippines." In *Philippine Post-Colonial Studies: Essays on Language and Literature*, ed. Christina Pantoja Hidalgo and Priscelina Patajo-Legasto. Manila: University of the Philippines, 1993.

Hess, Gary R. "The 'Hindu' in America: Immigration and Naturalization Policies and India, 1917–1946." *Pacific Historical Review* 38 (1969): 59–79. Reprinted in *Asian Indians, Filipinos, Other Asian Communities, and the Law*, ed. Charles McClain. New York: Garland, 1994.

Hing, Bill Ong. *Making and Remaking Asian America through Immigration Policy, 1850–1990*. Stanford: Stanford University Press, 1993.

Ho, Laura, Catherine Powell, and Leti Volpp. "(Dis)Assembling Women Workers' Rights Along the Global Assemblyline: Human Rights and the Garment Industry." *Harvard Civil Rights—Civil Liberties Law Review* 31, no. 2 (forthcoming).

Hong, Grace Kyungwon. "The Not-Working Class and Chinese Immigrant Labor: Discursive and Specular Projects of Containment in Bret Harte's *Overland Monthly* and Arnold Geuthe's Photographs of the Chinese Quarter." Unpublished manuscript, San Diego, California, 1995.

Hong, Grace, James Lee, David Maruyama, Jim Soong, and Gary Yee, eds. *Burning Cane*. Special issue. *Amerasia Journal* 17, no. 2 (1991).

hooks, bell. *Ain't I a Woman: Black Women and Feminism*. Boston: South End, 1981.

Horkheimer, Max, and Theodor W. Adorno. *The Dialectic of Enlightenment*. Trans. John Cumming. New York: Seabury, 1972.

Houchins, Lee, and Chang-su Houchins. "The Korean Experience in America, 1903–24." *Pacific Historical Review* 43 (1974): 548–75.

Hull, Gloria, Patricia Bell Scott, and Barbara Smith, eds. *All the Women Are White, All the Blacks Are Men, but Some of Us Are Brave*. New York: Feminist Press, 1982.

Hune, Shirley. "Politics of Chinese Exclusion: Legislative-Executive Conflict, 1876–1882." *Amerasia Journal* 9, no. 1 (1982): 5–27.

Ileto, Reynaldo. "Outlines of a Nonlinear Emplotment of Philippine History." In *Reflections on Development in Southeast Asia*, ed. Lim Teck Ghee. Singapore: ASEAN Economic Research Unit, Institute of Southeast Asian Studies, 1988.

Irigaray, Luce. *This Sex Which Is Not One*. Trans. Catherine Porter, with Carolyn Burke. Ithaca: Cornell University Press, 1985.

Irons, Peter. *Justice Delayed: The Record of the Japanese American Internment Cases*. Middletown: Wesleyan University Press, 1989.

Jaluague, Eleanor M. "Escaping Fantasy: Reconstructing Popular Memory and Consciousness in Lualhati Bautista's '*Gapo*." Unpublished manuscript, San Diego, California, 1994.

Jameson, Fredric. "Imaginary and Symbolic in Lacan: Marxism, Psychoanalytic Criticism, and the Problem of the Subject." *Yale French Studies* 55/56 (1977).

———. "Reification and Utopia in Mass Culture." *Social Text* 1, no. 1 (1979): 130–48.

———. *Postmodernism, or, The Cultural Logic of Late Capitalism.* Durham: Duke University Press, 1991.

Jayawardena, Kumari. *Feminism and Nationalism in the Third World.* London: Zed, 1986.

Jeffords, Susan. *The Remasculinization of America: Gender and the Vietnam War.* Bloomington: Indiana University Press, 1989.

Joaquin, Nick. *Culture and History: Occasional Notes on the Process of Philippine Becoming.* Manila: Solar Publishing, 1988.

Jun, Helen Heran. "Contingent Nationalisms: Renegotiating Borders in Korean and Korean American Oppositional Struggles." *positions* (forthcoming).

Kang, Laura Hyun Yi. "Compositional Subjects: Enfiguring Asian/American Women." Ph.D. diss., University of California, Santa Cruz, 1995.

Kaplan, Amy. "Left Alone with America: The Absence of Empire in the Study of American Culture." In *Cultures of United States Imperialism,* ed. Amy Kaplan and Donald E. Pease. Durham: Duke University Press, 1993.

Karst, Kenneth. *Belonging to America: Equal Citizenship and the Constitution.* New Haven: Yale University Press, 1989.

Kelley, Robin D. G. *Race Rebels: Culture, Politics, and the Black Working Class.* New York: Free Press, 1994.

Kettner, James. *The Development of the Concept of American Citizenship, 1608–1870.* Chapel Hill: University of North Carolina Press, 1978.

Kim, Elaine. *Asian American Literature: An Introduction to the Writings and Their Social Context.* Philadelphia: Temple University Press, 1982.

———. "'Such Opposite Creatures': Men and Women in Asian American Literature." *Michigan Quarterly Review* (Winter 1990): 68–93.

———. "Poised on the In-Between: A Korean American's Reflections on *Dictée.*" In *Writing Self/Writing Nation: Selected Essays on Theresa Hak Kyung Cha's DICTEE,* ed. Elaine Kim and Norma Alarcón. Berkeley: Third Woman Press, 1993.

———. "Home Is Where the Han Is." In *Reading Rodney King, Reading Urban Uprisings,* ed. Robert Gooding-Williams. New York: Routledge, 1993.

Kim, Elaine, and Norma Alarcón, eds. *Writing Self/Writing Nation: Selected Essays on Theresa Hak Kyung Cha's DICTEE.* Berkeley: Third Woman Press, 1993.

Kim, Min-Jung. "'Moment of Danger': Continuities and Discontinuities between Korean Nationalism and Korean American Nationalism." *positions* (forthcoming).

King, Deborah K. "Multiple Jeopardy, Multiple Consciousness: The Context of a Black Feminist Ideology." *Signs* 14, no. 1 (1988): 42–72.

Kingston, Maxine Hong. *The Woman Warrior.* New York: Random, 1975.

Kogawa, Joy. *Obasan.* Boston: David Godine, 1981.

Konvitz, Milton. *The Alien and the Asiatic in American Law.* Ithaca: Cornell University Press, 1946.

Kosasa-Terry, Geraldine E. "The Politics of 'Local' Identity in Hawai'i." Paper presented at the annual meeting of the Association for Asian American Studies Conference, San Jose, California, June 1992.

Kwong, Peter. *Chinatown, N.Y.: Labor and Politics, 1930–1950.* New York: Monthly Review Press, 1979.

Lacan, Jacques. *Ecrits.* Trans. Alan Sheridan. New York: Norton, 1977.

LaCapra, Dominick. *History and Criticism.* Ithaca: Cornell University Press, 1985.

Lai, Him Mark, Genny Lim, and Judy Yung, eds. *Island Poetry and History of Chinese Immigrants, 1910–1940.* San Francisco: Hoc Doi Chinese Cultural Foundation, 1980.

Laplanche, J., and J.-B. Pontalis. "Splitting of the Ego." In *The Language of Psycho-Analysis.* London: Hogarth, 1973.

Lasker, Bruno. *Filipino Immigration to the Continental United States.* Chicago: University of Chicago Press, 1931.

Layoun, Mary. "Fictional Formations and Deformations." *South Atlantic Quarterly* 87, no. 1 (Winter 1988): 53–73.

Lee, Chong-Sik. *The Politics of Korean Nationalism.* Berkeley: University of California Press, 1963.

Lefebvre, Henri. *The Production of Space.* Trans. Donald Nicholson-Smith. Cambridge: Basil Blackwell, 1991.

Lefevere, André, ed. *Translating Literature: The German Tradition.* Assen: Van Gorcum, 1977.

Leong, Russell. "To Open the Future." In *Moving the Image: Independent Asian Pacific American Media Arts,* ed. R. Leong. Los Angeles: UCLA Asian American Studies Center and Visual Communications, 1991.

Lim, Shirley Geok-lin, Mayumi Tsutakawa, and Margarita Donnelly, eds. *Forbidden Stitch: An Asian American Women's Anthology.* Corvallis, Oreg.: Calyx, 1989.

Lipsitz, George. *A Life in the Struggle: Ivory Perry and the Culture of Opposition.* Philadelphia: Temple University Press, 1988.

———. *Time Passages: Collective Memory and American Popular Culture.* Minneapolis: University of Minnesota Press, 1990.

———. *Dangerous Crossroads: Popular Music, Postmodernism and the Poetics of Place.* London: Verso, 1994.

———. "Civil Rights Rhetoric and White Identity Politics." In *Cultural Pluralism, Identity Politics, and the Law* (forthcoming).

Lloyd, David. *Nationalism and Minor Literature: James Clarence Mangan and the Emer-*

gence of Irish Cultural Nationalism. Berkeley: University of California Press, 1987.

———. "Genet's Genealogy: European Minorities and the Ends of Canon." In *The Nature and Context of Minority Discourse*, ed. Abdul JanMohamed and David Lloyd. New York: Oxford University Press, 1990.

———. "Analogies of the Aesthetic: The Politics of Culture and the Limits of Materialist Aesthetics." *New Formations* (Spring 1990): 109–26.

———. *Anomalous States: Irish Writing in the Postcolonial Moment*. Durham: Duke University Press, 1993.

Lloyd, David, and Lisa Lowe. *Worlds Aligned: The Politics of Culture in the Shadow of Capital* (forthcoming).

Loo, Chalsa. *Chinatown: Most Time, Hard Time*. New York: Praeger, 1991.

Loomba, Ania. "Criticism and Pedagogy in the Indian Classroom." In *The Lie of the Land: English Literary Studies in India*, ed. Rajeswari Sunder Rajan. Delhi: Oxford University Press, 1992.

Lorde, Audre. "The Master's Tools Will Never Dismantle the Master's House." In *This Bridge Called My Back: Writings by Radical Women of Color*, ed. Cherríe Moraga and Gloria Anzaldúa. Watertown, Mass.: Persephone, 1981.

Louie, Miriam Ching. "Immigrant Asian Women in Bay Area Garment Sweatshops: 'After Sewing, Laundry, Cleaning, and Cooking, I Have No Breath to Sing.'" *Amerasia Journal* 18 (1992): 14.

Lowe, Lisa. *Critical Terrains: French and British Orientalisms*. Ithaca: Cornell University Press, 1991.

Lowe, Lydia. "Quitting Time." *Ikon* 9, *Without Ceremony: A Special Issue by Asian Women United* (1988): 29.

———. "Paving the Way: Chinese Immigrant Workers and Community-Based Labor Organizing in Boston." *Amerasia Journal* 18, no. 1 (1992).

Luibheid, Eithne. "The 1965 Immigration and Nationality Act: An 'End' to Exclusion?" *positions* (forthcoming).

Lye, Colleen. "Toward an Asian (American) Cultural Studies: Postmodernism and the 'Peril of Yellow Capital and Labor.'" In *Privileging Positions: The Sites of Asian American Studies*, ed. Gary Y. Okihiro et al. Pullman: Washington State University Press, 1995.

Lyotard, Jean-François. *The Postmodern Condition: A Report on Knowledge*. Minneapolis: University of Minnesota Press, 1984.

MacKinnon, Catharine. "Feminism, Marxism, Method, and the State: An Agenda for Theory." *Signs* 7 (1982): 515–44.

Mani, Lata. "Multiple Mediations: Feminist Scholarship in the Age of Multinational Reception." *Inscriptions* 5 (1989): 1–23.

Marchetti, Gina. *Romance and the "Yellow Peril": Race, Sex, and Discursive Strategies in Hollywood Fiction*. Berkeley: University of California Press, 1993.

Marcuse, Herbert. "A Note on Dialectic." In *The Essential Frankfurt School Reader,* ed. Andrew Arato and Eike Gebhardt. New York: Continuum, 1988.

Marx, Karl. *Capital: A Critique of Political Economy.* Vol. 1. New York: International Publishers, 1967.

———. "On the Jewish Question." In *Marx-Engels Reader,* ed. Robert Tucker. New York: Norton, 1972.

———. *Grundisse.* Trans. Martin Nicolaus. New York: Penguin, 1973.

McClain, Charles. *In Search of Equality: The Chinese Struggle against Discrimination in Nineteenth-Century America.* Berkeley: University of California Press, 1994.

———, ed. *Asian Indians, Filipinos, Other Asian Communities, and the Law.* New York: Garland, 1994.

———, ed. *Japanese Immigrants and the American Law: The Alien Land Laws and Other Issues.* New York: Garland, 1994.

McCormick, Thomas J. *The China Market: America's Quest for Informal Empire, 1893–1901.* Chicago: Quadrangle, 1967.

———. *America's Half-Century: United States Foreign Policy in the Cold War and After.* 2d ed. Baltimore: Johns Hopkins University Press, 1995.

Melendy, H. Brett. "Filipinos in the United States." *Pacific Historical Review* 43 (1974): 99–117. Reprinted in *Asian Indians, Filipinos, Other Asian Communities, and the Law,* ed. Charles McClain. New York: Garland, 1994.

Mies, Maria. *Patriarchy and Accumulation on a World Scale: Women in the International Division of Labor.* London: Zed, 1986.

Mirikitani, Janice. "Breaking Tradition." *Ikon* 9, *Without Ceremony: A Special Issue by Asian Women United* (1988): 9–10.

Mitter, Swasti. *Common Fate, Common Bond: Women in the Global Economy.* London: Pluto, 1986.

Miyoshi, Masao. "A Borderless World? From Colonialism to Transnationalism and the Decline of the Nation-State." *Critical Inquiry* 19 (Summer 1993): 726–51.

Mohanty, Chandra Talpade. "Cartographies of Struggle." In *Third World Women and the Politics of Feminism,* ed. Chandra Talpade Mohanty, Ann Russo, and Lourdes Torres. Bloomington: Indiana University Press, 1991.

———. "Feminist Encounters: Locating the Politics of Experience." In *Destabilizing Theory,* ed. Michelle Barrett and Anne Philips. Stanford: Stanford University Press, 1992.

Moretti, Franco. *The Way of the World: The Bildungsroman in European Culture.* London: Verso, 1987.

Moy, James. *Marginal Sights: Staging the Chinese in America.* Iowa City: University of Iowa Press, 1993.

Muñoz, Carlos. *Youth, Identity, Power: The Chicano Movement.* New York: Verso, 1989.

Murashige, Michael S. "Race, Resistance, and Contestations of Urban Space." Ph.D. diss., Department of English, University of California, Los Angeles, 1995.

Nain, Gemma Tang. "Black Women, Sexism, and Racism: Black or Antiracist Feminism?" *Feminist Review*, no. 37 (Spring 1991): 1–22.

Nash, June, and Maria Patricia Fernandez-Kelly, eds. *Women in the International Division of Labor*. Albany: State University of New York Press, 1983.

Nee, Victor G., and Brett de Bary Nee. *Longtime Californ': A Documentary Study of an American Chinatown*. New York: Pantheon, 1972.

Ng, Fae Myenne. *Bone*. New York: Hyperion, 1993.

Nguyen, Viet Thanh. "Representing Reconciliation: Le Ly Hayslip between Viet Nam and the United States." *positions* (forthcoming).

Niranjana, Tejaswini. "'History, Really Beginning': The Compulsions of Post-Colonial Pedagogy." In *The Lie of the Land: English Literary Studies in India*, ed. Rajeswari Sunder Rajan. Delhi: Oxford University Press, 1992.

———. *Siting Translation: History, Post-Structuralism, and the Colonial Context*. Berkeley: University of California Press, 1992.

Okada, John. *No-No Boy*. 1957. Reprint, Seattle: University of Washington Press, 1976.

Okihiro, Gary Y. *Margins and Mainstreams: Asians in American History and Culture*. Seattle: University of Washington Press, 1994.

———. "Reading Asian Bodies, Reading Anxieties." Paper presented at Department of Ethnic Studies, University of California, San Diego, November 1995.

Oliver, Melvin L., and Thomas M. Shapiro. *Black Wealth, White Wealth: A New Perspective on Racial Inequality*. New York: Routledge, 1995.

Omatsu, Glenn. "The 'Four Prisons' and the Movements of Liberation: Asian American Activism from the 1960s to the 1990s." In *The State of Asian America: Activism and Resistance in the 1990s*, ed. Karin Aguilar-San Juan. Boston: South End, 1994.

Omi, Michael, and Howard Winant. *Racial Formation in the United States: From the 1960s to the 1990s*. New York: Routledge, 1994.

Ong, Aihwa. *Spirits of Resistance and Capitalist Discipline: Factory Women in Malaysia*. Albany: State University of New York Press, 1987.

———. "The Gender and Labor Politics of Postmodernity." *Annual Review of Anthropology* 20 (1991): 279–309.

Ong, Paul, Edna Bonacich, and Lucie Cheng, eds. *The New Asian Immigration in Los Angeles and Global Restructuring*. Philadelphia: Temple University Press, 1994.

Palumbo-Liu, David. "Wetbacks and Re-essentialized Confucians." Paper presented at the annual meeting of the Association for Asian American Studies, Oakland, Calif., June 1995.

———. "Universalisms and Minority Culture." *differences*, 7, no. 1 (1995): 188–208.

———. "Model Minority Discourse and the Ideology of Healing." In *Minority Discourse: Ideological Containment and Utopian/Heterotopian Potential*, ed. Abdul JanMohamed (forthcoming).

Pandey, Gyanendra. "Peasant Revolt and Indian Nationalism." In *Selected Subaltern Studies*, ed. Ranajit Guha and Gayatri Chakravorty Spivak. Oxford: Oxford University Press, 1988.

Pateman, Carole. *The Sexual Contract.* London: Polity, 1988.

Pearson, Charles H. *National Life and Character: A Forecast.* New York: Macmillan, 1893.

Prakash, Gyan. "Writing Post-Orientalist Histories of the Third World." *Society for Comparative Study of Society and History* 32, no. 2 (1990): 383–408.

Preston, William, Jr. *Aliens and Dissenters: Federal Suppression of Radicals.* Urbana: University of Illinois Press, 1963.

Pritchard, Earl H. "The Japanese Exclusion Bill of 1924." *Research Studies of the State College of Washington* 2 (1930): 65–77. Reprinted in *Japanese Immigrants and the American Law*, ed. Charles McClain. New York: Garland, 1994.

Rafael, Vicente L. *Contracting Colonialism: Translation and Christian Conversion in Tagalog Society under Early Spanish Rule.* Ithaca: Cornell University Press, 1988.

———. "Anticipating Nationhood: Collaboration and Rumor in the Japanese Occupation of Manila." *Diaspora* 1, no. 1 (Spring 1991): 67–82.

———. "Cultures of Area Studies in the United States." *Social Text* 41 (Winter 1994): 91–111.

———, ed. *Discrepant Histories: Translocal Essays on Filipino Cultures.* Philadelphia: Temple University Press, 1995.

———. "Taglish, or, the Phantom Power of the Lingua Franca." *Public Culture* 8, no. 1 (1995): 101–26.

Redclift, Nanneke, and M. Thea Sinclair, eds. *Working Women: International Perspectives on Labour and Gender Ideology.* London: Routledge, 1991.

Reich, Robert B. *The Work of Nations: Preparing Ourselves for Twenty-First-Century Capitalism.* New York: Knopf. 1991.

Reid, Roddey. *Families in Jeopardy: Regulating the Social Body in France, 1750–1910.* Stanford: Stanford University Press, 1993.

Riggs, Fred W. *Pressures on Congress: A Study of the Repeal of Chinese Exclusion.* New York: Columbia University Press, King's Crown Press, 1950.

Robinson, Michael. "Ideological Schism in the Korean Nationalist Movement, 1920–1930: Cultural Nationalism and the Radical Critique." *Journal of Korean Studies* 4 (1982–83): 241–68.

Roediger, David. *The Wages of Whiteness: Race and the Making of the American Working Class.* London: Verso, 1991.

———. *Towards the Abolition of Whiteness.* London: Verso, 1994.

Rogin, Michael. "Blackface, White Noise: The Jewish Jazz Singer Finds His Voice." *Critical Inquiry* 18 (Spring 1992): 417–53.

Rooney, Ellen. *Seductive Reasoning: Pluralism as the Problematic of Contemporary Literary Theory*. Ithaca: Cornell University Press, 1989.

Rosaldo, Michelle, and Louise Lamphere, eds. *Woman, Culture, and Society*. Stanford: Stanford University Press, 1974.

Rosenberg, Daniel. "The IWW and Organization of Asian Workers in Early Twentieth Century America." *Labor History* 36, no. 1 (Winter 1995): 77–87.

Rousseau, Jean-Jacques. Trans. Maurice Cranston. *The Social Contract*. Harmondsworth: Penguin, 1968.

Ryang, Sonia. "Historian-Judges of Korean Nationalism." *Ethnic and Racial Studies* 13, no. 4 (October 1990): 503–26.

Said, Edward. *Orientalism*. New York: Random, 1979.

———. *Culture and Imperialism*. New York: Knopf, 1993.

Saito, Leland. "Contrasting Patterns of Adaptation: Japanese Americans and Chinese Immigrants in Monterey Park." In *Bearing Dreams, Shaping Visions*, ed. Linda Revilla, Gail Nomura, Shawn Wong, and Shirley Hune. Pullman: Washington State University Press, 1993.

Sakai, Naoki. "Modernity and Its Critique: The Problem of Universalism and Particularism." *South Atlantic Quarterly* 87: 475–504.

Saldívar, José David. *The Dialectics of Our America: Genealogy, Cultural Critique, and Literary History*. Durham: Duke University Press, 1991.

———. *Border Matters: Remaking American Cultural Studies*. Berkeley: University of California Press, forthcoming.

Saldívar, Ramón. *Chicano Narrative: The Dialectics of Difference*. Madison: University of Wisconsin Press, 1990.

Sandoval, Chela. "U.S. Third World Feminism: The Theory and Method of Oppositional Consciousness in the Postmodern World." *Genders*, no. 10 (Spring 1991): 1–24.

Sangari, Kumkum. "The Politics of the Possible." In *The Nature and Context of Minority Discourse*, ed. Abdul JanMohamed and David Lloyd. New York: Oxford University Press, 1990.

Sangari, Kumkum, and Sudesh Vaid. *Recasting Women: Essays in Indian Colonial History*. New Brunswick: Rutgers University Press, 1990.

San Juan Jr., E. "Mapping the Boundaries: The Filipino Writer in the USA." *Journal of Ethnic Studies* 19, no. 1 (Spring 1991): 117–31.

Santner, Eric. *Stranded Objects: Mourning, Memory, and Film in Postwar Germany*. Ithaca: Cornell University Press, 1990.

Sapiro, Virginia. "Women, Citizenship, Nationality." *Politics and Society* 13 (1984): 1–26.

Sassoon, Anne Showstack. "Hegemony, War of Position, and Political Intervention." In *Approaches to Gramsci,* ed. Anne Showstack Sassoon. London: Writers and Readers, 1982.

Saxton, Alexander. *The Indispensable Enemy: Labor and the Anti-Chinese Movement in California.* Berkeley: University of California Press, 1971.

Schirmer, Daniel B., and Stephen Rosskamm Shalom, eds. *The Philippines Reader: A History of Colonialism, Neocolonialism, Dictatorship, and Resistance.* Boston: South End, 1987.

Scott, Ridley. *Blade Runner* (1982).

Sharpe, Jenny. *Allegories of Empire: The Figure of Woman in the Colonial Text.* Minneapolis: University of Minnesota, 1993.

Shibutani, Tamotsu. *The Derelicts of Company K.* Berkeley: University of California Press, 1978.

Shimakawa, Karen. "'made, not born': National Abjection and the Asian American Body on Stage." Ph.D. diss., University of Washington, 1994.

Smith, Paul. *Discerning the Subject.* Minneapolis: University of Minnesota Press, 1988.

Soja, Edward W. *Postmodern Geographies: The Reassertion of Space in Critical Social Theory.* London: Verso, 1989.

Sone, Monica. *Nisei Daughter.* Seattle: University of Washington Press, 1953.

Spivak, Gayatri Chakravorty. "Subaltern Studies: Deconstructing Historiography." In *In Other Worlds.* New York: Routledge, 1988.

Stanley, Peter. *A Nation in the Making: The Philippines and the United States, 1899–1921.* Cambridge: Harvard University Press, 1974.

Sturken, Marita. *Tangled Memories: The Vietnam War, the AIDS Epidemic, and the Politics of Remembering.* Berkeley: University of California Press, 1997.

Sumida, Stephen H. *And the View from the Shore: Literary Traditions of Hawai'i.* Seattle: University of Washington Press, 1991.

Takaki, Ronald. *Strangers from a Different Shore.* New York: William Morrow, 1989.

Tan, Amy. *The Joy Luck Club.* New York: G. P. Putnam, 1989.

Thompson, E. P. *The Making of the English Working Class.* Harmondsworth: Penguin, 1968.

Thomson, James C., Peter W. Stanley, and John Curtis Perry. *Sentimental Imperialists: The American Experience in East Asia.* New York: Harper, 1981.

Trask, Haunani-Kay. "Politics in the Pacific Islands: Imperialism and Native Self-Determination." *Amerasia* 16, no. 1 (1990): 1–19.

Trinh T. Minh-ha. *Woman, Native, Other: Writing Postcoloniality and Feminism.* Bloomington: Indiana University Press, 1989.

Truong, Monique Thuy-Dung. "Kelly." *Amerasia Journal* 17, no. 2 (1991): 41–48.

Tsurumi, E. Patricia. "Colonial Education in Korea and Japan." In *The Japanese Colo-*

nial Empire, 1895–1945, ed. Ramon H. Myers and Mark R. Peattie. Princeton: Princeton University Press, 1984.

Uno, Roberta, ed. *Unbroken Thread: An Anthology of Plays by Asian American Women*. Amherst: University of Massachusetts Press, 1993.

Viswanathan, Gauri. *Masks of Conquest: Literary Study and British Rule in India*. New York: Columbia University Press, 1989.

Volpp, Leti. "Immigration, Gender, and Violence: The Rest against the West." Paper presented at the annual meeting of the Association for Asian American Studies, Oakland, California, June 1995.

Wang, L. Ling-chi. "The Politics of Ethnic Identity and Empowerment: The Asian American Community since the 1960s." *Asian American Policy Review* (Spring 1991): 43–56.

———. "The Structure of Dual Domination: Toward a Paradigm for the Study of the Chinese Diaspora in the United States." *Amerasia Journal* 21, nos. 1 and 2 (1995): 149–169.

Wang, Peter. *A Great Wall*. 1985.

Wang, Wayne. *Dim Sum*. 1984.

White, Hayden. *Metahistory: The Historical Imagination in Nineteenth-Century Europe*. Baltimore: Johns Hopkins University Press, 1973.

White, Richard. *It's Your Misfortune and None of My Own*. Tulsa: University of Oklahoma Press, 1991.

Williams, Raymond. *Marxism and Literature*. Oxford: Oxford University Press, 1977.

Williams, William Appleman. *The Contours of American History*. Chicago: Quadrangle, 1966.

———. "The Frontier Thesis and American Foreign Policy." *Pacific Historical Review* 24 (November 1955): 379–95.

———. *The Tragedy of American Diplomacy*. Cleveland: World Publishing, 1959.

Women of the South Asian Descent Collective. *Our Feet Walk the Sky: Women of the South Asian Diaspora*. San Francisco: Aunt Lute Foundation, 1993.

Wong, Diane Yen-Mei, and Dennis Hayashi. "Behind Unmarked Doors: Developments in the Garment Industry." In *Making Waves: An Anthology of Writings by and about Asian American Women*, ed. Asian Women United of California. New York: Beacon, 1989.

Wong, Morrison G., and Charles Hirschman. "Labor Force Participation and Socioeconomic Attainment of Asian American Women." *Sociological Perspectives* 26, no. 4 (October 1983): 423–46.

Wong, Sau-ling Cynthia. *Reading Asian American Literature: From Necessity to Extravagance*. Princeton: Princeton University Press, 1993.

———. "Sugar Sisterhood: Situating the Amy Tan Phenomenon." In *The Ethnic Canon: Histories, Institutions, and Interventions*, ed. David Palumbo-Liu. Minneapolis: University of Minnesota Press, 1995.

Wong, Shelley Sunn. "Notes from Damaged Life: Asian American Literature and the Discourse of Wholeness." Ph.D. diss., Department of Ethnic Studies, University of California, Berkeley, 1993.

Woo, Deborah. "The Socioeconomic Status of Asian American Women in the Labor Force: An Alternative View." *Sociological Perspectives* 28, no. 3 (July 1985): 307–38.

Woodhull, Winifred. *Transfigurations of the Maghreb: Feminism, Decolonization, and Literature.* Minneapolis: University of Minnesota Press, 1993.

Yanagisako, Sylvia. *Transforming the Past: Kinship and Tradition among Japanese Americans.* Stanford: Stanford University Press, 1985.

Young, Marilyn. *The Vietnam Wars: 1945–1990.* New York: Harper, 1991.

Yung, Judy. *Unbound Feet: A Social History of Chinese Women in San Francisco.* Berkeley: University of California Press, 1995.

Zavarzadeh, Mas'ud, and Donald Morton, eds. *Theory, Pedagogy, Politics: Texts for Change.* Urbana: University of Illinois Press, 1991.

Index

abstract citizen. *See* citizenship: abstract

Adorno, Theodor W., 30–31, 184 n.24, 185 n.35, 195 n.67, 196 n.74, 205 n.5

aesthetic(s), 4, 32, 33, 44, 107, 157, 176, 205 n.5; aestheticization of racialized ethnic cultures, 9, 30, 86–96, 176; Asian American, 30–33, 44, 176; of infidelity, 32, 130, 152 (*see also* disidentification); modernist, 3–4, 31, 32, 50; postmodernist, 31–33, 107, 210 n.29; realist, 104, 107, 130

affirmative action, 26, 199 n.6

African American(s), 19, 23, 26, 35, 42, 90–91, 95, 160, 175; culture, 34; social movements, 22–24, 26; women, 162

AIDS (HIV), 26

Aiiieeeee!: An Anthology of Asian-American Writers (Chin et al.), 43, 50, 199 n.9

Alarcón, Norma, 212 n.7, 220 n.10

alien(s), 4, 6–14, 19–21, 69, 160, 173, 170. *See also* citizenship; immigrant(s): undocumented

Alien Land Laws. *See* laws

allegory, 35, 47, 57, 63, 77, 133, 169, 197 n.79

Althusser, Louis, 57, 92, 145–46, 150, 160; "Contradiction and Over-determination," 183 n.19, 191 n.44; "Ideology and Ideological State Apparatuses," 145–46, 215 n.24, 216 n.29; "The 'Piccolo Teatro': Bertolazzi and

Brecht," 217 n.35; *Reading 'Capital'* (with Etienne Balibar), 160

America(n), U.S.: capitalism, ix, 12–18, 40, 92–93, 158–61, 189 n.42; as construction, 2–4, 6, 9, 56–59; hegemony in postwar internationalism, 17–18; national culture, ix–x, 2–4, 6, 9, 13, 29–31, 34, 44, 48, 56–57, 65, 167; national history, 9, 27, 102, 105–7, 112; national identity, 9, 16, 56–59, 102–3; nation-state, 5–9, 10, 12–18, 21–22, 29, 33, 37, 47, 82, 143, 162, 170, 176

America Is in the Heart. See Bulosan, Carlos

Asia, ix, 4, 5, 15, 17–19, 89, 101, 103, 105, 159, 160, 165, 176; as capital, ix, 30, 84, 102, 190 n.42; as construction, 4, 18–19, 84–85, 101, 179 n.10 (*see also* orientalism); as labor, ix, 5, 7, 12–16, 189 n.42, 191 n.43; U.S. investment in, 8, 15–18, 103, 111, 159

Asian American(s), 4, 7, 10, 12, 14, 22–24, 26, 28, 30, 35, 43, 65–68, 82–83, 177 n.4; aesthetics, 30–33, 44; critique, 8–9, 28–29, 156; cultural identity, 38, 64, 70–72, 82, 158; cultural nationalism, 34, 38, 71, 75–76, 129, 171; cultural negativity, 31, 44; culture, ix–x, 4, 6, 12, 21, 22, 29, 30–36, 64–83, 156, 168–73; feminists, 71, 76; history, 5–29 passim, 100–127 passim; literary canon, 31–33, 42–54; post-1965 Asian immigrants, 16, 39, 103, 154–65, 189–90 n.42;

About the Author

Lisa Lowe is Professor in the Department of Literature at the University of California, San Diego. She is the author of *Critical Terrains: French and British Orientalisms.*

Library of Congress Cataloging-in-Publication Data
Lowe, Lisa.
Immigrant acts : on Asian American cultural politics / Lisa Lowe.
  p. cm.
Includes bibliographical references (p.) and index.
ISBN 0-8223-1858-x (cloth : alk. paper). — ISBN 0-8223-1864-4
(paper : alk. paper)
1. American literature—Asian American authors—History and
criticism—Theory, etc. 2. Politics and literature—United
States—History—20th century. 3. Asian Americans—
Intellectual life. 4. Asian Americans in literature.
5. Immigrants in literature. I. Title.
PS153.A84L69 1996
810.9'895—dc20   96-20952